CW01266737

BRITAIN'S NAVAL ROUTE TO GREATNESS

BRITAIN'S NAVAL ROUTE TO GREATNESS

1688-1815

JEREMY BLACK

AMBERLEY

For Michael and Judith Sheppard, in friendship

First published 2023

Amberley Publishing
The Hill, Stroud
Gloucestershire, GL5 4EP

www.amberley-books.com

Copyright © Jeremy Black, 2023

The right of Jeremy Black to be identified as the Author of this work has been asserted in accordance with the Copyright, Designs and Patents Act 1988.

ISBN 978 1 3981 1435 7 (hardback)
ISBN 978 1 3981 1436 4 (ebook)

All rights reserved. No part of this book may be reprinted or reproduced or utilised in any form or by any electronic, mechanical or other means, now known or hereafter invented, including photocopying and recording, or in any information storage or retrieval system, without the permission in writing from the Publishers.

British Library Cataloguing in Publication Data.
A catalogue record for this book is available from the British Library.

1 2 3 4 5 6 7 8 9 10

Typesetting by SJmagic DESIGN SERVICES, India.
Printed in the UK.

CONTENTS

Preface 7

1 From the Armada to the Glorious Revolution, 1588–1688 13
2 To Defend the Revolution, 1689–1716 30
3 Years of Limited Hostilities, 1717–38 51
4 War: From Problems to Victory, 1739–48 72
5 From Peace to Triumph, 1749–63 95
6 Deterrence and Defeat, 1764–83 126
7 Brinkmanship to the Fore, 1784–92 161
8 To Confront a Revolution, 1793–1802 170
9 Defeating an Emperor and Fighting a Republic, 1803–15 190
10 Conclusions 233

Postscript: Routes to Modernity? 254
Selected Further Reading 256
Notes 260

Preface

DAYS OF DECISIVENESS

… the greatest battle ever fought upon salt water … I saw the smoke banks on that October evening swirl slowly up over the Atlantic swell, and rise, and rise, until they had shredded into thinnest air, and lost themselves in the infinite blue of heaven. And with them rose the cloud which had hung over the country; and it also thinned and thinned, until God's own sun of peace and security was shining once more upon us, never more, we hope, to be bedimmed.

The closing sentences of Arthur Conan Doyle's novel *Rodney Stone* (1896), with the protagonist himself named after a great admiral, captured the strong sense of Nelson's 1805 victory at Trafalgar as a naval deliverance. That was how the 'long eighteenth century' was seen, with the House of Lords singing in Gilbert and Sullivan's *Iolanthe* (1882) in the song 'When Britain really ruled the waves' of how England had 'set the world ablaze' in 'Good King George's Golden Days' and everyone knowing that this was a reference to the reign of George III (1760–1820), the period of Nelsonian triumph. In 1940, the attack on the Italian fleet in Taranto was originally planned for Trafalgar Day, 21 October, the date that still resonates most in the service.

In 1688, England was successfully invaded by sea, launching William III of Orange on his successful conquest, first of England and then of the British Isles. However, throughout the period from the mid-1690s until World War Two, Britain was the leading naval power in the world; and this situation, one that required continual effort, was fundamental for British and global history. The Royal Navy was seen as crucial to British strength and security, and correctly so.

In this book, I will consider the navy's achievements and discuss the hows and whys of them. In doing so, I will be drawing on over four decades of my own work on Britain in this period, as well as on the relevant excellent detailed studies produced in recent decades by many other scholars. Attention will be devoted to battles, the moments of decisiveness, to the linkages between national strength and naval success, to the global role of the navy, to comparisons between the Royal Navy and both the army and foreign navies, and to the role of the Royal Navy in foreign policy and strategic thought.

This role helped set the 'tasking' of the navy, which is a key point as the navy did not exist to seek and win battle in any abstract sense, but was rather established in, and by, particular contexts. These were not simply a matter of the capabilities of ships. Strategy instead was 'outside-in', in the sense that it helped set the size of the navy that was developed and its purpose. This book accordingly devotes considerable space to strategy and its location in developing political contexts. Within these, operational art, to employ a modern concept and term, was developed in the naval context of the coordination of fleets, and in delegated squadrons and their use and management.

Naval success owed much to its primacy for Britain, whereas, for France and Spain, naval power was secondary to that on land, which, far more, was also the situation for the Indian rulers with whom Britain was in conflict. Drawing on the geographical needs for the self-defence of an island and from distrust of standing armies, this primacy was a matter of governmental emphasis but, even more, public politics, a politics that stretched from theatrical interludes to parliamentary debates. Admirals and naval battles were seen as heroic figures and occasions, and celebrated accordingly – a process that reached its apotheosis with Nelson's death in triumph at Trafalgar – and that helped explain the shock of failure. Furthermore, the extent to which the navy launched and sustained the army's amphibious operations ensured that it received some of the praise for episodes such as the capture of Quebec in 1759.

It is both important and too easy to move from the structural dimension of naval strength, and the trade-offs and constraints involved, to achievements on campaigns and in battle. There was clearly a close relationship between that strength and these achievements. This was not least that of the resilience that came from a pertinent naval infrastructure. Yet, there was also a need to fight for the victory; and much that was involved in this conflict rested on combat skills and contingent circumstances, rather than anything that came from an inherent resource base. This point, which was to be made by George III and exemplified by Nelson's victory over a larger Franco-Spanish fleet at Trafalgar, is more generally the case with military history, and emerges also from the consideration of other conflicts, not least due to asymmetries (differences) in goals. Clearly, the notion that war is won by the big battalions – notably so for naval war – enjoys much traction, but it is less than the complete account for military history. In particular, factors such as leadership, command quality, adroitness, able operational and strategic prioritisation, tactical skill, morale, resilience, persistence under fire and combat cohesion are not explained in these terms. Partly due to these factors, capacity, capability and competence vary in their impact and character.

At the same time as such abstraction, it is necessary, at every stage, to remember violence and risk. Most contemporaries did not experience this directly, but they could recover it through descriptions as by Tobias Smollett, a novelist who served as a medic in the Caribbean campaign in the early 1740s. His protagonist, Roderick Random, describes

> the head of the officer of the marines, who stood near me, being shot off, bounced from the deck athwart my face, leaving me well nigh blinded with brains ... a drummer ... received a great shot in his belly, which tore out his entrails, and he fell flat on my breast.

For war, *Roderick Random*, like the references to conflict elsewhere in Smollett's work, is a brilliant counterpoint to shallow heroism, instead capturing the truer qualities of care in such circumstances. The brutality of life on the fictional *Thunder* extends to the totally unnecessary clash with a French warship in which the casualties mentioned above occur. Although at war with Spain from 1739 in the War of Jenkins' Ear, Britain at that time was at peace, albeit an uneasy peace, with Spain's ally France. This continued until fighting with France began in 1743, while war between the two was declared in 1744. There was no need for Captain Oakum of the *Thunder* to attack the French warship, an attack in which the British lost 10 killed and 18 wounded, 'most part of whom afterwards died', as was generally the case with the wounded due to blood poisoning, but one that the dire circumstances on that ship would have exacerbated. The shallowness of bellicosity emerges clearly in this case:

> Captain Oakum, finding that he was like to gain neither honour nor advantage by the affair, pretending to be undeceived by seeing their colours; and hailing the ship with which he had fought all night, protested he believed them Spaniards.

Smollett's scathing pen was even more withering when it comes to the centrepiece of the 1741 British expedition, the attack on Cartagena in what is now Colombia, the key Spanish position in the southern Caribbean. As was indeed the case, Smollett presented this attack as a totally mishandled and very costly campaign. It therefore prefigured the complete British failure to relieve Minorca in 1756, an episode that was to feature in Smollett's *Adventures of an Atom*.

The War of Jenkins' Ear itself drew heavily on false expectations about the vulnerability of the Spanish empire to attack; but, aside from the serious inherent problems of amphibious operations given the multiple constraints of the period, there were the particular factors at play in 1741. As Smollett brought out, with heavy and repeated irony about being fair to the enemy (a situation totally different from the treatment of the sailors), there were unnecessary delays on the part of the British in mounting the attack. These delays not only helped the Spaniards to prepare but were also especially serious for the British given the difficulties of operating in the Tropics. The exposure to disease, notably the yellow fever that proved particularly deadly for this expedition, was a key problem. There was also a very serious failure of co-operation between the army and naval commanders, one that sapped the dynamism necessary for success and, moreover, caused failures in key attacks. Smollett also published *A Journal of the Expedition to Carthagena*, a factual work on what he had handled in *Roderick Random*, in which he concluded,

> Thus ended, in damage and disgrace, the ever-memorable expedition to Carthagena, undertaken with an armament, which, if properly conducted, might have not only ruined the Spanish settlements in America, but even reduced the whole West Indies under the dominion of Great Britain.

This sense of naval power and maritime potential resonated throughout the period.

It is a great pleasure to acknowledge the kind help of Denver Brunsman, Samantha Cavell, Patrick Deane, Grayson Ditchfield, Mike Duffy, Richard Harding, Steve Pfaff, Mark Stevens and Peter Ward who have commented on earlier drafts, providing stimulus, encouragement and correction. They are not responsible for any errors that remain. Dedicating this book to Michael and Judith reflects my pleasure in their friendship.

I

FROM THE ARMADA TO THE GLORIOUS REVOLUTION
1588–1688

The nineteenth century was in the shadow of Nelson's triumph at Trafalgar in 1805, with naval achievement and capability assessed and discussed in a context that resonated with this past glory. Indeed, the public went into World War One (1914–18) seeking to repeat Trafalgar, only to find the battle of Jutland (1916) no imitation: the bold attack of the British battlecruisers proved very costly, British losses were heavier than German ones, and the achievement there was strategic, in discouraging further German fleet sorties, rather than operational or tactical.

To a degree, the aftermath of Trafalgar was a reiteration of the impact of the defeat of the Spanish Armada in 1588 on subsequent English (from 1707 British) thought about the navy. Thus, in January 1746, when a French invasion in favour of the Jacobites threatened, though it was not in the event mounted, the diplomat Robert Trevor observed, 'Their *armada* keeps hovering over our coast.'[1] The Spanish invasion attempt was a formidable, albeit misconceived and mismanaged, project. Its defeat owed much to its inherent contradictions, but English naval attacks also played a significant role, and they, alongside the apparently providential role of the storms that badly damaged the Armada, took a key part in the public memorialisation of the episode.

The defeat of the Armada, however, conveyed a sense of naval capability that did not match the limitations of both vessels and naval warfare, nor the disaster of the English expedition against Lisbon in 1589. The wooden warship equipped with cannon was the single most costly, powerful and advanced weapon system, until replaced with its metal-built successors from the 1850s. Yet, wooden warships faced many constraints in terms of provision, maintenance, manning and operation. The construction of large warships used largely unmechanised processes, was an immense task and needed large quantities of wood. The capital investment in the ships and their equipment, notably armament, was formidable; as was the need for maintenance, for wood, rigging and canvas rotted, while cannon corroded. There was also the need for a large, skilled and reliable crew, not least to man rigging and operate the cannon.

The construction and logistical infrastructure of a fleet constituted the major 'industrial' activity of the period, with a requirement for a commensurate administrative effort to support it. Naval construction helped Britain's early leadership in the industrial age, while the way the navy was financed and the use of private contractors suggested practices that yielded economic advantages compared with competing states. That the effort was judged worthwhile in England in particular reflected the nature of its strategic culture. There, and elsewhere, the main driving forces behind the great expansion of the navies were political: intense international power struggles dominated by warfare involving battle fleets, as well as pressure from domestic interests supporting maritime power.

The character of naval conflict changed from the sixteenth century, beginning a pattern that lasted throughout the 'Age of Fighting Sail' which came to an end in the nineteenth century. The rising importance of firepower had led to a shift, initially slow and incomplete, towards stand-off tactics in which ships less frequently came into direct contact; and seizure by boarding therefore became more difficult. Furthermore, the process of modification and improvement in naval ordnance made gunnery more accurate, deadly and effective, especially the major drop in the cost of cannon, and significant improvements in gunpowder.

Although truly effective ways of deploying naval firepower were not found until the seventeenth century, this shift had important implications for naval battle tactics and further encouraged the development of warships primarily as artillery platforms. England constructed purpose-built warships on new technological lines in the 1570s, which were essentially for the defensive task of dominating the English Channel against possible Spanish attack, although they were hired out by Elizabeth I (r. 1559–1603) for commerce raiding against Spain on an *ad hoc* basis. The latter process was an aspect of the nature of the English naval effort as an uneasy co-operation between government and private maritime interests, one that remained the case, albeit to a varying extent in the period covered by this book. While Elizabeth's attempt to make war pay for itself was naïve as well as understandable, the ability to draw on privateers proved an important aspect of English naval capability, providing a pool of highly capable leaders and battle-trained seamen. Begun in 1585, the war with Spain, which continued until 1604, illustrated the limitations of naval power for both sides, notably vulnerability to storms, the problems of combined operations, as in the lack of coordination between Spain's fleet and invasion army in 1588 and the unsuccessful English expedition against Lisbon in 1589, and the heavy supply demands posed by large fleets.

Yet, the defeat of the Armada in 1588 also demonstrated the growing technical skill of English seamanship and naval warfare, not least gunnery using compact four-wheeled gun carriages, as well as effective command. After harassing the Spanish fleet in its passage along the Channel, the English were able to use fireships to disrupt it off Calais and then to inflict considerable damage in a running battle off Gravelines. A strong southwesterly wind, seen as a 'Protestant wind', drove the Armada, which had no deep-water base in which to take shelter, into the North Sea. Rather than risking a return voyage up the Channel in the face of winds and English opposition, the Armada returned home to Spain round Scotland and Ireland. It lost 28 ships to unseasonably violent storms that drove vessels onto the rocky coasts, with a heavy loss as well of manpower.

Aside from the problems of ensuring repeated success, as was to be shown in 1589, English naval power proved difficult to sustain. The withdrawal of royal support under James I (r. 1603–25), and his antagonism towards English piracy and privateering, removed the underpinning of naval capacity. Indeed, the highly unsuccessful expeditions of the 1620s against Spanish and French targets Cadiz and La Rochelle showed that within a quarter-century of Elizabeth's reign, the naval capability of England had been severely diminished, with a dramatic decrease in the competence of its commanders. At the same time, there had been a significant build-up in the number and skills of the wider population of sailors.[2]

In the 1630s, the contrary pressures of naval politics saw the remembered virtues of Elizabethan maritime strength but also strong distrust of Charles I's plans for naval expansion, financed by means of Ship Money.[3] Both in a continuance, but also in very contrasting circumstances, the republican 'Rump' parliamentary government that replaced Charles (r. 1625–49) after the Civil War developed a formidable naval power which, building on expansion during the Civil War, became the largest in the world by 1650. Furthermore, the earlier dependence on large merchantmen ended with the establishment of a substantial state navy.[4] Short-term deficit financing was used, generally successfully, in the 1640s and 1650s, though the system faced serious problems by 1659 as a result of the costs of war with Spain.[5]

The English were to find their naval wars with the Dutch in the seventeenth century more of a pattern for those in the eighteenth with the French, than the example set by war with Spain from 1585 to 1604. There were four Anglo-Dutch wars between 1652 and 1688, with only the last, very brief, one yielding a decisive result; but the lack of such decisiveness was not too different from the pattern of conflict on land. The first three Anglo-Dutch wars saw fleet actions in European wars, fought with heavy guns, as well as commerce raiding and strikes at colonial centres. Attempts to preserve or cut trade links were crucial to the financial and economic viability of both powers. In the First Anglo-Dutch War (1652–4), English victories closed the Channel to Dutch trade, which helped lead the Dutch to negotiate peace. Both sides greatly increased their naval strength with the construction of new and larger ships. Larger ships generally meant a more robust hull which could resist gunfire more effectively. These ships were also an indication of an incredible commitment in the context of an early modern economy that was still largely agrarian.

Nature of Naval Warfare

The development of line-ahead tactics was an important change that maximised broadside power and ensured that broadsides could be used throughout a battle, rather than just in the initial stages, as well as offering ships a degree of mutual protection, not least against vulnerability in the stern. The stress on cohesion reflected a move away from battle as a series of struggles between individual ships as part of a more general mêlée. In part there was a degree of copying the Dutch, but there was also a transfer of military models to sea, as English commanders with experience of combat on land, notably during the Civil War, sought to apply its lessons and to devise a formation that permitted control and co-operation during battle. In turn, fighting instructions and line tactics instilled discipline and operational control, rather than risk, and encouraged a new stage in fighting as a unit that permitted more effective firepower, one that was further enhanced when merchantmen ceased to appear in the line of battle.[6] However, the specifications and seaworthiness of individual ships, and the nature of conflict at sea, made it very difficult to maintain cohesion once ships became closely engaged.

English warships were not alone in becoming more heavily gunned. Instead of relying on converted merchantmen, there was an increased use for fleet operations of purpose-built warships that were heavily gunned and built accordingly with strong hulls. Heavier shot was fired, and broadside firepower increased with the development of improved tracks which used the gun's recoil to speed reloading onboard. There was also a professionalisation of naval officership, senior ratings and infrastructure, one linked to the central role of the state, including in the organisation of private activity and support, notably privateering.[7]

As the specifications of warships thereafter changed relatively little, and notably so in the closing decades of the seventeenth century, ships remained in service. Indeed warships could stay in the line of battle for decades as long as they were kept seaworthy. That was far from easy, but a deterioration in sailing characteristics alone did not mean that warships were discarded unless it became very serious.

In turn, this situation could make it difficult for a squadron to act as an effective unit. Moreover, repair, reconstruction on the old base or like-for-like replacements were all problematic. While prone to complain in the aftermath of the indecisive battle of Toulon in 1744, Admiral Thomas Mathews had good cause. Of *Chichester*, he wrote,

> [A]s for the rest of her ports [gunports] they were caulked in when she first fitted out and have never been opened since, nor will they ever be, except in a mill-pond ... it would have been more for His Majesty's service (abstracted from good husbandry) that she had been burnt, than to have repaired her at such a monstrous expense; a commanding officer has a bad time of it with such a number of bad men of war, and those ill manned ... when it is not in his power to engage the enemy, when he is superior to them, nor to escape when he is inferior.[8]

Naval operations and combat faced serious limitations during this period and thereafter. This was true of all types of operations, from amphibious assaults or battle to blockade, commerce protection and small-ship actions. For the first, Charles, 3rd Duke of Marlborough observed in 1758 of amphibious attacks on France,

> I wish Mr Bligh had made the same unalterable determination that I did, which was to trust as little as possible to the winds which all the admirals in Europe cannot command. Therefore always to the best of my knowledge to be two days nearer to my ships than the enemy's army.[9]

As far as battle was concerned, Captain John Jervis was to write to the Secretary of the Admiralty in 1778,

> I have often told you, that two fleets of equal force can never produce decisive events, unless they are equally determined to fight it out, or the commander-in-chief of one of them *bitches* it so as to misconduct his line.[10]

The importance of numbers in a line-of-battle order discouraged the numerically inferior navy from engaging, not least as their opponents could, as it were, try to curve the line in order to bring greater pressure to bear. Yet, if the two navies were fairly evenly matched, it was difficult to obtain a decisive result, because the line-ahead formations that the mounting of guns on the broadside of warships produced were powerful defensive positions, while wooden warships could take a lot of battering. It was not easy to sink them, not least because it was difficult to depress guns so as to hole them below the waterline.

Because the overwhelming majority of the cannon on ships of the line fired from the sides and not forward, warships could not simultaneously advance on and fire at an opponent, while half the cannon could not be brought to bear when two lines were engaged. Moreover, inaccurate gunnery, not least due to windage (the gap between shot and the inside of barrels), the limitations of smoothbores, and problems with irregular shot and varied gunpowder charges, did not help with their firepower, and encouraged firing from a short range. The enhancements offered by rifled cannon did not come until the nineteenth century. Guns were loaded, aimed and fired by hand, which required coming into range. Despite all these caveats, if a cannon ball hit it could do tremendous damage, which was the rationale of the line of battle.

Lacking, by modern standards, deep keels, sailing vessels suffered from limited seaworthiness. Furthermore, the operational problems of working sailing ships for combat were very different from those that steam-powered vessels were to encounter. The optimal conditions for sailing ships were to come from windward across a sea which was relatively flat. It was more difficult to range guns in a swell, not least as the gunports provided only limited movability in any direction for the cannon.

Limitations on manoeuvrability of both ships and guns ensured that ships were deployed in line in order to maximise their firepower. Moreover, skill, in handling ships in line or in battle, entailed balancing the wind between the sails of the three masts in order to achieve control over manoeuvrability and speed.[11] Line tactics and fighting instructions were designed to encourage an organisational cohesion that permitted more effective firepower, mutual support and flexibility in the uncertainty of battle, but tactical practice conformed to theory (usually geometrical[12]) even less at sea than on land, due in part to the major impact of weather and wind on manoeuvrability. Although experience, standardisation of both ships and guns, and design improvements all enhanced performance, there were still significant limitations, not least in terms of standardisation, as the sailing characteristics and, separately, fighting skill and determination of individual ships turned out to be far from uniform.[13] Widespread differences in the wear and tear of sails and hulls, and of marine growth on hulls, even among ships of the same size and age, affected operations and made a facility of repair and maintenance in dock very important. As a result of the range of operating problems and tactical factors, success in naval engagements was particularly impressive. This should be borne in mind in assessing the discussion of both battles and warfare by subsequent naval theorists, notably Alfred Thayer Mahan in the late nineteenth century.

Sir Charles Wager, the First Lord of the Admiralty, an experienced commander, told the House of Commons in January 1734 that it was not easy to intercept Spanish treasure fleets and referred to

> the great seas that roll there in the winter ... at that time of the year [the fleets] might have passed even within my view, without its being in my power either to come up with them, or to fire a gun at them: but gentlemen often censure other people's actions, because they know nothing of the matter about what they take upon them to criticise.

Moreover, the nature of communications ensured not only that the sheer scale of naval battle posed major problems, but also that, once detached, ships were difficult to recall speedily, which, always a concern for England, became a far greater problem as more ships were sent to trans-oceanic stations. Reacting to, or predicting, the likely moves of opponents based in a number of places, and operating at the strategic, operational and tactical levels in an absence of reliable information, the British were continually moving ships between their squadrons.

The unpredictable constraints of the weather were also an issue. George, 2nd Earl of Bristol, envoy in Turin, reported in 1756: 'The French say that His Majesty's fleet cannot hold the sea long as the winter is approaching, and that when Sir Edward Hawke retires into port, their communication will be again opened with Minorca without their risking an engagement.'[14] Thus, France would be enabled to maintain its control of its recent Mediterranean conquest. Moreover, that month, the First Lord of the Admiralty drew the attention of ministerial colleagues to the dire consequences of maintaining the blockade of the French Atlantic port of Brest into the winter, explaining 'that the crews of the ships are very sickly, that the ships must necessarily return in order to be refitted, and that, upon the whole, the fleet would run the utmost hazard, were it to continue cruising off Brest, beyond the middle of the next month'.[15] In December 1796, a French invasion fleet for Ireland was able to leave Brest in large part because the British blockading squadron had been disrupted by gales, only for the French in turn to be hit by the latter.

Wind-powered warships were dependent, at all levels, on the weather. Ships could only sail up to a certain angle to the wind. Too much or insufficient wind were serious problems, while reliance on the wind alone made inshore naval operations very chancy. French ships could only leave Brest with an easterly wind, which was not that prevalent, and this helped the British blockaders. If westerly winds were strong enough to drive the British fleet from station, they also kept the French in port. Blockaders, however, faced serious limitations in the surveillance as well as command and control capabilities of naval power. These limitations made it very difficult to 'see' or control in any strategic sense, and certainly limited the value of any blockade. In 1708, a French invasion force left Dunkirk in the face of a larger British blockading squadron by making use of the mist. In January 1756, the Jacobites felt able to propose that the French invade England between Rye and Winchelsea, carried from Dieppe and Boulogne in small ships, while the British fleet, it was claimed, would be held back from the defence of the coast by adverse winds.[16]

A very different instance of naval vulnerability was provided by the sinking of four ships on rocks near the Isles of Scilly in 1707 with nearly 2,000 sailors killed, including all of the 800, not least the commander, Sir Cloudesley Shovell, on the flagship

Association. About 3,500 sailors were lost alongside four warships when a storm hit a British fleet off Newfoundland in September 1782.

Delay was also a factor, as in the unsuccessful expedition against Charleston, South Carolina, in early 1776, which sailed from Cork in early February, assembled off Cape Fear in North Carolina, and did not attack Sullivan's Island off Charleston until 28 June. Lieutenant-General Earl Cornwallis, who had sailed from Cork on 10 February, reported on 27 March,

> ... our voyage hitherto has been very unsuccessful; the wind has been almost always contrary, and, till the first of this month, constant and most violent gales of wind ... I fear there is no chance of our arrival on the American coast before the end of next month at the soonest, and the assembling the fleet off Cape Fear, where there is no port, may be a work of some time.[17]

In the event, although the first ships reached the anchorage on 18 April, Cornwallis did not do so until 3 May. The sand bar at Cape Fear was found to block the entrance of ships of deep draught into the river. In turn, due to an unexpected shallowness of nearby waters, three ships ran aground in the attack on Sullivan's Island. This was an instance of the major issues posed by ship handling in poorly charted inshore waters. Entering and leaving anchorages could prove particularly dangerous.

In contrast to contrary winds, calms in late July 1777 delayed the force sailing from New York to the Chesapeake. It sailed on 23 July and did not land at Elkton until 25 August. Contrary winds and calms both reflected not only the particular circumstances of individual sailing environments but also their annual climate routine. Furthermore, the latter could interact with the virulence of disease, or just illness, and the activity of their vectors. Thus, the autumnal storms of the North Atlantic were apt to interact with a cold spell that encouraged some infections, and the same was differently true of summer calms in the Caribbean, although the hurricane season was a major factor there.

There was the possibility of improved responses, in part due to better knowledge and to incremental changes in healthcare, ship design and rigging. Yet there was nothing like the situation described by Captain Sir Edward Corcoran in Gilbert and Sullivan's *Utopia Limited* (1893):

Unbend your sails and lower your yards,
Unstep your masts – you'll never want 'em more.
Though we're no longer hearts of oak,
Yet we can steer and we can stoke,
And thanks to coal, and thanks to coke,
We never run a ship ashore!

Throughout our period, geography posed issues for all powers, sometimes to the advantage of Britain, but often not. Thus, Alexander Straton, a diplomat, observed in 1783, with reference to the location of a major Spanish port: 'If we do not sail before them, the situation of Cadiz relative to the East and West Indies gives them a decided superiority in point of passage,'[18] meaning the time taken.

1665–87

In a lesson that was instructive, by comparison and contrast, for 1688–1815, the English found it difficult to sustain the position achieved in the 1650s, even though, unlike the army, it was not linked in its reputation and political resonance with domestic oppression. Indeed, in the 1660s, thanks to French and Dutch shipbuilding, the English went from leading to third most important naval power.[19] Moreover, in 1665-7, despite heavy blows on the Dutch, notably in the battle of Lowestoft (1665) and the Two Days Battle (1666), the Second Anglo-Dutch War involved the humiliation of a successful Dutch raid on the English warships anchored in the River Medway. There was no comparable humiliation in the Third Anglo-Dutch War (1672-4), but nor was it a victory: the Dutch fought a successful defensive war against an alliance of England and France, a task that anticipated unsuccessful later Franco-Spanish assaults on Britain. If English naval strength revived in the late 1670s, thanks to a major shipbuilding programme, the French navy still remained larger then and in the 1680s. Indeed, in the early 1680s, during a period of political chaos in England, there was a rapid deterioration in the state of naval materiel and finances as attested by the fine naval administrator Samuel Pepys.

The Anglo-Dutch Wars occurred as part of a period from 1652 to 1692 in which England, the Dutch, France and Spain vied for naval superiority, and built warships and developed supporting infrastructures accordingly. Naval success was designed to serve strategic goals, permitting or preventing invasion, while naval strength was regarded as crucial for trade protection and as important for prestige. The achievements of the battlefleet, the ships of the line, both defensive and offensive, had to be secured by the action of smaller, faster ships, notably in trade interception but also protection.

Foreign naval strength posed a triple problem for the British. First, it affected naval strategy, operations and tactics greatly, by discouraging an adventurous strategy, forcing a concentration of naval strength in home waters, and making the avoidance of the loss of warships a key element. Secondly, foreign naval strength ensured a need for high rates of preparedness and for a prophylactic programme of naval construction and repair able to cope with anticipated developments. The resulting pressure on the dockyards and on expenditure posed major administrative and political pressures. Even if Britain had a clearer incentive to prioritise the navy compared with other powers, that did not mean that it would succeed in mastering the challenges and manage the burdens of naval supremacy.

Thirdly, there was the issue of assessing foreign naval strength and intentions. Much effort was put into both, but the quality of the information gathered varied, on occasion the British were seriously surprised, as in 1666 and 1688 by the Dutch and in 1744 by the Brest squadron, while uncertainty over French plans handicapped British operations, as in 1741, 1747, 1756 and more generally. This uncertainty had operational and strategic consequences, as well as leading to serious difficulties in assessing the most sensible level of naval construction and preparedness, a problem exacerbated by the often kaleidoscopic unpredictabilities of the international situation. Had Britain had to consider only one opponent, then naval planning might have been easier.

Naval Disaster

A century after the Armada was seen the ultimate debacle of English naval power, one even worse than the failures in 1756 and 1781 to relieve besieged English forces at Minorca and Yorktown respectively, although, as a reminder of the selective nature of the historical record, one that was not to be publicly interpreted as such. In 1688, William III of Orange prepared to invade England and overthrow his uncle and father-in-law, James II and VII of Scotland (r. 1685-8), but faced the limitations of naval power. His first invasion attempt, in mid-October, was defeated by storms at sea, with the loss of many supplies, including over 1,000 horses which were especially liable to break their legs in storms. Louis XIV of France (r. 1643–1715) offered his cousin James naval assistance, but, concerned about the international implications, James responded in an equivocal fashion.

William's second attempt was far more successful, and England was invaded despite its possession of a large and impressive navy. A strong northeasterly wind prevented the English fleet, then lying at the Gunfleet off Harwich, from leaving their anchorage, but allowed William, this time going to the south of this fleet, to sail into the Channel. By the time the English finally set out on 3 November, the main Dutch force was already passing Dover. It was commanded by Arthur Herbert, who had been dismissed by James for his political beliefs. William landed at Brixham in Devon on 5 November, at which time the pursuing fleet was no nearer than Beachy Head. Even so, a successful attack would have weakened William, as with the successful attack on the Spanish fleet off Sicily in 1718 (see chapter three). However, at a Council of War held that day the English captains decided not to attack what they believed would be a larger Dutch force. Disenchanted with James, some of the captains were less than fervent in their hostility to William. Thereafter, first storms and then bad weather prevented the English fleet from acting until it surrendered to William's authority on 13 December.

The most ignominious naval campaign in English naval history owed much to a defensive, reactive mentality that reflected division and discontent among the captains as well as England being formally at peace.[20] It also demonstrated the primacy of politics, both international and domestic, in the challenges facing the English navy, and in the way in which its history was remembered and presented.

The sailing-ship navies. Relative size as percentage of total size

	1680	1690	1700	1710	1720	1730
Britain	29.3	25.1	25.8	26.4	28.3	28.1
France	29.9	28.5	25.7	22.4	7.8	10.8
Netherlands	14.5	13.7	14.9	15.6	12.9	1.2
Spain	3.4	6.0	2.6	1.3	3.6	10.8

	1740	1750	1760	1770	1780	1785
Britain	29.5	36.5	37.6	32.3	28.8	30.5
France	13.8	15.2	15.6	20.2	21.7	18.4
Netherlands	9.8	8.2	6.2	7.3	5.6	8.5
Spain	13.8	5.4	13.7	15.2	15.7	14.5

Source: Jan Glete, *Navies and Nations* (1993), I, 242, 312.

2

TO DEFEND THE REVOLUTION
1689–1716

The system established as a result of the Glorious Revolution of 1688–9 was particularly vulnerable as a result of two factors. First was the strong enmity of Louis XIV of France (r. 1643–1715), whose navy was the largest in the world in the 1680s and early 1690s. Secondly, there was the extent of opposition to the new system in the British Isles and the support, instead, for the Jacobite cause, that of the exiled James II of England (VII of Scotland), which was backed by Louis.

There was a particularly intense naval crisis in 1689–92. In 1689, after the indecisive battle of Bantry Bay (1 May), in which Arthur Herbert, now First Lord of the Admiralty, and 22 ships of the line were unable to defeat a French fleet of 24 ships of the line covering a landing of French troops in Ireland to support James, the English had to return to Portsmouth for repairs, because there was no dry docking in the Channel further west. This situation gave the French a major advantage, as, from their Atlantic bases at Brest and Rochefort, they could challenge the English in the Channel and in Irish waters, and could also attack shipping routes to England as they focused on the Channel, notably those from the Mediterranean, Indian Ocean, Caribbean and North America. At the same time, the French bases were primarily built for war with Spain in the Bay of Biscay, and there was no Channel base large enough to match Portsmouth. Much French dockyard building was at Toulon in order to dominate the western Mediterranean.

Two months after Bantry Bay, the French threat was accentuated when the able Anne-Hilarion, Count of Tourville evaded the English fleet off Brittany to lead much of the Toulon (Mediterranean) fleet into Brest. This created a threatening concentration of French strength that was not matched in subsequent conflicts and notably not in the crises of 1744–6, 1759, 1778–9 and 1805, in each case when the Toulon and Brest fleets remained separate. Divisions between fleets posed a major problem of strategy, whether in peacetime preparation or wartime concentration.

In 1690, the French successfully escorted another force of troops to Ireland, and were also victorious off Beachy Head on 30 June. Tourville greatly outnumbered the Anglo-Dutch fleet, which was affected by the determination of the Earl of Torrington (the ennobled Herbert) not to risk his English ships for fear that doing so might expose England to invasion. Torrington had been ordered to engage, in part to cover English trade, but he hung back – possibly with good reason, but, nevertheless, ensuring that the Dutch in the van were badly pummelled. Tourville was also successful in the pursuit, and a number of allied warships ran aground and were burnt. Imprisoned in the Tower of London and court-martialled, Torrington was acquitted, but lost his position as First Lord of the Admiralty and did not again hold command.[1]

Yet, as so often, operational success did not have major strategic effects. In part, this was because the success did not match the preferences derived from strategic culture. Tourville, whose instructions when he left Brest were to attack Portsmouth and then sail on to blockade the Thames, was unable to exploit the victory, while worry about the lack of a Channel base led him to come down to Torbay where he burned Teignmouth. The French did not have an invasion force ready and Louis was more concerned about the conflict in the Spanish Netherlands (Belgium). As in 1588, 1744-6 and 1805, any combination of forces for an invasion was made difficult because of the separation between troops in or near Belgium and warships further west, in this case in Brest.

Instead, the most significant use of naval power in 1689–91 was in Ireland, where both English and French warships supported the units they had sent there, respectively against and in support of James II. Londonderry, then under siege by supporters of James, was relieved by the English fleet in 1689 after the boom across the River Foyle blocking the harbour had been broken. James was urged by the French to play a waiting game rather than risk battle, to burn Dublin, destroy all the food and forage in William's path, and wait for a French fleet to interrupt William's seaborne supply route. Grasping Dublin's symbolic and strategic significance, and fearing the consequences of delay, James instead chose in 1690 to fight at the Boyne, only to be heavily defeated by William and then to lose Dublin. In what was to prove a consistent situation, the French fleet were able to support opposition in Ireland by sailing to the southern or western coasts, but not to break the Irish Sea axis of English intervention in Ireland. William had been able to land in Ireland earlier in 1690.

The French sought to exploit their naval (and land) strength by invading England in 1692, but secrecy was lost, delays in the invasion preparations hindered Tourville, and he was compromised by a failure to unite the French naval forces and by rigid instructions enforcing conflict even if outnumbered. A far larger Anglo-Dutch fleet under Admiral Edward Russell, naval commander-in-chief from December 1690, attacked the French on 29 May 1692 off Barfleur on the Cotentin peninsula. Russell was able to gain the initiative, but the French fought well before withdrawing. In all, 22 of the French warships reached St Malo through the hazardous Race (the strait between Alderney and the Cotentin), but many of the damaged warships took shelter under the forts at St Vaast and Ile Tatihou in the bay of La Hougue on the east side of the Cotentin peninsula. They were attacked and burned on 2 June by small boats sent in by Vice-Admiral Sir George Rooke. One of the most successful small-boat operations of the period, it was made possible by the division and demoralisation among the French fleet caused by their earlier pummelling from the Anglo-Dutch fleet. In all, 15 warships and the transports were destroyed. The resonance of the battle of Barfleur-La Hougue was seen throughout the 'Age of Fighting Sail'. Thus, in about 1778, Benjamin West produced a painting of the battle of La Hougue that was engraved by William Woollett in 1781.

Given the difficulties of forcing battle on opponents who did not want to fight, it was unsurprising that planning for this, as for many other battles, was very much *ad hoc*. Yet, with the training of a fleet as a unit, rather than as single ships, the need for planning increased. However, once cannon had opened fire, the details of a battle generally became obscure. This reflected the extent to which cannon were using black powder, which produced copious quantities of smoke as well as hanging in the air with a grittiness that affected sight and breathing. Furthermore, the lack of standardised timepieces contributed to the difficulties of recording and recovering detail.

That Barfleur was one of the most important naval battles of the period indicates the extent to which battles interacted with the strategic context, in this case the contrary pressures on French resources and (differently) attention. Under pressure also from the economic crisis of 1693–4, which hit French government finances, the French refocused their naval strategy from the *guerre d'escadre*, the war of squadrons, in which they had sought battle, to the *guerre de course*, in which attacks on trade took top priority. While the battlefleet losses were largely replaced by France, it was not used.

This was a response to the English victory at Barfleur, but more was at stake, not only in terms of the army versus navy equation, but also with reference to what the French could achieve at sea. Tourville took large fleets to sea in 1693 and 1694, but achieved little. The war in Ireland was over, an invasion of England appeared a less promising prospect, and when planned in 1696 it was thwarted by a formidable English fleet off Dunkirk, and there was little for the French to achieve in the Mediterranean with their fleet. This was not only because much of the French fleet was in Brest. Unlike England, France, which had a far larger army as well as significant defences for coastal cities, notably Brest, did not need a fleet for defensive purposes. Indeed, the English had scant success with attacks on the French ports of St Malo, Brest, Calais and Dunkirk.

The English had more success in demonstrating power by means of sending a fleet under Russell (from that May First Lord of the Admiralty) to the Mediterranean in 1694, which was followed by its wintering at the allied port of Cadiz. In contrast, from 1700, Spain was not to be such an ally again for England/Britain until after the French invasion of 1808. The interests of Austria, France and Spain in the western Mediterranean ensured that into the 1740s it was the, or at least a, cockpit of

European diplomacy, which meant that the deployment of naval power there was significant. In the 1670s, this had entailed Dutch, French and Spanish fleets in Sicilian waters, but now the English were to play a role. English warships had been to the area previously, especially under Robert Blake in the 1650s, and, thereafter, to protect trade against the Barbary pirates of North Africa. In contrast, although that remained a factor, from 1694 such naval deployment was more closely linked to strategic co-operation or confrontation with other European states. At the same time, this deployment was made without any confidence about French capability or intentions, or indeed the English response. Thus, in September 1695, on his appointment to command the fleet sent to the Mediterranean, Sir George Rooke was ordered that

> in case the French fleet or any part of it now in the Mediterranean shall pass the Streights [of Gibraltar], in order to come into these seas, you take care to follow with, or send after them, at least, an equal force of the ships that shall be under your command, with regard to the number and nature of the French ships, either to engage, or stop them, or in default thereof to come away for England for the strengthening of His Majesty's fleet here.

The following January, in light of reports that the Toulon fleet was 'to come early into these seas', Rooke was instructed to return to England unless he obtained good information that the French plan had been laid aside.[2]

There was also the deployment of naval forces more widely. The wealth of the Indies attracted governmental attention, and the accessibility of the Caribbean coasts to amphibious operations, and the extent to which warships provided firepower, troop-carrying capacity and logistics, made this focus a matter of opportunity as well as need. Warships appeared able to fulfil their roles. Eight small ships of the line under Commodore Lawrence Wright arrived in the Caribbean in 1690, a contrast to the large forces deployed in home waters. However, an expedition against the French-ruled island of Guadeloupe in 1691 was thwarted, in part by the arrival of a French squadron. In turn, seeking to protect Jamaica, the English fought off, and successfully withdrew from, a much larger French fleet off La Désirade in 1692. Yellow fever hit English attacks on Martinique in 1693 and Saint-Domingue in 1695, while renewed threats to Jamaica encouraged England to send fleets to the Caribbean in 1694 and 1696, a process greatly eased by the changing naval situation in Europe.

Naval action alone was inadequate because of its dependence on wind and current, the need for bases, and the inherently transient nature of blockades.[3] Instead, it was necessary to capture the bases of other powers in order to limit their options, but that was a task that involved a very different capability to that of naval action alone. At the same time, naval captains benefited financially from the prize money obtained from captures and also from taking part in shipping goods on their warships and thus providing protection.

In turn, French commerce raiding hit English trade hard, and thus affected the economy and public finances, contributing to the major financial crisis in 1696. The loss in 1693 of over 80 merchantmen, when the Smyrna (Izmir) convoy taking out goods to the Mediterranean under an Anglo-Dutch convoy was intercepted by a far larger French fleet off Lagos in Portugal, caused a political and financial crisis which led to the dismissal from their joint command of the navy of three admirals.

The effectiveness of English naval operations varied, but there was a common theme of gaining the initiative, mounting attacks, protecting English trade and attacking that of France. This activity rested in part on a rapid and expensive programme of dockyard construction, for poor seaworthiness and the need to repair damage, which meant that the largest warships could not operate too far from their bases at this time, restricted the scope for major fleet operations. Portsmouth, which already had two dry docks that acted as a double dock, was expanded with the creation of two new dry docks and two wet docks. At Plymouth, where the naval facilities had hitherto been primitive, a new dockyard was constructed including a dry dock and a wet dock. Initially, in 1689, it was decided that the Plymouth dry dock should be capable of receiving up to third-rates (ships of the line mounting between 60 and 90 guns), but, in 1691, the dock contract was upgraded so as to be able to take the biggest ships of the line.[4]

The expansion of facilities at Portsmouth and Plymouth supplemented the earlier focus on the Medway and the Thames, at Chatham, Sheerness, Deptford and Woolwich, and was linked to a reconceptualisation of naval needs. In particular, conflict with France and more especially competition with France over Ireland in 1689–91, and the vulnerability to invasion of south-west England and more generally the south coast, threw the western naval bases into higher relief.[5]

An Interlude of Peace

Peace with France in 1697 was followed by naval demobilisation, with ships docked, their sails taken down and cannon moved into store, the officers switched to half pay and the ratings shed. This, however, was not as sweeping nor as politically sensitive as the situation with troop numbers. Moreover, peace did not mean that the navy was inactive. Ships were sent to Newfoundland to protect the English fisheries after recent French seizures of positions on the coast. In addition, alongside peace with France, a degree of confidence led in 1700 to the dispatch of a joint Anglo-Dutch fleet under Admiral George Rooke to the Sound where, bombarding Copenhagen, it helped to enforce a settlement of Dano-Swedish differences favourable to the latter, and thus protected English political and commercial interests. The co-operation with Dutch warships was another demonstration of the importance for naval purposes and power of the Glorious Revolution and the accession of William III.

The War of the Spanish Succession, 1702–13

The death of Charles II of Spain in 1700 led, from 1701, to a conflict over his childless succession between Austrian and French claimants. England joined the Austrian side in 1702, fighting until the Peace of Utrecht in 1713. The Dutch were an ally throughout, even though the death of William III in 1702 ended common rulership.

English naval strength was only fitfully contested by the French during the War of the Spanish Succession, in large part because their expenditure continued to be dominated by the army. This enabled the English to inhibit French invasion planning, to maintain control of maritime routes to the Low Countries, the crucial axis of the alliance, and to project power, especially into the Mediterranean.

The English, nevertheless, had to balance their commitments in the Mediterranean with those in Atlantic waters, especially the Channel, an issue that was to be found throughout the period. Naval strategy was in large part an exercise in prioritisation, and the latter entailed uncertainties and risks. Thus, in 1702, there was opposition to Austrian pressure for the dispatch of naval forces to attack Spanish-ruled Naples, a target which the Austrians were seeking to conquer and that was vulnerable to naval attack, as the British were to show on several occasions up to 1815. However, William Blathwayt, the Secretary-at-War, informed George Stepney, the envoy in Vienna, that it was necessary to retain superiority in the Channel, and that if a squadron of only 12 warships was sent to the Mediterranean it would be challenged by the threat posed by the French fleet in Toulon.[6] Detached squadrons could indeed be exposed to larger opposing forces, but, if a larger fleet was sent, that could lead to vulnerabilities elsewhere.

Rather than such a dispatch, the English in 1702 sought both to concentrate their fleet, thus lessening its vulnerability, and also to use it for a number of purposes. The latter was a common remedy, but repeatedly suffered from the danger of a failure to settle on and achieve any one in particular. In 1702, there was an attempt to intercept the Spanish treasure fleet from the New World, and thereby deliver a major blow to the financial liquidity of the Bourbons. By thus deploying the fleet in Channel and Atlantic waters, the English were able also to keep an eye on the French fleet in Brest and therefore protect Ireland and the Channel. The latter was indeed achieved in 1702, although there had been no real threat.

Less positively, while such a concentration had left the Smyrna convoy vulnerable to French attack in 1693, the treasure fleet was not intercepted at sea. In August 1702, French warships that had been sent to the Caribbean to convoy the treasure ships fought off Vice-Admiral John Benbow off Santa Maria in a running action. Before Benbow was fatally injured by chain shot, he had lost control of his captains, and most failed to give him sufficient support in the battle. As a result, two were court-martialled and shot. The same year, an English expedition against St Augustine, the main Spanish base in Florida, failed when it was relieved by a fleet from Havana, the major Spanish naval base in the Americas.

Rooke failed to capture Cadiz in an amphibious attack in 1702. However, failure was remedied by a success that created a positive impression of naval capability, when the treasure fleet was attacked at anchorage at Vigo on the Spanish coast. It was protected by a boom and strong batteries, but the southern battery was captured by an amphibious force and the boom broken by the *Torbay* under heavy fire on 12 October. The following engagement was decisively won by Rooke's Anglo-Dutch fleet and the French and Spaniards set fire to their ships. In turn, allied naval strength helped lead Portugal to change sides from France in 1703, which was important not only to naval forward-projection into the Mediterranean but also for operations in the Atlantic and Indian oceans.

But for the English navy, there would have been no war in Iberia, not least because the threat of naval action, underlined by the fleet's success at Vigo in 1702, led Portugal to abandon its French alliance in 1703. Fearing the consequences of English enmity, especially in terms of the crucial trade with Brazil, Pedro II had pressed for French naval assistance. The French envoy advised Louis XIV in 1701 that Lisbon must never be without some French warships in sight, and the arrival of a fleet of 18 ships gave the government some confidence and invalidated English threats. However, French naval protection was limited and requests to send ships to protect Brazil and the Portuguese bases in India were refused. In 1702, the French envoy was told that the alliance would end if an Anglo-Dutch fleet arrived before requested aid from France, but the French were unable to fulfil their promises. They could not supply the cannon they had promised for the defence of Lisbon because they did not dare to transport them from La Rochelle by sea. The British success at Vigo impressed the Portuguese, and in January 1703 the French navy was so inferior to that of the Maritime Powers (England and the United Provinces) that convoys between Europe and America were not safe.[7]

Similarly, France's role in Baltic and Italian diplomacy was lessened by her naval weakness. The degree to which the French emphasised privateering therefore was of considerable importance in military-diplomatic capability, representing a lessening of the ability to use military strength for diplomatic ends. This was a serious weakness for France, as the difficulty of achieving total victory ensured that success in war tended to go to the power that could preserve its own allies while disrupting the rival coalitions of states, and France's ability to do so was lessened by her naval weakness.

Thanks in part to the availability of a position at Lisbon, the English fleet under Sir Cloudesley Shovell entered the Mediterranean in 1703, encouraging Victor Amadeus II of Savoy–Piedmont to abandon Louis XIV. The English fleet pressed on to operate more generally in Spain, initially supporting the capture of Gibraltar in 1704, which prompted French attempts to regain the position. The major naval battle of the war, that of Malaga on 13 August 1704, reflected the importance of the western Mediterranean to both powers. An Anglo-Dutch fleet of 53 ships under Rooke protected Gibraltar from a 50-strong French fleet under the Count of Toulouse. This battle is not well remembered in the annals of British naval triumphs, which in part reflects the Nelsonian tariff of judgment in terms of ships sunk or captured. At Malaga, no ships were sunk, casualties were heavy on both sides, and several English ships ran out of ammunition. A gap in the allied line between van and centre closed before the French could exploit it. Toulouse wanted to renew the battle the next day, but his council of war forced him to return to Toulon. Although tactically indecisive, the battle was important operationally and strategically as it helped limit major French fleet actions in the region. This was the last large battle in the war, and the allied fleet thereafter held the initiative in the Mediterranean while the French navy languished.[8]

The Bourbons attacked Gibraltar by land as well as sea, initially mounting a siege in 1704 when the English squadron under Vice-Admiral Sir John Leake, instructed to cover Gibraltar, was taking on supplies in Lisbon, a frequent need that had operational consequences. Returning to Gibraltar that October, Leake surprised a smaller French squadron whose ships were all captured or destroyed. Leake then returned to Lisbon to convoy a fleet of troop transports for Gibraltar, arriving back in March 1705 when, again, a small French squadron was captured or destroyed. The remainder of the French fleet, then sheltering from a storm in Malaga Roads, retreated to Toulon before Leake could catch them. These naval blows led the French to abandon the siege.

This pattern of naval activity then expanded, prefiguring the role the British were later to attempt in the Mediterranean. In 1705, the English fleet supported the successful siege of Barcelona, landing cannon and seamen. The following year, the arrival of the fleet led the French to abandon their siege of Barcelona: the French fleet did not stay to fight the English. In 1706, the fleet, under Leake, went on to assist in the capture of Alicante, Majorca and Ibiza.

These operations posed significant support requirements and over a very sustained period. Again, this prefigured later commitments. As was always the case in such circumstances, there was a learning curve, but also the need to relearn the relevant skills. In part, this reflected the degree to which naval requirements did not operate in a vacuum but in an interactive context in which there were other active components, notably the nature of the opposition in terms of composition, capability, goals and moves, and the support obtainable by both ships from allies and neutrals. In turn, the last could be affected by English naval activity. Thus, in 1701, one of the under secretaries, John Ellis, wrote to Stepney, expressing interest in the possibility of using Adriatic ports made available by Austria, adding,

> I cannot but join with you in thinking that nothing considerable can be done in that part of the world, without a force at sea in the Mediterranean, to procure respect from the princes and inhabitants of the coast, and to set them at liberty from the apprehension and constraints they lie under from the marine power of France and Spain in conjunction.[9]

Allies posed many issues from the strategic to the tactical and logistical. These issues also focused on the question of respective priorities. Thus, in 1705, when the English considered naval operations against Toulon, Victor Amadeus II of Savoy–Piedmont instead pressed for their help in regaining his principal port, Nice, from the French. Two years later, George Byng reported from Lisbon that he could not spare ships to look out for French vessels carrying silver from Veracruz in Mexico expected at Cadiz, 'the King of Spain [the Habsburg candidate] pressing for a squadron to come into the Mediterranean to cover that coast from the attempts of the enemy'.[10] The problems of alliance strategy were certainly present in the 1707 campaign against Toulon, when the Austrians instead sent many of their crack army units against Naples. At the same time, Anglo-Dutch naval dominance of the western basin of the Mediterranean prevented the Toulon fleet from deploying its strength in Italian waters as it had done in the 1640s and 1670s.

In the event, in 1707, the Anglo-Dutch fleet under Admiral Sir Cloudesley Shovell supported the Austro-Savoyard invading forces in their crossing of the River Var and later covered their retreat. In terms of a knock-out blow, Toulon, though besieged as well as bombarded by the Anglo-Dutch fleet, which also provided cannon, supplies and medical care for the besiegers, was not captured. If it had been, it would have proved a vulnerable target to French counterattack, as in 1793. The situation was more promising in naval terms, however, for the French destroyed most of their warships in the harbour, and thus further improved the English naval position. In addition, unlike after Trafalgar, the French, from 1709, built no more ships of the line during the war. In 1709, Byng, then off Toulon, reported that the French 'only design small squadrons for their convoys and cruisers'.[11] Moreover, revictualling at sea was successfully employed in 1705 to support the English fleet maintaining a close watch on Brest in order to prevent its fleet from sailing to the Mediterranean.[12]

The position of the English in the Mediterranean in the latter period of the War of the Spanish Succession prefigured that in later conflicts, and notably in the contrast between the ability to have only a limited impact on France itself, and greater success elsewhere. In the first case, there was a repetition of earlier English failures elsewhere in France. In part in an effort to help the Camisards, Huguenot (French Protestant) rebels in the Cevennes, major raids were launched on the Provençal coast in 1707 and 1710, the second leading to the capture of the port of Cette. However, this capture was only temporary, as the build-up of French forces thwarted any English attempt to exploit their initial success. More significantly, the fleet, under Leake, took part in the capture of Minorca and Sardinia in 1708, thus lessening the chance that Spain, with French assistance, would be able to deploy forces forward and seek to recapture Naples. The British fleet was also thereby provided with more bases in the Mediterranean.

The fleet held the allied war effort together, transporting troops, money, supplies and dispatches, although it, in turn, required a major effort in supply and maintenance. Returning from the Mediterranean in 1709, Admiral Sir John Jennings reported, 'If I was rightly informed, neither Sir George Byng could propose to have put to sea with the fleet, nor the army in Catalonia have kept the field without the stores, provisions, and corn I carried with me.'[13] Admirals were confident of naval capability. In 1709, Jennings proposed an attack on Cadiz using ships to batter the forts, estimating he would need 24 of the line, of which eight would protect the landing. He abandoned the idea in light of reports of stronger defences, but nonetheless pressed for blockade:

Could I make up eight sail I should gladly put to sea, to endeavour to block up Cadiz, which at this time is under very great necessity for want of provisions in the place, where we are advised that oppression and ill usage with extreme want has made the inhabitants ripe for a revolt.[14]

Noting that there were 19 British warships of 50 guns or more in the Mediterranean, Byng added that he could not 'at present think we can hurt [the French] more than by alarming their coasts, hindering their commerce, and endeavouring to intercept their ships with corn from the Levant and Barbary'; while John Norris was sent to the Sound to stop the movement of Baltic grain to France.[15] Confidence was not only voiced by admirals. Charles, 4th Earl of Manchester, envoy in Venice, reported in 1708 that 'ten of our men of war would take all their galleys and ships'.[16] There were also frequent attacks on French commerce. Indeed, largely thanks to the British, nearly 1,800 ships and barges insured at Marseilles were captured. Conversely,

French privateering bases, especially St Malo and Dunkirk, proved difficult to contain, and the British suffered greatly from privateering. In the Mediterranean, as elsewhere, the British devoted much time to protecting trade from the often damaging raids of privateers.

Only limited success against Toulon in 1707 was, albeit very differently, matched by failure against Québec in 1711. This was due in part to poor navigation in the St Lawrence River, which led to troopships running aground with serious losses. The key element lacking, however, was any French ability to check the advancing fleet. Moreover, however successful, it was primarily a case of the English launching attacks. This was not a matter of 'command of the sea', for such a concept had only limited meaning let alone practicality, but rather of naval capability. By 1713, Britain was clearly able to demonstrate this.

The trend in relative naval power was apparent in the Caribbean where the French, although they could now use Havana as a base, did not take the initiative as much as the British in fleet terms, although they conducted damaging raids on British islands as well as launching devastating privateering attacks. In 1708, a strong Spanish treasure fleet was attacked off Cartagena by Rear-Admiral Charles Wager. The flagship, the *San José*, blew up after its powder magazine was hit and most of its crew were killed. Despite damage to the *Expedition*, Wager pushed on to bombard another ship into surrender. The captains of two other warships were court-martialled for failing to help Wager sufficiently. Most of the Spanish treasure went down with the *San José*, which became allegedly the world's richest shipwreck, with cargo valued in 2018 at about £15 billion; but Wager still gained considerable spoils.

Britain's role in the Anglo-Dutch alliance became more pronounced because the Dutch navy was affected by a lack of willingness to invest sufficiently in it or to reform its institutions,[17] and also in part by an understandable focus on the army fighting against the French in neighbouring Belgium. As a result, the Dutch played a smaller role against France at sea in the 1700s than had been envisaged in the 1689 agreement with Britain.[18] This was to continue to be the case thereafter, for example in 1718–20.

Meanwhile, there was a change in ship design and specification that increased operational and tactical effectiveness. Improvements in seaworthiness, stemming in part from the abandonment of earlier top-heavy and clumsy designs, increased the capability of warships, both to take part in all-weather blockades and to operate across the oceans. The emphasis on maximizing firepower in the late seventeenth century led to a development of three-decker capability. In the early eighteenth century, the focus instead was on stability, range and versatility, which led to a move towards two-deckers, while three-deckers became important anew for the bruising confrontations of the late eighteenth century. At the same time, there were different emphases in procurement and usage, including the extent to which ships were expected to cruise to the Mediterranean and to take part in line-of-battle artillery exchange.[19]

After the War

The terms of the Peace of Utrecht in 1713 were a reflection of British naval success, with the gains made, notably Gibraltar, Minorca and Nova Scotia, those obtained by amphibious operations secured by naval strength and superiority; as demonstrated most clearly by success in 1704–5 in defence of the new gain of Gibraltar. In 1713, the navy carried Britain's ally Victor Amadeus II of Savoy–Piedmont and 6,000 of his troops to take possession of Sicily. An age of British naval hegemony had begun, with the moves of other powers in the Mediterranean seen as depending in part on the navy.[20] At the same time, the terms reflected the potential naval threat from France, with provisions for the degradation of Dunkirk which had served as a major privateering base, as well, in 1708, as the base for an invasion attempt. Yet, as Captain Chadwick in the *Ferret* observed in 1715, Brest now only held a weak force.[21]

The war also saw the navy more politically grounded than in the 1690s when the politics of naval command had been highly divisive. In the War of the Spanish Succession, the government, which was dominated until 1710 by a shifting coalition of Whigs and some Tories, backed the navy alongside the army, while the opposition Tories endorsed a 'blue water' policy of only limited interventionism on the Continent, a stance they pushed to the fore when in power from 1710. Whatever the limitations of the policy, 'blue water' gained traction as a result of the costs of land campaigns and their failure to deliver a verdict, and it became closely identified with the Tories. Jonathan Swift's *The Conduct of the Allies* (1711) proved a crucial expression of Tory views on strategy, and notably of the support for navalism:

> It was the kingdom's misfortune that the sea was not the Duke of Marlborough's element, otherwise the whole force of the war would infallibly have been bestowed there, infinitely to the advantage of his country, which would then have gone hand in hand with his own.[22]

Swift also argued that victory and profit could both have been obtained by a maritime strategy:

> And what a noble field of honour and profit had we before us, wherein to employ the best of our strength, which,

against all the maxims of British policy, we suffered to lie wholly neglected? I have sometimes wondered how it came to pass, that the style of Maritime Powers, by which our allies, in a sort of contemptuous manner, usually couple us with the Dutch, did never put us in mind of the sea; and while some politicians were showing us the way to Spain by Flanders, others by Savoy or Naples, that the West Indies should never come into their heads. With half the charge we have been at, we might have maintained our original quota of forty thousand men in Flanders, and at the same time, by our fleets and naval forces have so distressed the Spaniards in the North and South Seas of America as to prevent any returns of money from thence, except in our own bottoms. This is what best became us to do as a Maritime Power. This, with any common-degree of success, would soon have compelled France to the necessities of a peace, and Spain to acknowledge the Archduke.[23]

Navalism, however, could have appeared vulnerable because 1714 brought the death of Queen Anne, the end of the Tory ministry, and the accession, as George I, of the Elector of Hanover. He was committed to Continental power politics and had a background of army service, as well as being more closely linked to the Whigs. The army also was to the fore in opposing the Jacobite rising of 1715–16 in Scotland and northern England. Moreover, British naval power could not prevent the Jacobite claimant 'James III and VII' landing at Peterhead in December 1715.

At the same time, the strength of the navy was a factor providing security against the possibility of France intervening on James' behalf, and both the navy and the lack of such intervention contributed to a sense of Jacobite isolation and failure. Earlier in 1708, at a time of war, the navy's presence off Dunkirk had not prevented a French attempt in the face of a pursuing British squadron to sail out and attempt a pro-Jacobite invasion of Scotland, but the swift abandoning of this attempt showed that it was not possible to stage a landing in the face of a superior fleet.[24]

Throughout, the role of the navy in defence of the Revolution Settlement and Protestantism was clear, and very directly so in the case of Jacobitism. Indeed, beating for volunteers in Tower Street, London in 1715, Captain Pearse of the *Phoenix* heard some of the mob cry, 'God Damn King George', and a drumhead was kicked in.[25] The place of naval issues in the realm of political debate was entirely appropriate as it was this political world that defined the navy's role, the challenges it had to face, and the resources that would be placed at its disposal. Only in part because its limitations were not always apparent to commentators, it is easy to appreciate why the navy proved a far easier political 'sell' than the army. That, however, also posed problems in terms of the discussion of its capability, problems that were to be repeatedly apparent over the following two decades.

3

YEARS OF LIMITED HOSTILITIES
1717–38

The capture of ten Spanish ships of the line and the destruction of four more off Cape Passaro in south-east Sicily on 11 August 1718 was a dramatic display of British strength and success against a poorly deployed Spanish fleet. Having defeated the Spanish rear, the pursuing British attacked the Spanish centre, suppressing it by superior broadsides which led to successive surrenders, many after long fights. The British followed up by successfully attacking other Spanish ships off Sicily.[1]

This victory, achieved while the two powers were not yet at war, led to euphoria about naval capabilities, the *Weekly Journal* on 18 October declaring, 'This single action renders the King of Great Britain as much master of the Mediterranean as he has always been acknowledged to be sovereign over the British seas.' A pamphlet added, 'The late action ... is become the entertainment of most conversations.'[2] Indeed, however implausibly, Sir David Dalrymple MP, the Lord Advocate for Scotland, was not alone in comparing the Spanish fleet to the Armada of 1588.[3] A sense of power and longevity was also seen in Josiah Burchett's *A Complete History of the most remarkable transactions at sea* (1720). Dedicated to Sir Charles Wager, the First Lord of the Admiralty, Thomas Lediard's *The Naval History of England* (1735) presented the revival of naval success after the Glorious Revolution as looking back to a national tradition and emphasised the importance of naval power for British trade.

The years between the War of the Spanish Succession (1702–13) and the outbreak of the War of Jenkins' Ear in 1739 do not tend to receive much attention in popular naval history, but they were years of significant achievement not only in campaigning but also in developing the institutional scale and sophistication of the navy.[4] In part, these years receive insufficient coverage because Britain's prime naval opponent was Spain, not France; but Spain, although much weaker than Britain at sea, remained a power, both in Europe and in the Atlantic. The relative ease of British victory off Cape Passaro in 1718, far more dramatic in its results than any since Barfleur in 1692, and, albeit on a smaller scale, more complete, showed that the challenge posed by Spain can be underestimated.

Indeed, the year after Cape Passaro, Spain was able to mount a diversionary attack on Britain, designed in part as a classic instance of the indirect use of naval power for strategic goals, to prevent the British from thwarting Spain in the Mediterranean. This attack revealed how little Passaro deterred further Spanish naval action, a point of which the British government was well aware. The rising of 1719 showed the vulnerability of Britain to invasion, as the main expeditionary force, under the leading Jacobite general, James, 2nd Duke of Ormonde, sailed from Cadiz with 5,000 troops in March. Cardinal Giulio Alberoni, the leading Spanish minister, wrote to Ormonde,

In order to prevent a landing, it is necessary to have ships and they take time to arm ... when we talked of the project we have laid a great stress on speedy expedition but we cannot command the winds ... the British coast is too long to defend effectively.[5]

It was difficult to find fleets once they had moved away from shore, which led to uncertainty and rumours once the fleet had sailed for Britain,[6] a situation that was to be repeated on subsequent occasions. In the event, a violent storm off Cape Finisterre at the end of March damaged and dispersed the fleet. Sent separately, three frigates and five transports carried about 400 Spanish troops to Stornoway in the Western Isles, and they were then able to move to the mainland. However, their main magazine was destroyed by British frigates, an instance of the degree to which the penetration of the landmass by sea lochs, and the narrow nature of the coastal strip, made western Scotland especially vulnerable to naval power. The Spanish troops and their Jacobite supporters were subsequently defeated on land by a larger British force.

From 1715, the British also sent warships to the Baltic in order to prevent Charles XII of Sweden from intervening on behalf of the Jacobites, as well as to advance Hanoverian interests against Sweden's European empire, and to protect British trade from Swedish attack.[7] Sweden had North Sea access from Gothenburg and was a significant and longstanding second-level naval power. In late 1716, the Swedish envoy argued that Swedish forces should invade Britain in March when easterly winds were prevalent, permitting an invasion across the North Sea.[8] This sense of vulnerability was well ventilated among the British public.[9]

In turn, political divisions within Britain led to governmental concern about likely opposition attacks on the dispatch of warships to the Baltic, largely on the basis of these supporting Hanoverian expansionism. In the event, in 1718, the parliamentary assault came on the fleet sent to the Mediterranean. This was a challenge the ministry easily survived, but the political sensitivity of a Mediterranean deployment was apparent from the outset. In October 1714, Charles, 2nd Viscount Townshend wrote in his own hand to James, Viscount Stanhope, his fellow Secretary of State, a letter the latter kept in his private papers, reporting that George had told Townshend

> that he cannot agree to what you propose in relation to his obliging himself in conjunction with the States to keep constantly a squadron of ships in the Mediterranean for the defence of the Emperor's territories in Italy, for though His Majesty may think it necessary at this present juncture to keep a squadron in those parts, yet to oblige himself to be constantly and in all events at this charge, is not, in his Majesty's opinion reasonable, besides such an engagement cannot be entered into without the consent of the States General [Dutch Parliament] where there is no secret, and as soon as it was known it would be looked upon here as a direct step towards a new war.[10]

In turn, Stanhope sought an enhancement of naval capability as an aspect of a war and peace strategy, writing in 1718,

> I hope measures are taken in England for a squadron's wintering in the Mediterranean, upon that will depend everything, for at the same time, that we should leave a door open to negotiate with Spain ... I think it absolutely necessary to redouble our vigour upon their hanging back, and so let them see, that what shall not be compassed by fair means will certainly be done by force.[11]

John Norris was the key commander in the Baltic, his instructions both reflecting changing British priorities and giving them form. Thus, in August 1718, he was ordered to prevent any possible joint action by Sweden and Russia by stopping their warships in the Sound so as to block any invasion of Britain.[12] In 1718, Norris, who like many military figures was an MP, joined the Board of Admiralty. When Sweden and Britain changed policy and became allies after the death of Charles XII in November 1718, Norris became commander of a fleet sent to the Baltic to protect Sweden from Russian attack and there was rising concern in the British press and among ministers about Russian naval plans. In June 1719, the Baltic squadron comprised 13 ships carrying 698 cannon.[13]

The problems of 1719–20 in the Baltic were a far cry from 1690–2 when France had effectively challenged Britain for control of the Channel, or in 1718 and 1719 when there were Spanish fleets at sea and plans to invade Britain. The British were confident that their navy would prevent Russia from dominating the Baltic and attacking Britain's allies, but that did not mean that it would be possible to force Peter the Great (r. 1682–1725) to restore his conquests from Sweden. Naval advice clashed with political hopes and pressure to act against the Russian fleet, leading James Craggs, a Secretary of State, to complain unfairly: 'Sir John Norris has in a manner protested against it [naval action]. He has now 17 ships of the line … he comes out like all your blusterers a very very little man.' Soon after Craggs revealed links to the parliamentary position: 'If Sir John Norris would be pleased to take the Czar and destroy his fleet, I should not much fear his allies next session.'[14]

In a common theme, deployment at a distance led to concern about the number of ships available for home service, while the difficult navigational conditions off eastern Sweden, the ability of the Russian fleet to take shelter in Reval (Tallinn), and the complexities of arranging co-operation with the Swedes all posed difficulties. In practice, the blusterers were politicians who had convinced themselves that British strength would lead to assured outcomes. The British faced the same problems they were to confront in the Baltic during the Ochakov Crisis of 1791 and again during the Crimean War (1854–6), namely the difficulty of intimidating Russia; or, for that matter, achieving victory if the Russians were unwilling to come out of harbour and fight.

In part, the same was true of the Mediterranean where the headline news of British victory did not match the problems faced in translating success into foreign policy achievements. In 1718, it was hoped that the threat of naval action would persuade Spain not to invade Sicily, but Philip V (r. 1700–46) called Britain's bluff. His 36,000-strong invasion force landed well before Passaro, and it captured Palermo, the capital of Sicily, nearly a month before the battle, while the latter did not ensure the defeat of this force. Indeed, the 1718–20 crisis in the Mediterranean revealed what was to come to the fore on subsequent occasions, for example in 1756 when Minorca was invaded by French forces, namely that, without a permanent squadron in the Mediterranean, British intervention would come too late.

It was easier to try to direct an expedition closer to home, especially one across the Channel. In late 1719, a force ordered to attack Corunna, a key naval base in the infrastructure of any Spanish invasion, was delayed by the weather.[15] As the target appeared too strong, Vigo was attacked instead, with the shipping and stores there destroyed. The contrast with the Spanish expedition to Scotland earlier in the year was readily apparent, while success at Vigo repeated that of the British attack on a Spanish treasure fleet there in 1702, and thus demonstrated a continual military potency.

In the Mediterranean in particular, but more generally in power politics, foreign policy commitments, especially treaty obligations, required naval force, indeed often were dependent on it. However, the capabilities of naval preparation and warfare did not permit as rapid a mobilisation and deployment of naval forces as politicians envisaged. This contrast may have owed something to the extent to which key governmental figures, notably George I (r. 1714–27) and George II (r. 1727–60), but also Secretaries of State, particularly James, 1st Earl Stanhope (1716–17, 1718–21) and William, 1st Earl of Harrington (1730–42, 1744–46), had served in armies, whereas there were no naval equivalents. However, the Lords of the Admiralty provided cohesion to the direction of the navy, while the consistent presence of the First Lord on the Council helped ensure that it could act as an effective vehicle for discussing strategy, as in June 1739 when war with Spain was planned.[16]

Furthermore, a successful naval strategy that matched political expectations required Mediterranean bases and their ancillary workers capable of serving to base, repair and victual a major squadron. Neither Gibraltar nor Minorca was suitable. Gibraltar was small, some of the bay was exposed to Spanish artillery fire, and there was a serious shortage of fresh water. Minorca was vulnerable to attacks by the Toulon squadron. Both Gibraltar and Minorca were dependent for grain on precarious supplies from the Barbary States of Morocco, Algiers and Tunis. Britain thus lacked the well-positioned, well-supported naval base in the Mediterranean that its foreign policy required.

Yet, this assessment must be more than a matter of the limitations that Britain could and should have overcome, because that approach presupposes that Britain was the key player able to control the situation if it brought the right force to it. In practice, that approach underplayed both the limitations of naval power and, linked to that but separate from it, the extent of independent agency that existed for other powers, not only opponents but also neutrals and allies. These factors were to be seen repeatedly. There was also an awareness of the multiple commitments facing British naval power. Thus, the Lords Justices governing Britain for George I (then in Hanover) reported in 1719,

> Should all the ships we have go to the Baltic, it is certain we cannot get any more ships to defend our own coast or insult that of Spain, which is esteemed to be the same thing, and we shall be open to any attempts of the Cardinal's without a possibility of defending ourselves, who I am afraid is but too exactly and too constantly informed of our circumstances and conditions.[17]

Nevertheless, in British diplomatic, political and popular circles, there was still considerable faith in naval power. The politics of naval bombardment were frequently advanced. In 1717–18, the bombardment of the Papal port of Civitavecchia was considered in order to ensure the release of the Earl of Peterborough who was held captive by the Papacy. The idea recurred in 1727 when 'James III and VIII' was sheltered in the Papal city of Avignon. The use of naval force against Lisbon, Genoa and Livorno was also proposed in the 1720s, and the idea was to recur. In 1725, Townshend suggested that, if Spain seized the goods of British merchants, a squadron of 15 or 16 warships and of bomb vessels be sent to demand satisfaction or take reprisals, and there was also discussion of the dispatch of a squadron to the Caribbean.[18] Townshend saw a squadron in the Mediterranean as a way to threaten links between Austria and Spain, as well as the Austrian position in Sicily.[19] In 1726, there were rumours of plans for a possible British bombardment of Cadiz, Malaga, Alicante,

Barcelona or Naples, none of which, in the event, occurred. It proved easier to get naval estimates through Parliament than army ones, as in November 1724 when the opposition forced a division on the army estimates but not the naval.

In practice, alongside fears about pro-Jacobite invasions, not least from France at the time of the Atterbury Plot of 1722, British governments were cautious about naval deployments, in part because they were more concerned to retain the navy for use as a factor in great-power confrontations. This entailed protecting Britain from the threat of invasion as in 1726–7, 1731 and 1733. There was also the need to protect Britain's allies, notably Sweden from the risk of Russian attack in 1726–7 and Portugal from that of Spanish attack in 1735–7, although in 1723, in part concerned about costs, Sir Robert Walpole, First Lord of the Treasury from 1721 to 1742, opposed the dispatch of a fleet to the Baltic on behalf of Denmark against Russian intimidation.[20]

There was also the use of the navy for more clearly offensive purposes, notably blockading the Spanish treasure fleet in Porto Bello in 1726, and thus hitting the liquidity of Britain's then opponents Spain and its allies Austria and Russia. In an instance of the carefully calibrated use of intimidatory pressure, the commander, Vice-Admiral Francis Hosier, was instructed to inform the Spanish authorities that there would only be an attack if the treasure fleet sailed or British goods were seized. Indeed, Hosier's blockade helped British trade in the region, ensuring that silver was brought back to Britain,[21] although Hosier and many of the sailors died from disease. The galleons were not able to sail until 1728. The *British Journal* of 24 May 1729 claimed that, thanks to Hosier's operations in the Caribbean, Spanish credit had collapsed, adding,

> This produced an alteration in that court; they signed and ratified Preliminaries; they raised the siege of Gibraltar; they

opened the Congress of Soissons, and restored effects of a very great value to the South Sea Company. None of which would have been done if our fleets had not blocked up their harbours and detained their galleons in the West Indies.

There was also consideration of attacks on Cadiz in 1727 and 1729, and on Austrian possessions in Italy, notably in 1726 and 1730. A Council of War held on *Torbay* near Cadiz in May 1727 discussed whether it was practicable to attack the Spanish squadron in Cadiz Bay, deciding

> that if it practicable with any number of ships to go into the Bay of Cadiz on such an enterprise, it is not with the number we have, the fortifications of that place having been much augmented ... and did not think fit to go on with any ships within the Bay of Cadiz till the troops had landed and taken possession of the fortifications on both sides, and especially since the safety of Gibraltar depends in some measure on this squadron continuing master in these areas, which an evil accident in such an attempt, that very probably might happen, would prevent.

The council stressed the need to prevent a junction of the Cadiz and Ferrol squadrons, adding 'that the best relief this squadron can give to Gibraltar is to continue masters of the sea'.[22]

In turn, recognising the weakness of Austria as a naval power, the Jacobites pressed, from late 1724, for an invasion from Ostend in the Austrian Netherlands (Belgium) in fishing boats and small ships, winning surprise by avoiding a major naval expedition.[23] Indeed, France suggested to its ally Britain that the latter send warships into the Channel 'to prevent any sudden attempt that might be made in favour of the Pretender'.[24] The threat of a sudden invasion attempt could not be dismissed lightly, and the British ministry was well aware of the danger posed by Ostend.[25]

British naval activity in European waters in 1725–7 acted to deter ideas of invasion, for example by making Spain, from which an invasion was discussed, fear an attack on its Biscayan ports. Townshend wrote with considerable satisfaction,

> Whilst one of his [George I's] fleets is preserving the tranquility of the North [Baltic] against the ambitious and pernicious designs of the Czarina, and another is keeping the Spanish treasure in the West Indies and thereby preventing the Emperor and Spain from disturbing the peace of the South, the very report of a third squadron going out has caused such alarm and confusion in the Austrian Netherlands, and has put Spain, in the low and miserable condition of their finances, to the trouble and expense of marching their troops and fortifying their seaport towns.[26]

Indeed, Britain's decision not to intervene in 1733–5 in the War of Polish Succession (in fact a war involving much of Europe) was of value to Spain which, partly as a result, proved far more successful in its Italian campaigning and power politics than in 1707 or 1718–20.

Separately, the period saw a successful British attack on piracy. This made investment less risky and more profitable, which increased the significance of the navy, and thus of the state, as the guarantor of trade; a situation that was different from that for much of the seventeenth century when both the navy and the state were less powerful. Peace in 1713 had brought fewer opportunities for naval employment and for privateering, which encouraged a turn to piracy. The threat from buccaneering to trade helped lead the navy to try to stamp it out, while peace freed the navy for that role, which led to wide-ranging operations not only in the Caribbean but also more generally, for example off West Africa and North America. Edward Thatch, a British-born privateer during the recent war, turned to piracy and took the name 'Blackbeard', basing himself in the Bahamas, only to be killed off the North Carolina coast in 1718. Operations against piracy, which required speedy ships commanded by resourceful captains, were but part of a more widespread process that included not only the effective application of intelligence but also a policy combination between colonies and London predicated on a commercial imperial Atlantic. This combination was as significant as naval operations.[27]

In international terms, however, the political aspect was challenging for Britain. First, foreign powers were not necessarily fearful of British naval power, indeed far from it, and British commentators were well aware of this; Britain's allies could press against the use of naval action, as France successfully did in 1727.[28] Secondly, there was the domestic political audience. The threat of action could be played up, but there could also be derision, as in 1729, about the costs and lack of action of fleets that did not sail or sailed but did not fight. Naval armaments were very expensive. Indeed, in 1718 and 1726, they deterred the Dutch from providing the naval assistance that was sought. There was an appreciation of the frictions of naval power, as with *Mist's Weekly Journal*, an opposition newspaper which, in the issue of 4 June 1726, referred to the need in wartime to return to Britain for supplies and to repair ships if there was damage from storms or conflict, but added,

> Would not our trade thereby be rendered very precarious? Or would it be possible to execute any great design which

required the attendance of a fleet? And would not the naval power of England in a short time look much less to be feared than it does at present, to the princes of Europe?

Governmental views were divided. Writing himself, rather than using a secretary, Horatio Walpole pressed Newcastle in 1726:

I do not love expensive alarms, without real action; nor can I see the great use of Sir John Jennings appearing off of Naples; it will make a noise, but when he comes home again without doing anything, I do not think the laugh will be on our side either in England, or in Europe ... the sending a fleet into the Mediterranean to prevent an [Austrian] encampment in Silesia will appear ridiculous, if that fleet shall do nothing more.[29]

From off Cadiz in 1727, Sir Charles Wager pointed out that having sufficient warships both to protect merchantmen from privateers and to hinder the trade of opponents was costly.[30] At the same time, it was essential to prepare the fleet for 'any action that may be rendered necessary',[31] as in 1729 in response to Spanish naval preparations, when a fleet was ordered to assemble off Spithead. This episode exposed the uncertainty of naval intelligence, in this case about both Spanish readiness and intentions, and a lack of agreement among ministers. The Lords of the Council, left in charge in London when George II went to Hanover, worried that Spain intended to dupe Britain in negotiations. Concerned at the prospect of having nothing definite to present to Parliament, they argued that Spain should be persuaded to settle by the delivery of an ultimatum supported by the threat of naval action including possibly a blockade and an attack on Puerto Rico.[32] In contrast, Townshend, the Secretary of State with George, regarding this course as hasty and likely to anger Britain's allies, delayed matters by persuading the Dutch to add a squadron to the Spithead fleet, thereby also ensuring problems in obtaining co-operation.[33]

The decision not to use the fleet for conflict kept its potential strength a mystery, and therefore enhanced its value as a diplomatic counter internationally and a political one domestically. This also meant that unrealistic public estimations of naval capacity could be maintained, notably talk of seizing the Spanish empire. In practice, the naval campaign of 1726 had showed the vulnerability of British forces in the Caribbean to disease, as was again to be brutally demonstrated in 1741. Had a broader assault been attempted in the 1720s then there would almost certainly have been failure, which might well have compromised public attitudes toward 'blue water' operations. Instead, there remained a contrast between public attitudes – not least, as in *The Pacifick Fleet: A New Ballad* (1729), cynicism about a failure to act – and ministerial scepticism and disinclination to accept the risks and costs of naval warfare.

This contrast continued in the 1730s, a period in which the international naval situation completely changed. The cause – the collapse of the Anglo-French alliance in 1731 – was an abrupt demonstration of the dependence of naval capability on political circumstances. The immediate response was a war panic at the prospect of a French invasion on behalf of the Jacobites. The medium term was repeated concern about not only French intentions but also a Franco-Spanish alignment. One such alignment was achieved in 1733, only to be sundered in late 1735 and not to resume until the early 1740s. The longer-term consequence was a realisation that naval superiority and strategic security would require war with France if, as seemed likely, there was no reconciliation.

British foreign policy was dependent on alliances and the state of international relations, but this was not taken sufficiently into account in the public sphere when discussing naval strategy. The French alliance had permitted the dramatic display of naval capability in 1726, and was the basis for the planned naval attacks on Spain in 1727 and 1729. The ending of the alliance forced a recasting of naval strategy, one that opposition polemicists felt able to deride because they did not grasp the diplomatic bases of naval capability. The pressure from public assumptions was acute, Under Secretary Charles Delafaye observing in 1729,

> ... the protection of trade and navigation ... were you to hear how people talk in all manner of places and conversations you would conclude there is scarce a man in England but would sell the coat off his back to venture his life to be revenged of the Spaniards.[34]

There were repeated changes in international relations. The collapse of the Anglo-French entente in 1731, caused substantially by the unilateral negotiation of an Anglo-Austrian alliance, and the transformation of entente into hostility, were followed in 1733 by French success in reversing Britain's achievement of 1731, when it had won Spain's accession to the new alliance with Austria. This both changed the strategic and political situation, and posed the problems over British security and foreign policy that a generation of politicians had become accustomed to fudging and tackling with rhetoric. From 1731 onwards, fear of war with France increased and rumours of imminent hostilities circulated frequently. By 1733, the French envoy, Chavigny, could suggest to Paris a French invasion of Britain in support of the Jacobites. At that stage, the level of British preparedness was low, with very few warships ready to sail other than a small squadron designed to intimidate the Barbary States, the privateers of North Africa.

Indeed, a sustained and serious mid-century crisis began in 1731 and lasted until the decisive defeat of the French navy at Lagos and Quiberon Bay scotched French invasion plans in 1759. It was a period of acute vulnerability and of serious fears about potential invasion on a number of occasions, including 1744–6 and 1756–7. Ministries also suffered domestically as a result of adverse wartime developments, which played a significant role in the fall of the Walpole and Newcastle ministries in 1742 and 1756 respectively. Although it would be mistaken to suggest that the entire period was characterised by anxiety, and this was certainly not true of 1749–52, nevertheless the adverse international situation limited domestic political opposition, to an extent that was true of neither the 1720s nor the 1760s.

As a consequence, the 1730s saw much espionage as well as defensive naval mobilisations and deployments. These were primarily designed against apparent French threats. In 1731, Newcastle ordered the dispatch of spies to the naval bases at Toulon, Brest, Port and Rochefort, while the sloop *Ferret* reported on the Channel ports.[35] Three years later, he wrote to the Lord Lieutenant of Ireland,

> The French are getting a fleet together at Brest, and taking up transport ships along their coast, in order most probably to send them to Danzig [Gdansk] … However, common prudence requires, in our present situation, that the necessary precautions should be taken, to make us secure against the worst that can possibly happen.[36]

In the event, the French sailed for Danzig where, once landed, their force was to be defeated by the Russians.

In practice, navies were far more limited as invasion forces than was to be the case in the Age of Steam, let alone that of air power. It was far harder to damage shore emplacements than warships. Moreover, although bomb vessels could provide indirect fire, naval support was gravely limited if troops were drawn up beyond the landing beach. For any invasion, the French would be dependent on flat-bottomed boats, a substantial number of which would be required to land any appreciable force. It was difficult to transport cavalry in such vessels, and, until a port was taken, any invasion force could anticipate being short of cavalry, a crucial element in the fast-moving campaign that would be required if France was to exploit a landing. The Channel did not offer an environment comparable to the Baltic, where shallow waters saw the manoeuvrable galley provide the sole efficient assault craft of the age.

Nevertheless, there had been successful invasions, including of Britain in 1688 and of Sardinia in 1717, and the best forms of deterrence for Britain were, first, naval strength, as in 1692, and, even more, France having other concerns. An anonymous memorandum in the French archives suggested that, on 1 January 1734, of the 124 ships of the British navy, 90 were in a good state.[37] The early spring saw a rapid preparation of many of these ships for sea. This success was a matter of politics and administration, albeit with a sceptical Chavigny suggesting that the British were so short of sailors that it would affect their operational effectiveness.[38] The British were indeed short of sailors,[39] but their situation was helped by a concentration in home waters with no equivalent to the Mediterranean and Caribbean commitments seen in 1744–5, whereas France and Spain were busy fighting Austria in Italy, and France also doing so on the Rhine. Philip, 4th Earl of Chesterfield told the Lords in March 1734,

> We are certainly in greater danger of being suddenly invaded by our neighbours, when they have their troops unemployed and quartered upon the sea coasts, than when all their troops are marched many hundred miles from their sea coast, and employed against another enemy; and surely they may more suddenly fit out a fleet proper for that purpose, when none of their ships of war are employed elsewhere, than when they were obliged to keep many of them in seas very far distant from this island.[40]

In turn, the French government feared British attacks, and notably so in 1731.[41]

The multiplicity of factors that affected the consideration of naval operations was shown in 1734 when Thomas Robinson explained to the Austrian Chancellor 'what could hinder His Majesty to send a fleet into the Mediterranean ... I said the very preservation of the nation, while a French fleet lay already equipped over against our coast: and when he said we had ships enough,' Robinson stressed the shortage of sailors.[42] In turn, Harrington, Newcastle's counterpart as Secretary of State, emphasised that the admirals had been consulted:

> All our best seamen are clear in their opinion that the sending ships thither at this season would have been of infinite prejudice to the fleet itself, and of no manner of advantage to the Emperor for these must not only have come too late to prevent any embarkation from Spain, but have been rendered unfit for service afterwards by the damages they would suffer by wintering in those seas.[43]

The selective quotation of sources so that only one particular factor is emphasised is of limited value.

In addition, there was British concern about Spanish preparations, concern that looked back to the new role taken by the Spanish fleet from the late 1710s. Thus, in the late summer of 1727, reports that the Spaniards intended to mount a pro-Jacobite invasion of the British Isles led to the strengthening of the fleet in Spanish waters with ships from Norris's fleet, which was recalled from the Baltic. Townshend ordered Wager to destroy the Spanish fleet if it should sail toward Britain and to seize the Spanish treasure ships.[44] In the end, Spain backed down, largely due to France supporting Britain. In 1732, rumours about the destination of a Spanish expedition that, in the event, went to Oran led to British governmental surveillance.

In 1735, there was far more acute British concern about a possible Spanish invasion of Britain's ally and key commercial partner, Portugal, a connection essential to Britain's maritime and naval position in the Atlantic. This led to a major deployment to the Tagus, with 30 ships under Norris anchoring there on 9 June. This would have prevented any Spanish naval attack on Lisbon, as had successfully happened in 1580, but could have done nothing against any overland assault. That was blocked instead by the collapse of the Franco-Spanish alliance in 1735 and by Spain's concern about Italian developments. The notion, however, of displaced concentration was seen in 'a scrub report whispered about by the low Jacobites here, that we are to be invaded by 10,000 men and many ships from Brest, now our fleet is gone to the coast of Portugal'.[45] In practice, France had other commitments.

The fleet, which remained until April 1737, encouraged an optimistic tone in British discussion of naval power. Thus, the *London Daily Post* of 23 August 1735 claimed that, after visiting the fleet, John V of Portugal had remarked that 'it was no wonder the English fleet reigned masters of the sea'. Another London paper, the *Hyp-Doctor* of 23 December 1735, declared, 'Spain is awed by Sir John Norris.'

Moreover, press reports were reprinted in provincial papers. This was part of the more general process in which sea power helped in the construction of national identity, while that identity in turn helped ensure that there was a commitment to sea power.[46] The *Newcastle Courant* of 7 June 1735 reported,

> The fleet under his [Norris's] command consists of 25 ships of the line, is mounted with 1756 guns and manned with 12,455 seamen, all chosen men, and who, it is said, desire nothing more than an opportunity to revenge themselves on the Spaniards for the vile treatment some have met with from them.

While to a degree formulaic and an aspect of the sense of sailors as true patriots, this reference to their views captured the extent to which these could play a role in morale.

In the event, conflict did not begin until 1739, and then with Spain and not France. In the meanwhile, the 1730s were significant for showing how being the world's foremost naval power did not prevent serious problems of strategic and operational assessment and assumptions. Indeed, the outbreak of war in 1739 was linked to the earlier failure to translate British naval superiority to Spanish acquiescence as had been anticipated by Britain, with a diplomat named Robert Trevor writing to a counterpart, 'You ought not to be surprised at these pacific appearances when I tell you England has at present 107 ships of war ... actually in commission.'[47] However, other factors and issues proved more significant, and the British were unsuccessful in intimidating Spain by sending a fleet under Admiral Nicholas Haddock to Spanish waters. A war that did not develop as hoped was the consequence. Moreover, although France was neutral in 1739, it was still a threat. That year, Walpole told the Attorney General that the French squadron at Brest might not act against Britain but 'could not be neglected. That, by this means, they will put us to the expense of a war and the running away with our trade.'[48] The outcome was far from predictable.

4

WAR: FROM PROBLEMS TO VICTORY
1739–48

All difficulties that could be apprehended in Parliament will by this be removed, the pride of France a little humbled, and I hope our allies so far encouraged, that your Royal Highness will find them willing and able to exert themselves for their own safety and support.[1]

The Second Battle of Cape Finisterre left the easily excitable Thomas, Duke of Newcastle, Secretary of State for the Southern Department, in no doubt in writing to William, Duke of Cumberland, British Captain General commanding in the Low Countries against French invaders. Fought on 14 October 1747, the battle saw the talented and energetic Rear-Admiral Edward Hawke win a brilliant naval action. Concerned to re-open their trade with their colonies and those of Spain in the Caribbean, and thus help both the economy and public finances, France sent eight ships of the line from the Brest fleet, under the Marquis de l'Etenduère, to protect a large convoy. They were intercepted by Hawke with fourteen more lightly gunned ships of the line.

Hawke followed the tactics used by George Anson in the First Battle of Cape Finisterre on 3 May 1747, closing with the French as fast as possible and thereafter fighting a series of individual actions. This was done by Hawke in order to beat the French quickly and enable pursuit of the convoy with the loot that offered, not least in prize money. The French fought well, but the British benefited from having taken the initiative, and from abandoning the rigid tactics of a line in order to direct heavier concentrations of gunfire on individual French ships. Six of the French ships were forced to surrender and the French also lost 4,000 sailors, a crucial limitation of their maritime strength. As a consequence of these battles, in the first of which the French had four ships of the line, four frigates, six merchantmen, and 3,000 sailors captured, the French fleet could no longer escort major convoys bound for French colonies, which destroyed the logic of the French imperial system, while the victory also made French action on behalf of the Jacobites less plausible.

These victories, however, came late in the war with France and there was no comparable victory in that with Spain which had begun earlier. The war, nevertheless, for Britain saw a recovery from the failures of its early stages and an ability to take the initiative with a good chance of success. This was accompanied by the turn to a new generation of dynamic naval leaders, notably Anson and Hawke. Moreover, with growing political support, there was also administrative sophistication and infrastructure.[2]

In the meanwhile, there had been repeated concern about the naval situation, and naval activity had not matched British hopes, either governmental or popular. There had been successes, especially the naval role in the capture of Porto Bello from Spain and Louisbourg from France, in 1739 and 1745 respectively, but there had also been much disappointment.

In particular, the only major naval battle prior to the two in 1747, that off Toulon on 11 February 1744, had been indecisive, leading to political controversy within Britain; although it was not easy to decide how best to engage a Franco-Spanish fleet when Britain was not yet formally at war with France, even if their armies had fought at Dettingen in modern-day Germany in June 1743. The British pressed the Spaniards hard off Toulon, while the French exchanged fire at a range from which they could not inflict much damage. The British rear, under Vice-Admiral Richard Lestock, did not engage due to Lestock's determination to keep the line. Lestock and the commander, Admiral Thomas Matthews, had had disagreements and Lestock was wilfully unhelpful, but Matthews had given contradictory instructions. The net effect was that the British squandered their numerical advantage. The French were able to come to the assistance of the Spaniards, the British withdrew, and when they returned to pursue the Bourbon fleet on 12 February, the latter was able to retire with the loss of only one already badly damaged ship, the Spanish *Poder*; the damage it suffered was a testimony to the impact of British broadsides. Matthews was cashiered.[3]

The battle discredited the 80-gun ships of the line: lacking the firepower of 90- and 100-gun three-deckers, they appeared undergunned for their limited seaworthiness, and this threw critical light on the state of naval force-structure, and notably on the Admiralty's care of the fleet during the previous peacetime years. Indeed, Matthews offered a warning about the conventional practice of judging naval effectiveness in terms of gun numbers:

> Nor can ships which cannot make use of their lower tiers of guns, though they mount ninety and eighty guns, do the duty expected (by the ignorant) against the 74 and 64 gun ships of France who can fire theirs ... there is no proportion of metal, our lightly gunned ships having but twelve and six pounders, whereas some of the enemy's seventy-four gun ships

carry forty, eighteen and nine pounders ... the rest of them, thirty two, eighteen and nine; their ships of sixty four guns have twenty four, eighteen and nine pounds, which makes even them better men of war than our eighty gun ships that cannot make use of their lower tiers which they will ever seldom be able to do... I have now but two ships of ninety and three of eighty guns, that can make use of their lower tiers of guns, if it blows a cap full of wind ... I do not judge that I have a sufficient force to withstand the conjunct [French and Spanish] fleet when joined by the squadron from Brest.[4]

Nevertheless, the Franco-Spanish fleet in the Mediterranean did not subsequently mount a comparable challenge.

The location of battles provides one indication of naval confrontation and sensitivity, but it is not a complete guide. Indeed, the dispatch of British warships to the Caribbean, more than in earlier wars, and conflict there from 1739 were both significant, although they involved amphibious operations, notably against Porto-Bello (1739) and Cartagena (1741), rather than fleet action. Whereas in 1718–20 Spanish operations in the Mediterranean had provided an obvious and vulnerable focus for British naval action, this option was closed until 1741 when Spain attacked Austria. Unlike in the War of the Spanish Succession, there was no civil war in Spain in which to intervene with amphibious attacks, and Portugal was not an ally. Strategy yet again was defined primarily in terms of geopolitical options and political priorities.[5]

François Fagel, in effect the Dutch foreign minister, observed in August 1739, at the start of the war,

Many people here are of Admiral Wager's opinion, that the English fleets will not be able to do great harm to Spain in

Europe, the Spaniards having but little navigation in these parts. In the West Indies indeed there is more likelihood of getting the advantage over them, but this is also liable to much hazard and may raise the jealousy of the French and other nations.[6]

Success at Porto-Bello that November was to be much celebrated in Britain. Becalmed alongside one of the three defending forts, the six British ships of the line silenced it with a heavy fire, before landing sailors and marines who, climbing through the embrasures, took the surrender of the poorly defended position, which was followed by that of the other forts and town. The four small Spanish warships there were captured or destroyed.

In 1740, Newcastle informed Edward Vernon, the naval commander in the Caribbean,

> The King [George II] does not think it proper to prescribe any particular service to be undertaken by you, but leaves it entirely to your discretion to act against the Spaniards, in such manner, and in such places, as shall appear to you best to answer the ends proposed by His Majesty's orders to you, which were to distress and annoy the Spaniards in the most effectual manner, by taking their ships, and possessing yourself of such of their places and settlements as you should think practicable to attempt.

Vernon was told that he would be kept 'greatly superior to any force that either is, or may be sent by the Spaniards to the West Indies'.[7] In the event, the dispatch of a French fleet to the Caribbean that year to prevent hostile British acts served as a limiting factor, even deterrent, and in political as well as military terms. Jean-Frédéric, Count of Maurepas, the active

Minister of the Marine from 1723 until 1749, was seen by the critical Marquis d'Argenson as seeking war at sea in order to further the navy's position.[8] 'The truth is,' noted Newcastle, 'the French preparations do necessarily oblige us to keep such a fleet here as is in other respects useless and might be much more advantageously employed elsewhere.'[9] Thus, by keeping a fleet there, the French limited what the British could hope to achieve against Spain. At any rate, Vernon and his colleagues did not win the expected successes against Spanish possessions both in the Caribbean and more widely. Thus, the naval blockade of St Augustine, Florida by five frigates and three sloops failed to prevent the arrival of Spanish supply ships that breached the siege.

There was a lack of naval battles with France and Spain not only in the Caribbean but also off North America and in the Indian Ocean, where, most notably in 1748, Boscawen relieved Fort St David near Cuddalore in India having decided that Mauritius would be too difficult to attack. This lack in part reflected caution. In June 1746, the British fleet in the Indian Ocean, seven warships under Commodore Edward Peyton, broke off an action with a larger French force under Mahé de la Bourdonnais off Negapatam and withdrew, leading to the French being able to capture Madras (Chennai) and Peyton being sent home under arrest. Moreover, his successor, Thomas Griffin, was court-martialled for negligence for failing to engage a French squadron.

The situation in home waters was even more challenging, as their security was the prime necessity in protection against invasion. This requirement ensured that Vernon received very different instructions in 1741 when the return to European waters of the Brest fleet led to an instruction to 'send home forthwith' many of his ships.[10] Sixteen of the line were indeed sent back, which enabled an increase in the British presence in home waters.

Unlike in the previous war between the two powers, and despite British concerns, there was no Spanish invasion attempt, which denied the British the opportunity for a major naval clash and therefore possible victory. However, anxieties about such an attempt reflected a sense of vulnerability. After reports in 1739 about a planned invasion from Corunna, William, 3rd Duke of Devonshire, the Lord Lieutenant of Ireland, expressed concern:

> The west side of Ireland is the properest for the Spaniards if they attempt to make a descent on Ireland because they may sail wide of the Channel in the Western Ocean and so avoid the British fleets.[11]

However, no such invasion was intended, as Spanish priorities focused instead on the Mediterranean and American waters.

In order to strike at the heart of British power, France, in contrast, planned an invasion of southern England on behalf of the Jacobites in 1744. The plan was to send the Brest fleet to cruise off the Isle of Wight in order to prevent the British from leaving Spithead or, if they did, to engage them in the western Channel. Five of the Brest ships were to sail to Dunkirk and escort Maurice of Saxe's invasion force of 10,000 troops to the Thames. Dudley Ryder, the Attorney General, recorded,

> News came that the Brest squadron of 21 sails were come within the chop of the Channel, and seemed to be sailing northwards and had 30,000 spare arms. Intelligence also came that the Pretender's eldest was gone from Italy and suspected he was gone to Brest.[12]

Sir James Lowther MP commented on the difficulty the Admiralty was encountering in raising seamen. François de Bussy, a senior

French official in British pay, revealed the entire invasion plan in return for £2,000, leading Britain to request 6,000 Dutch troops and Dutch warships to convoy the transports to the Thames. Moreover, British troops were summoned from Ireland and the Austrian Netherlands, and units already in southern England marched toward the coast, including Lord John Sackville, who had recently faced the anger of his parents for making Lady Frances Leveson Gower pregnant and had been obliged to marry her two days after she gave birth.

The two fleets came in sight of each other off Dungeness and anchored, preparing for battle next day, but a strong gale that night drove most of the British ships out to sea, while, with fewer losses, the smaller French fleet was able to run before the wind to Brest. The same storm hit Dunkirk, destroying many transports, as did a second storm there.

Many, for example Colonel Cuthbert Ellison, saw the hand of Providence at work in the end of the invasion.[13] Concluding that the danger was past, the Admiralty ordered Norris to send several ships to reinforce Mathews in the Mediterranean, much to the anger of Norris, although the strategic rationale was clear, namely the fear that the Toulon fleet might join its Brest counterpart.

The vulnerability to invasion indicated in 1744 was to be underlined in 1745–6 when the Jacobite rising under Bonnie Prince Charlie led anew to French preparations for invasion. The prince's arrival in Scottish waters on a frigate, the *Doutelle*, reflected the failure of blockade. Embarking at St Nazaire, and initially delayed by contrary winds at the mouth of the Loire, the *Doutelle* rendezvoused with the 64-gunner *Elisabeth*, which was carrying arms and 700 troops, only for the two ships to encounter *Lion*, a British 60-gunner, 100 miles west of the Lizard. A four-hour action left the *Lion* a dismasted wreck with 45 killed and 107 wounded out of a complement of 400, but the badly damaged *Elisabeth* was in no state to continue the voyage and only the *Doutelle*, which had not taken part, sailed on for Scotland.

The British government was soon concerned about reports of Spanish naval preparations, as well as French ones at Brest and Dunkirk, and some warships were recalled from the Mediterranean. The failure to defeat the French fleet in 1744 therefore had serious consequences in 1745. Unlike in 1715, when there had been the previous large Jacobite rising, France was at war with Britain, its navy was in a strong state, it was undefeated, and it had a series of possible invasion bases. Brest dominated the Channel in the event of westerly winds, while, separately, significant French forces were kept near the frontier with the Austrian Netherlands (Belgium), and these could be readily moved to the Channel ports. For these reasons, France could enjoy the initiative, although sufficient transports were far harder to assemble, and winds were at the beck and call of no state. This strategic situation put a premium for Britain on the destruction of the French navy, lending military relevance to the sense of humiliation and dissatisfaction that followed failures to achieve this end.

The nature of naval operations in the age of sail, however, was not conducive to forcing an unwilling opponent to fight in a position of inferiority. Moreover, there was an awareness that defensive naval deployments could only achieve so much. Despite much British activity, there was no sense of any command of the sea. In August 1745, Newcastle's private secretary, Andrew Stone, observed, 'We hope we shall soon have a pretty strong squadron in the Channel. But I know too well, the great delays and uncertainties that service is liable to, to depend very much on it.'[14] Indeed, the navy proved unable to capture most of the French ships sent to Scotland in 1745–6 and the ministry was concerned about the French troops that might be sent there.[15]

However, no supporting French invasion was launched due to weather, British naval deterrence and other French concerns, but the British navy had to prepare for the risk.

Over 1,000 French troops arrived in north-east Scotland from Dunkirk in late November 1745. The north-eastern coast appeared to be the logistical key to the Highlands, for the British occupation of the ports of Montrose, Stonehaven and Aberdeen would make it harder for the French to send reinforcements and supplies. Thus, as with the French seizure in 1745 of Ostend, a possible invasion base, ports were a key strategic asset.

Fog could help the Jacobites. In March 1746, they gathered together a fishing fleet at Findhorn and, in a thick fog that provided cover from the warships in the Moray Firth blockading Inverness, the Jacobites landed on the north side of the Dornoch Firth, dispersing the local pro-Hanoverian Highlanders.

On the whole, however, the British blockade struck home. Thus, in the spring of 1746, the French sent 396,000 écus in three ships in response to requests from Bonnie Prince Charlie for financial help. *L'Emeraude* reached Aberdeen just before Cumberland's army and had to leave the port without landing its cargo. The French squadron returned safely to Dunkirk with the exception of *L'Aventurier*, which landed some supplies at Peterhead before being forced to run aground by three British warships. The ship was burned, the crew escaped and Bonnie Prince Charlie was provided with a small sum of money, but this was no substitute for the 1,000 troops the squadron had carried. Sent later, the small and fast *Prince Charles* carried money and arms. Intercepted in the Pentland Firth, the ship sought to escape by sailing into shallow waters near Tongue, only to be seriously damaged by the *Sheerness*'s cannon. The crew landed with the money but was captured.

In December 1745, Newcastle instructed Cumberland to limit his pursuit of Bonnie Prince Charlie in order to deal with a potential invasion.[16] Indeed, in October, the French government had decided to prepare an invasion and also promised assistance to the Jacobites. Thanks to their excellent naval intelligence, not least the network of agents organised by Richard Wolters,[17] the British were aware of preparations but Vernon felt that he had insufficient warships, clashing with the Secretary of the Admiralty, who argued that he had more than the French. Vernon drew attention to the winds, not least that they might help the Brest fleet cover an invasion:

> With a southerly wind it is very practicable for them to get by unobserved by our ships to the westward, and, if the others were ready to sail with them when they had slipped by, and they too strong for me, they might execute their descent before their Lordships could have time to provide a preventive remedy against it ... My particular promise ... is to watch the coasts of Kent and Sussex, and therefore, if with a southerly wind we should put to sea, without certain advice of the enemy being at sea, and which way they were gone, if it comes to overblow for one night southerly we must be driven to the northward by it, and, of course, leave the coasts of Sussex and Kent exposed to the enemy's attempts, which their constant spies the smugglers would not fail to give them advice of.[18]

Generally less alarmist, the British ministry relied on the navy, and not only to thwart invasion but also to align with the army. In particular, as troops returned from Flanders, they were sent to the Midlands or Newcastle, rather than to the south coast.

The sense that a Jacobite triumph would have transformed the naval situation was struck by Henry Fielding, a pro-government writer, in the *True Patriot* of 7 January 1746 when he offered a dream of what would have happened had the Jacobites been successful. This included, 25 days after the proclamation of the Stuart king:

> This day the Gazette informs us, that Portsmouth, Berwick and Plymouth were delivered into the hands of French commissaries, as cautionary towns [held to ensure compliance with agreements]; and also twenty ships of the line, with their guns and rigging, pursuant to treaty.

In the event, Bonnie Prince Charlie was totally defeated that April at Culloden.

For the remainder of the War of the Austrian Succession, Britain's naval strength contrasted with the dismal progress of the campaigns on land in the Low Countries. In consequence, and in marked contrast to the situation during the War of the Spanish Succession, there was the hope that naval success could compensate for Continental defeats. This expectation placed a new politico-strategic responsibility on the navy, for it was now required to obtain trans-oceanic advantages, an obligation that necessitated a mastery of home and European waters that would permit the dispatch of major naval forces to support such expeditions. In part, these ideas were of long standing, reflecting a traditional optimistic public assessment of naval capability, but the political need for them can be traced to 1745. It was then that the hopes of defeating France on the Continent that had been so marked in 1742–3, especially after victory at Dettingen, were replaced by the realisation that it would be difficult to stop the French triumphing by land.

Meanwhile, a new front had opened up. In 1744, French warships based in Louisbourg on Cape Breton Island had attacked the British in Nova Scotia, but in 1745, New England militia struck back, supported by the small British Leeward Islands squadron under Commodore Peter Warren. His support testified to a capacity to ensure an integrated character for the British military effort in the New World, with warships rotated between the Caribbean in the winter and North American waters in the summer. In turn, this capacity created an expectation that such integration would be the case, yet also, as was to be seen in the failure of the Yorktown campaign of 1781, serious problems of command and control. While the French were attacked on land, Warren blockaded the harbour of Louisbourg, hitting the food available to the defenders, before forcing his way into it in June.

This capture was rapidly followed by the idea of its exchange for French gains in the Austrian Netherlands, which placed an immediate strategic task on the navy, that of the defence of Cape Breton, which meant keeping French warships in their harbours or defeating them if they sailed out. Newcastle complained about this in 1746:

> Should they go to North America, and make conquests there, we shall lose the means of making peace or war. For when once they have either retaken Cape Breton or taken Newfoundland or Nova Scotia (which will be the equivalent for it) we have no longer in our hands the means of purchasing peace of France; or of inducing this nation to carry on the war.[19]

Until the two British victories off Cape Finisterre in 1747, the British lacked a clear margin of naval superiority, and the French fleet in Brest retained the strategic initiative because the port could not be blockaded effectively. Indeed, in the summer of 1746, the Brest fleet, which the British had feared would mount a landing on the west coast of Scotland, was able to sail for Nova Scotia. Moreover, with the French fleet as yet undefeated, the British chose not to attack Canada in 1746 but rather to assault the French port of Lorient, the base of the *Compagnie des Indes*, which ensured that the British were able to maintain their fleet in European waters. Luckily for the British, the squadron of ten ships of the line sent by France to Nova Scotia was wrecked by bad weather, disease (typhus and typhoid) and inadequate supplies, returning to France with heavy losses. This illustrated the difficulties of amphibious operations, and the particular organisational and operational problems facing the French in mounting trans-Atlantic expeditions.

From 1747, Britain kept more warships to the west of the Channel, and this was very important in ensuring success in the two battles off Cape Finisterre, as well as in hitting French overseas trade. Naval victories in turn affected – or, as significantly, were believed to affect – the political situation, Lady Elizabeth Yorke, the daughter of Lord Chancellor Hardwicke, observing of the Second Battle of Cape Finisterre:

> Admiral Hawke has likewise disappointed the designs of more than the French, it having been intended by the opposition to begin their attack this session by falling upon the Admiralty; now it is thought that this scheme must be defeated, since after the late repeated successes, such an attempt cannot be very popular or successful.[20]

Victories in 1747 transformed the earlier invasion threats of 1744–6 which recurred in January 1747,[21] and the danger in

1746 that Cape Breton would be lost, into a completely different political, strategic and diplomatic situation. Thus, Vice-Admiral Sir Peter Warren, the captor of Louisbourg in 1745, was second-in-command at the First Battle of Cape Finisterre, after which the Freedom of the City of London was conferred on him and he was elected MP for the prestigious seat of Westminster. The angry debates over naval policy that had characterised the earlier years of the war ended, so that John, 4th Earl of Sandwich, who had played a role at the Admiralty from 1744, could write in November 1747, 'It is plain that our fleet has honour and great support.'[22] This was an important pledge to naval commanders of continued backing.

The British were also a major presence in the Mediterranean, not least as an assistance to Austria and the kingdom of Sardinia (Savoy–Piedmont). The threat of naval action affected French, Neapolitan and Spanish moves, especially the movement of reinforcements and supplies to Spanish units in Italy, particularly in 1742 when the Franco-Spanish fleet intended to convoy a new force of Spanish troops to Italy was blockaded in Toulon. Indeed, assumptions were such that the failure by Admiral Haddock in 1741 to prevent Spanish forces designed to attack Austrian Italy from landing there was falsely attributed to a neutrality agreement on behalf of Hanover. Spain's European empire was dependent on maritime links. In 1743, the Genoese envoy in Paris told the French foreign minister that the British were absolute masters of the Mediterranean and that it was necessary to bear their affronts in silence, while John, Lord Carteret, the chief minister, informed the House of Lords that, thanks to the British fleet, the Spanish army in Italy would be destroyed due to lack of food.[23]

Moreover, Britain benefited from allies with ports and armies of their own. It was far easier for squadrons to operate in support of independently based land forces, rather than to have to transport and supply them, as with amphibious assaults on the French coast. British success, in practice, was mixed. When, in 1745, the British tried to bombard Genoa, they found the Genoese galleys deployed in line, sufficiently close in to remain protected by coastal artillery, but far enough out to prevent the British bombarding the city. After firing about 60 shots, the British left.

Meanwhile, the British pressure on French and Spanish trade was worldwide. There were important prestige captures, notably the treasure-laden Manila galleon *Neustra Señora de Covadonga* off the Philippines in 1743 by Anson, who was then on a circumnavigation of the world; a large French merchantman in the Straits of Malacca in 1744; and three large French East Indiamen in the East Indies in January 1745. Later that year, Warren captured several large French merchantmen at Louisbourg by keeping the French flag flying after the base had been seized and waiting for them to sail in. In the winter of 1747–8, George Pocock captured 30 merchantmen in the West Indies. Warships based at English Harbour, Antigua, a naval base developed from 1728, successfully blockaded Martinique in 1746–7.

Aside from naval action, there was also privateering, which entailed a fusion of patriotism and profit. Indeed, more than 6,600 prizes were taken in 1702–83, nearly half by privateers. The prospect of privateering profits was important in mobilizing support for imperial warfare within the colonial mercantile community.

British forces, however, were not always successful. Thus, in August 1746 a squadron under Captain Cornelius Mitchell confronted a weaker French squadron escorting a convoy through the Windward Passage, but Mitchell abjectly failed to press the attack, for which he was court-martialled and cashiered. On the whole, however, it was the British who were on the attack. At the very close of the war, in October 1748, Rear-Admiral Charles Knowles, the commander-in-chief on the Jamaica Station, seeking a Spanish treasure fleet, engaged the Spanish Havana squadron off the city. The British fleet lacked cohesion, and the failure of some of the ships to engage led to recriminations and court martials. However, the Spanish warships proved less effective in close action. One of them was captured, the flagship was driven ashore, and another ship was badly damaged.

At the same time, it was necessary to protect British trade from privateers. This was a problem throughout, and particularly in British waters and in the Caribbean. Moreover, it led to complaints about naval priorities including from those who were politically prominent such as Sir James Lowther MP, the developer of the port of Whitehaven in Cumbria on the Irish Sea, who wrote thither from London in 1739:

> We shall hardly be pestered for some time with Spanish privateers to meddle with our ships going to Dublin and Drogheda, but there is a vast clamour in the City [of London], that we have no men of war out on the south and south west parts of Ireland, and in the mouth of the Channel, to hinder our merchant ships from falling into the hands of the Spaniards. They are very angry also that so many thousand men are kept on board of 90, 80 and 70 gun ships in harbour to no manner of purpose, which if put on board ships of 50, 40 30 and 20 guns would destroy all the ships the Spaniards could fit out against us. They say the men of war that are out do nothing but look after a few rich prizes expected from the West Indies and let the Spaniards ruin all our trade in the Streights [of Gibraltar].[24]

There was also damage in the Americas. Thus, the agricultural staple trades of the Carolinas, the Chesapeake and, especially, the Caribbean all sustained serious losses, and in 1747–8 French and Spanish privateers off the Delaware Capes brought Philadelphia's trade to a halt.

The warfare of the period overwhelmingly displayed the significance of naval power to British strategic capability. This was so obvious that it was almost taken for granted, but continual effort was necessary to maintain this effectiveness, in terms of preparing, deploying and sustaining warships and the related manpower and infrastructure. A classic instance was the deployment of British forces on the Continent from 1742 against France, the ability to supply and reinforce them, and, in 1745, to bring them back in the face of Jacobite rebellion, only to return them thereafter. The British were also able to take for granted the movement of troops and supplies up the east coast of Britain. Another aspect of the dominance of the North Sea was the assertive British role in support of the imposition of Orangist control in the key Dutch provinces of Holland and Zealand in 1747 in order to further the war with France. In this instance, George II was happy to maintain a squadron in Dutch waters even against the advice of the Admiralty.

The continued significance of political circumstances for naval strategy and operations were shown in the discussions in 1746 about an amphibious operation against Canada. Hopes were high for imperial expansion, with John, 4th Duke of Bedford, the politically powerful First Lord of the Admiralty from 1744 to 1748, the leading advocate, and William Pitt the Elder a supporter. This campaign, to which the Cabinet agreed in April, was the return from Newcastle to the 'New Allies' group of politicians, notably Bedford and John, 4th Earl of Sandwich, who effectively acted as Bedford's deputy and succeeded him as First Lord, for their support for a continuation of the war on the Continent, as such an operation helped the British effort seem 'national'. However, the continued Jacobite threat and the experience of failure in 1711 (Quebec) and 1741 (Cartagena) induced caution about launching the Canada plan. This was officially attributed to adverse winds, but in practice arose from the as yet undefeated nature of the French fleet, the continued French capacity to mount invasions, and the need to win the political support of Newcastle, who was committed to the war on the Continent.[25]

It was not only strategic and operational problems that were magnified with deployment at a distance, and these deployments were significant in scale in the Caribbean, the Mediterranean, and, to a lesser extent, the Indian Ocean. Yet, the war showed that the navy could be an effective fighting force and administrative body in all three. In the Caribbean, failures, notably at Cartagena in 1741, were not primarily due to administrative deficiencies, although victualling created problems. The difficulties of operating in the Caribbean were not new, but the size of the forces were, and therefore the quantity of supplies required. Separately, the Admiralty's failure to keep the fleet in the Caribbean adequately manned was a reflection of the degree to which it had not yet solved the problem of manning in general, a problem that was considerably exacerbated by the effects of disease. More positively, the Sick and Hurt Board supplied all the medicines it was asked to, the Admiralty consented to the building of a new hospital, and the sick were given the best treatment that the medical knowledge of the day allowed, the last a problem as the nature of the diseases was not understood. In addition, although convoying was poorly organised, the men on the spot were generally able to make good the administrative deficiencies that were revealed. British warships in the Caribbean could fulfil their operational role, and that was the decisive test of a naval administration.[26]

The improvement of naval bases in Jamaica and Antigua provided the relevant infrastructure. The facilities for refitting and repair provided by such bases were important to sustaining naval strength, which was a difficult task, not least as a consequence of the natural decay of what were organic working parts. The longevity of a typical ship of the line was about 12 to 17 years, longevity defined as the time between launch and the need for at least middling repair. In turn, a complex combination of factors, beginning first with the cutting of the timber, its storage, the mode of construction, weather conditions, the service of the ship, notably in terms of water temperatures and storm pressure, and its care while in reserve, determined the longevity of a ship and the amount of repair that it was likely to need.

The demands of the war also put pressure on naval manning, not least as there was no permanent force of naval personnel. Instead, the permanent navy consisted of ships and officers, with relatively few sailors. The formation of a reserve of seamen was proposed without result. The Register Act of 1696, which provided for a voluntary register of seamen, proved unworkable and was repealed in 1710, and subsequent proposals for legislative action met resistance. As a result, naval efficiency was measured in the ability to create fighting teams for existing ships once mobilisation was ordered, and then to ensure their effectiveness for, and in, combat.

The enlistment of volunteers was important. In mid-century, landsmen, nearly all of whom were volunteers, made up almost one-third of the navy's wartime strength. However, the navy continued to be dependent on the press gang.[27] By law, this method of compulsory service through seizure applied only to professional seamen. Yet, the legal situation was both abused and arbitrary, and this was widely understood, not least affecting the protagonist in Tobias Smollett's popular novel *Roderick Random* (1749). Although not pressed, Smollett had served in the Caribbean on the Cartagena expedition of 1741. The press led to violence, bribery, legal disputes and much misery, and was one of the most dramatic impositions of the state on the population. In November 1747, in Boston while between assignments in the Caribbean, Rear-Admiral Charles Knowles caused the largest disturbance against British imperial authority in the American colonies in the generation before the contentious Stamp Act by pressing Massachusetts seamen.[28]

More seriously, the system was only partially successful.[29] On many occasions, naval preparations and operations were handicapped by a lack of sailors. Possibly, however, there was no better option, in the absence of any training structure for the navy, and given the difficulty of making recruitment attractive when length of service was until the end of the war, which was generally very distant. The government never seriously considered paying sailors more; unsurprisingly so, given the size of the navy, and in light of concern over naval expenditure. The Bourbon alternative – the French and Spanish registrations of potential sailors – was not obviously superior and, in practice, led to evasion and a shortage of sailors, the latter a major problem for the Bourbon fleets in the attrition of conflict with Britain.

Very differently, George II in 1743 had rejected an attempt by the Admiralty to increase the number of admirals to take note of changes in naval organisation and tasking since the time of Charles II. However, soon after, he proved willing to accept more than one flag officer of each rank, in addition to practices that made the retirement of elderly captains much easier, and thus created opportunities for younger, more energetic counterparts.

The navy ended the war in 1748 in a rich glow of success, at the same time as the disadvantages of alliance politics and of a Continental military commitment were fully demonstrated by the French advance into the United Provinces (Netherlands). The economic dimension appeared particularly significant, Newcastle observing of the French in March that 'their trade is absolutely ruined'.[30] French exports became scarce, for example wine in Berlin, the trade with her colonies largely ceased, and France itself suffered due to difficulties in importing grain, with resulting increases in price.[31]

The political direction was clear. A renewed shift towards 'blue water' attitudes became more apparent from mid-century, and ambitious politicians rushed to identify themselves accordingly. In Parliament, William Pitt, newly admitted to the ministry, pressed the case for a strong navy in April 1746, declaring, 'I hope I shall never so far differ from myself, as not to say that our naval power is what we must expect peace with France from,' adding he had 'always thought it the policy of this nation to be as strong at sea as possible ... I wish the navy was greater.'[32] In 1747, Pitt, now Paymaster of the Forces, visited Portsmouth, touring the dockyard and the warships.

In turn, the opposition very much endorsed navalism. On 21 January 1748, the *Westminster Journal* declared, 'No peace can be sold to us which is not founded on the reduction, at least, of the French commerce, and the ruin of the naval power of France.' Velters Cornewall, a Tory MP recruited by Frederick, Prince of Wales for his bipartisan opposition movement, pressed the case in the Commons on 8 February for a naval war.[33]

The year 1748 saw the publication to great success of an account of Anson's circumnavigation, and, amid much support for navalism, there was a belief that a naval war was possible. This, however, was not viable. The War of the Austrian Succession had entailed serious disappointments in the conflict with Spain and shown that naval strength did not protect British interests in the Low Countries and Hanover. Indeed, there was a short-lived governmental interest in gaining Ostend, a possible invasion port, as part of the peace, or at least providing troops for its garrison, although this was not pursued.

In domestic political terms, navalism was a more acceptable strategy, not least because it lessened the need for co-operation with allies. As yet, however, not least due to the Hanoverian interests of George II, government remained committed to alliances on the Continent. This was to provide the key strategic context for post-war British foreign policy, but not for British maritime strategy in the next war. Indeed, the contrast helped exemplify the significance of politics for naval tasking. In 1748–56, it was reasonable to assume that peacetime alliances would ensure that war would require a powerful aid to the military operations and geopolitical alignments of allies, especially Austria and Sardinia (Savoy–Piedmont) in the western Mediterranean. Instead, Britain was to be allied to Prussia but not to provide such assistance in the Baltic, both due to a British concentration on France and because Britain did not go to war with Prussia's Baltic opponents, Russia and Sweden. Thus, yet again, the primacy of politics emerged clearly.

5

FROM PEACE TO TRIUMPH
1749–63

On 20 November 1759, rocky Quiberon Bay on the coast of Brittany saw the decisive mid-century battle, one that brought to an end French plans for an invasion of Britain. Trapped by Edward Hawke and 24 ships of the line while still off the Breton coast, 21 French ships of the line had taken refuge in the bay, counting on its shoaly waters and strong swell to deter British attack on a late November day as the light dimmed.

The British had scant knowledge of the bay's rocks and the wind was ferocious, but Hawke, showing decisiveness and an aggressive determination for battle, ordered his ships to 'form as they chased, that no time might be lost in the pursuit'. He boldly sailed into the bay's confined space, overhauled the French rear division, and forced a general close action. In this, the well-tried and experienced British ships, captains and crew won out over a French fleet that was unable to form a line. British seamanship and gunnery proved superior in this confused engagement and seven French ships of the line were captured, sunk or wrecked. French casualties were heavy, not least when the *Superbe* sank with the loss of its entire crew of 630 after two broadsides from Hawke's *Royal George*. The British lost about 400 dead, the French about 2,500. This was a classic instance of battle arising despite an attempt by one side to avoid it. In his report, Hawke observed,

> The commanders and companies of such as did come up with the rear of the French, on the 20th, behaved with the greatest intrepidity, and gave the strongest proof of a true British spirit ... When I consider the season of the year, the hard gales on the day of action, a flying enemy, the shortness of the day, and the coast we are on, I can boldly affirm, that all that could possibly be done, has been done.

Although the experience from the previous war was in practice very important for British operational capability, including the command skills and fighting style shown in 1747 and 1759, this outcome had scarcely seemed inevitable a decade earlier. Then, as a result of long war service, including damaging operations in the Caribbean, the battle fleet in good condition had been greatly reduced, and the dockyards could not cope with requirements for repair and replacement. The 1749 visitation of the royal dockyards revealed corruption and inefficiency.

Moreover, France and Spain were actively rebuilding their navies, unlike after the War of the Spanish Succession when France had failed to match Spain in so doing. Indeed, in 1746–55, the two powers launched more warships than Britain. In 1749, Vernon wrote to Sir Francis Dashwood, a fellow MP,

> I look on the fate of this country to be drawing to a speedy period whenever France shall attain to a superior maritime power to Britain ... whenever they think themselves so, the

first blow they will strike, will be to strip us of every one of our sugar colonies ... and the natural consequence of that will be that you will by the same blow, lose all your American colonies as to their dependence on Britain.[1]

Naval concerns were given more political weight by the role of naval officers in Parliament. Thus, in 1750, Rear-Admiral Charles Knowles MP pressed ministers on the vulnerability of Jamaica.[2] More generally, the Admiralty was part of the political system. Thus, Sandwich was removed as First Lord in June 1751 as part of the Pelhams (Newcastle and his brother Henry Pelham) getting John, 4th Duke of Bedford, Sandwich's key ally, out as Secretary of State. Sandwich was succeeded by Anson, a Pelham ally, who served until 1756 and then again from 1757 until 1762. Ministers were divided over policy as well as patronage. In a House of Lords debate on the subsidy treaty with the Elector of Saxony, Newcastle attacked the reliance only on 'our wooden walls'.[3] Writing to his closest ally, Philip, 1st Earl of Hardwicke, Newcastle tried to contextualise his navalism in 1749:

> The necessity of keeping up our marine to the height. It has been the doctrine I have preached ever since the peace [1748]. Without that, all alliances, all subsidies, will signify nothing: but a known, established, avowed superiority at sea will give weight to an inferior alliance upon the Continent; and, perhaps, upon the whole, put us near upon an equality; at least, so near, as that no attempt will be made upon us. But a naval force (though carried so high) unsupported with even the appearance of a force upon the Continent, will be of little use. It will provoke; but not effectively prevent. It may, indeed, be more easily carried here, as coinciding with the notion of the Tories; but it will end, in a few years, in

nothing. France will outdo us by sea, when they have nothing to fear by land; and they can have nothing to fear there, if we can have nothing to oppose them ... our marine should protect our alliances upon the Continent; and they, by diverting the expense of France, enable us to maintain our superiority at sea.[4]

However, other Whig politicians did not agree, not least those concerned about Nova Scotia, notably George, 2nd Earl of Halifax, the President of the Board of Trade from 1748 to 1761, Bedford and Sandwich.[5] In January 1751, Pitt, then Paymaster General, attacked the ministry's attempt to reduce the naval establishment from 10,000 to 8,000 sailors, voting with the opposition, only to lose. However, as ever, more was involved than just 'blue water' versus Continental. For example, Halifax pressed in 1751 for the stationing of two warships off Nova Scotia, a measure opposed by the Admiralty, in part on cost grounds.[6] There were also repeated attacks on the ministry for failing to prevent France from repairing Dunkirk, a dangerous privateering base and possible invasion support, the condition of which was regulated by treaty.

Yet, despite frequent opposition criticisms, the ministry sought to maintain a strong navy. In particular, it kept a close eye on French naval developments which were the prime target of British espionage. Furthermore, the problem of excessive demands on the British dockyards was overcome in the early 1750s, not least through using the private sector to build new ships. In the long term, improved infrastructure and better naval construction lessened the problems of cyclical decay.[7]

Prefiguring the situation in the 1790s, 1880s and 1930s, there was an awareness that British naval power might not be equal to all the demands that could be placed upon it, but, more positively, the situation was eased by differences between France and Spain. As a consequence, the government focused on the threat from France rather than from the two Bourbon powers and sought to placate Spain, deciding for example in 1750 not to send two frigates to explore the Pacific.

The most sensitive Anglo-French issue in North America for a while was Nova Scotia, which raised the issues of naval power, oceanic geopolitics and maritime trade, and in a way in which the interior of North America did not. In June 1753, Newcastle wrote to Joseph Yorke, the envoy in The Hague, 'The King will not suffer anything to be done that may tend to secure France, in case of war, against the superiority of His Majesty's fleet in any part of the world.'[8] This included India, where, in 1755, visiting *Kent*, Muhammad Ali Khan, Nawab of the Carnatic, a British ally, was reported 'greatly surprised at its size and number of guns'.[9] A foreign source for the views of an Indian ruler is perforce unreliable, but there is no direct information on the latter and, certainly, no Indian state had a comparable warship.

Naval strength was often mentioned in British diplomatic correspondence, Newcastle writing to Robert Keith, envoy in Vienna, in October 1753,

> His Majesty's fleet (though at a very great expense), is in a better condition, than it ever was known to be, in time of peace: and the great effect which the superiority of the King's navy the last war had towards obtaining the peace shows how necessary and effectual the keeping up that fleet may be for the preservation of it.[10]

In practice, the powers of central and eastern Europe (Austria, Prussia and Russia) were less impressed. Naval power proved of limited value in supporting British goals in its diplomacy, notably the Imperial Election Scheme (the plan for an agreed suggestion to the position of Holy Roman Empire) and the efforts to deter a Prussian attack on Hanover. When he succeeded to East Friesland in 1744, Frederick the Great (II) of Prussia acquired Emden, a port that gave far easier access to the Atlantic than the earlier Prussian ports on the Baltic, but he lacked the resources and interest to develop Prussia as a naval power and had a smaller navy than Prussia had had in the 1680s.

Alongside opposition politicians arguing for a focus on the navy, there were ministers concerned to maintain Britain's European allies. In 1749, told by a Savoy–Piedmont minister that he 'had heard we were going to put our naval force upon a better foot than ever, and that we intended for the future to place our chief strength in it', the envoy in Turin replied that the British government thought it could only preserve the balance of power in co-operation with allies.[11] Indeed, the response of the ministry to the drift in 1754–6 to war with France over North American differences was a determination to strengthen Britain's Continental alliances.

Far from there being any notion that maritime strength could bring conquests that would compensate for Continental vulnerability, the ministry based its diplomacy on the defence of Hanover, a goal very dear to the heart of George II. At the same time, there was public criticism of government policy, and this was given an historical context. A quasi-Athenian focus on naval strength appeared particularly attractive to Tories critical of Continental interventionism, such as the political writer John Shebbeare in 1755–7.[12] This argument became an aspect of a British tendency to see naval strength as particular to more liberal societies, which looked back to the presentation of Athens, Venice and the Dutch, finding prosperity, strength and progress in terms of maritime activity and naval power. This theme, which was to be developed by David Hume, was not only pursued by Tories but also by Whigs such as Sir John Barnard, a longstanding MP for the City of London, who told Newcastle in 1755 that he

> agreed to that in a national view it would be melancholy to see the French in possession of Flanders, Holland and that extended coast which might fall a sacrifice to their conquests; but as to Hanover he seemed to think that we might more easily procure a restitution of it by pushing our conquests at sea and in America than preserve it by endeavouring to support a Continental war.[13]

Newcastle himself, opposing the idea of ceding Gibraltar and Minorca as part of a peace settlement, had written to Sandwich in 1747:

> How shall you and I pass our time, who are known to be so much for the trade and commerce, and maritime interests of this country, if we give up, upon any account, our maritime possessions in the Mediterranean.[14]

Diplomacy as a prop to power, however, failed. Britain lost its alliance with Austria and Russia in 1756. Moreover, although the naval mobilisation performed relatively smoothly, the naval war with France initially went badly wrong. In 1755, Admiral Edward Boscawen was sent to block the dispatch of 3,650 French troop reinforcements to Canada,[15] a step that led the Marquis of Mirepoix, the French ambassador, to recommend his recall as well as to underline to the British the danger of a clash at sea.[16] The British, in contrast, argued that it was unsurprising, due to the outbreak of conflict already in the Ohio Country, that they should try to stop the dispatch of reinforcements.

Sailing from Spithead on 21 April, Boscawen was sent more ships when the size of the French squadron that had sailed from Brest on 3 May was ascertained. On 10 June, Boscawen attacked, capturing two ships and 800 troops, but, partly due to fog, most of the French sailed on to Canada. To the concern of British ministers,[17] there was no equivalent to the successful peacetime attack on a Spanish fleet off Sicily in 1718. Moreover, Boscawen's move proved crucial to the deterioration in relations between the two powers. In addition, the emphasis on naval manpower ensured that in 1755, before war was formally declared in 1756, the navy began seizing French vessels so that their fleet would lack sailors and there would be insufficient ships to mount an invasion.[18]

In 1756, there was an even more serious naval failure, one that was in part a matter of command flaws, but that also reflected a degree of caution on the part of the British government and Admiralty arising from French and Spanish naval strength. Anson focused on the threat of a French invasion, but this caution did not match public expectations. The British government had hoped, and the public expected, that the arrival in the Mediterranean of a fleet under Admiral John Byng would render French naval preparations at Toulon ineffective.[19] However, instead, the French moved quickly, landing troops on the nearby British Mediterranean island base of Minorca on 18 April. This expedition was a dramatic step which demonstrated the French ability to set the agenda. As a result of such a clearly hostile move, which lacked the ambivalence of developments in North America, war on France was declared on 17 May.

The French invasion was made more significant, in terms both of international relations and of British politics, by the abject failure of Byng to compensate for it by relieving the Minorca garrison besieged in Fort St Philip. Byng's fleet had sailed late and was short of sailors, while some of his ships were in poor repair. Indeed, in fairness to Byng, the abject failure was the culmination of a series of missteps that accompanied the growing crisis.[20] On 20 May, 30 miles off Minorca, Byng was unable to defeat a French fleet of comparable size. The British manoeuvred to take full advantage of the wind, while the French remained on the defensive. Contrary to the well-established rules of eighteenth-century naval warfare, the fleets were not parallel as they approached one another on the same tack. Instead, Byng was converging on Galissonière's fleet at an angle, so that the two vans were closer together than the two rears. This track allowed the French to concentrate their broadsides on Byng's van before the entire British line could come into action. One of these broadsides shot away the topmast of the *Intrepid*, causing it to stop, thereby threatening to entangle Byng's remaining ships. Instead of breaking his line and passing round the damaged ship to continue his attack, Byng chose to stop to dress the line of his fleet. As the rear of his force therefore attempted to sort itself out, it was beyond effective cannon range of the French and unable to influence the battle. There had been a failure to concert operations between the parts of Byng's force. The van, commanded by Rear-Admiral Temple West, had engaged the French at close quarters and was badly pummelled by heavy, raking French broadsides. By the time Byng had readied the rear of his fleet, West's force was mangled and the British fleet was in no condition to renew its attack.

That night, the fleets further separated. After refitting his ships, Byng conducted a council of war with his captains on 24 May. In light of its weakened state, the council was 'unanimously of the opinion that the fleet should immediately proceed to Gibraltar', the nearest British position. This was a decision that sealed the fate of the now deserted garrison on Minorca.

The political impact was greater because there had been earlier reports first of failure, and then of a victorious Byng relieving Minorca. William, Earl of Bath commented, 'One moment all the world is calling our admirals rascals and cowards, and then we are elated to the skies with a little false news, and our fleet it is said did their duty as they ought.'[21] The net effect was to generate not only a public storm in Britain, but also a collapse of confidence in, and on the part of, the ministry. As Newcastle had noted in 1755, 'Sea war, no continent, no subsidy [to foreign powers] is almost the universal language.'[22] What had been reasonable, and certainly defensible – strategic and operational decisions by the ministry and its agents, based on the assessment of resources and threats – had unravelled due to the pressure of events. When news of Byng's defeat was finally confirmed in Britain, he was abused at length in print, while his effigy was burned in many cities. A series of public displays of a lack of confidence drove this agitation home.

Court-martialled, Byng was found guilty of failing to do his utmost to relieve Fort St Philip or to destroy the French warships, and was sentenced to death. The court added a recommendation for a royal pardon because they (correctly) did not believe that his failure had arisen from cowardice or disaffection. This recommendation led to a renewed outburst of public anger. The navy was not supposed to fail, and a strong belief in naval invincibility was the bedrock of public faith in the government. If the British could not rule the waves, Britain itself might be conquered. If the navy would not do its duty, who would? This point was driven home because Byng's father had won the striking victory over a Spanish fleet off Sicily in 1718, the battle of Cape Passaro. William Hotham, later an admiral, observed the furore in

Bath: 'People's violence in general, and the ladies in particular, is to me something very shocking.'[23]

In practice, the failure to press home the attack on the French was a command decision that had more to do with the navy's rigid adherence to the Permanent Fighting Instructions and the legacy of the battle of Toulon in 1744, than with the inability of the commanders. Moreover, as a key strategic element, the wish to preserve forces in home waters against a threatened French invasion greatly affected the number of ships that could be spared for Byng. If the government had acted in accordance with French plans, keeping more warships in home waters than was, in the event, necessary, that did not mean that its response was inherently wrong; it was only poorly implemented, or unsuccessful. The latter was an important distinction, but one that left (and leaves) room for contention.

The public's rage over the loss of Minorca, combined with the political vulnerability of the Newcastle government, ensured that there was little possibility of a fair allocation of responsibility. Byng's supporters claimed that the ministry was making the admiral a scapegoat for its own negligence, a view also taken by Pitt, and there was sympathy for Byng.[24]

Despite this, Byng was publicly shot on the *Monarch* in the Solent on 14 March 1757, with men from other ships in boats around in what was a major display of retribution for failure. This led to a passage in Voltaire's novel *Candide* (1759): '*Dans ce pays-ci il est bon de tuer de temps en temps un amiral pour encourager les autres* (in this country, it is good to kill an admiral from time to time to encourage the others).' In fact, no other admirals were shot in this fashion.

Leaving aside the alleged negligence, the accusation of scapegoating was reasonable. In 1756, as with the battle of Ushant in 1778, the individual ships' companies were newly recruited or pressed, their captains were still working up and determining the capacities of their crews and ships, and the admiral was still working up and determining the capacities of his captains, who were equally unsure of their commanders. These battles also indicated how admirals had only limited control once battles had begun, with fighting instructions and orders limited by wind, the poor manoeuvrability of warships, and the responses of individual captains.

British agents had reported the danger of a large-scale invasion of Britain,[25] and the French government certainly began to receive a new tranche of Jacobite memoranda advocating such action.[26] Moreover, the risk of invasion had kept most of the navy in home waters, blockading the French fleet, and thus unable to support Byng. This posed a relationship between European and trans-oceanic tasks very different to that offered by Continental interventionism, but, again, with a trade-off between these tasks. Moreover, until the prospect of French invasion was addressed, there would only be so much strength that it was possible to commit to either Continental or trans-oceanic enterprises. In 1756, Henry Fox, one of the Secretaries of State, observed,

> If invasion or threats of invasion from France can effect the keeping of our fleet and troops at home, while they send regular troops, with their fleets to North America, the object of the war will be lost the first year of it.[27]

Bedford, then Lord Lieutenant of Ireland, followed up three years later by voicing his opposition to sending troops from there to India:

> Though I do not think in the present situation of affairs, whilst there is so great a fleet at sea, and descents are daily

making upon different parts of the French coasts, that there is any fear of an immediate invasion of Ireland, yet when the season of the year shall render it imprudent to carry on these operations under the protection of a great fleet any longer, it is very possible, under the favour of long nights, for the French to throw over in small craft such a number of troops as may surprise Cork or other considerable seaports on the neighbouring coasts to them.

Bedford correctly added that the British fleet could be shut up in the Channel by a westerly or a southwesterly wind.[28] This point, however, was politically problematic given the widespread unwillingness in public discussion to appreciate the consequences of British vulnerability. In addition, the British task was complicated by Dutch neutrality, unlike in 1689–97, 1702–13 and 1744–8, for this neutrality deprived Britain of the assistance of the Dutch navy. Moreover, with Austria now France's ally, concern about France using the Austrian Netherlands (Belgium) for an invasion of Britain, and perhaps gaining territory there, came to play a role, with particular anxiety about Nieuwpoort, which could serve as an invasion port.

In the aftermath of the loss of Minorca, its reacquisition by means of the cession of Gibraltar to Spain was considered. This underlined the extent to which military failure brought up unwelcome questions of prioritisation. The navy's difficulties were increased by the loss of Minorca as there was no comparable base for it, nor, indeed, any in the Mediterranean east of Gibraltar.

Although this was the nadir of British naval humiliation, it was not the end of it. In 1757, there was the failure in late September of a British expedition against the French Atlantic naval base of Rochefort, an expedition intended to challenge the articulation of France's trans-oceanic system. This failure, which owed much to poor intelligence, inadequate co-operation between naval and army commanders, and indifferent and hesitant generalship, led to much criticism of the ministry. The failure also indicated the problems facing the policy of coastal expeditions, problems that were of conception as well as implementation. The political controversy after Rochefort, which included a Commission of Enquiry into the conduct of the generals, did not gain the traction of that after Minorca the previous year, in part because there was no comparable humiliation and in part because Pitt was in the ministry. Nevertheless, there was a significant political cost.[29] However, failure at Rochefort owed more to the army.

Indeed, in 1757, there was an impressive display of naval power, while 'failure' in part was a matter of an inability to meet all the demands placed upon Britain, not least from Prussia. Robert, 4th Earl of Holdernesse, Pitt's colleague as Secretary of State, explained why it was not possible to send a fleet to the Baltic:

> ... the strength of the English marine is not equal perhaps to what is thought abroad, owing to the great want of sailors; and yet His Majesty must have a squadron in the Mediterranean, equal at least to the [French] Toulon fleet; one in the Channel, to keep the squadrons of Brest and Rochefort in respect; one in North America; a considerable one in the West Indies, which from the nature of the trade winds is necessarily divided, and one in the East Indies ... It will give you but a melancholy prospect to see the French Marine so very near equal to that of England.[30]

On the other hand, a large concentration of French warships helped explain the abandonment of the planned British expedition against Louisbourg in 1757. The British attempt to hinder French maritime operations, especially to prevent France reinforcing her colonies, by maintaining a naval presence off Brest, had been unsuccessful. The French navy had sailed from its west coast ports relatively freely, and their merchant and supply convoys had continued to operate. Yet, French trade was under increasing pressure from British warships, both in European waters and further afield. For example, in the Gulf of Mexico, most ships bound for New Orleans were captured, and this weakened the French colony of Louisiana, not least by increasing discontent among the Native Americans who could be given fewer trade goods as inducements to maintain their support. Moreover, the French fleet that sailed to Louisbourg in 1757 was then devastated by an outbreak of typhus which it then brought back to Brest and thence to Rochefort. The typhus killed thousands of sailors and civilians in those ports and crippled the French navy for 1758.

In 1758, the ability of the British navy to act both as an offensive operational force and as a restraint on French trade was fully demonstrated. Louisbourg fell to an amphibious expedition. In the colonies, the lack of siege trains of heavy artillery led frequently to a reliance on the cannon of supporting warships when attacking coastal positions, the cannon either fired from the ships or manhandled ashore and fired by sailors. French insurance premiums for ships to Quebec rose from about 5 per cent in 1755 to 50 per cent or more in 1758, and were seldom obtainable in 1759, a year in which many of the French merchantmen sent to Canada were captured.[31] With the capture of Louisbourg, insurance rates on British trade to America correspondingly fell greatly, those on West Indies sugar falling later that year. French commerce dried up by the end of 1758, while the rise of captures by the British navy was indicative of its superiority in most Western waters.

Also in 1758, Commodore Charles Holmes sailed up the unbuoyed channel of the River Ems, and by cutting the supplies of the French garrison at captured Emden led to its withdrawal, which provided the British with a landing port in Continental Europe. Holmes thereafter supported the deployment of British troops in Germany. At the same time, there was a careful watch on the French ports, albeit not with an outcome that pleased critical politicians such as Charles Townshend:

> Nobody can be so foolish as to expect any success ... from that majestic navy which is once more crying the hours off Brest under Lord Anson, who, with the deportment, punctuality and terror of a London watchman, knocks every night at every French seaport in the Channel to see that all is home and quiet within his station. The admiral is, I fear, better suited to this service than the fleet, which might have been sent upon real duty.[32]

Individual French warships proved vulnerable to the increasingly insistent British naval pressure in European waters, and the cumulative effect weakened the French. The large number of warships captured by Britain and incorporated into its navy played a major role in affecting the balance of naval strength. This incorporation aided the process by which the British changed the nature of its navy, copying the Bourbon large two-deckers. These were more manoeuvrable than the small three-decker 80- and 90-gun ships that had been so important earlier in the century.

The thesis of Edward Gibbon that a similarity in weaponry would prevent any one European power from achieving a position of hegemony was completely inaccurate as far as the maritime and extra-European world was concerned, for the navy was in fact very similar to its opponents in the weaponry employed. Supported by Anson, as First Lord of the Admiralty, Sir Thomas Slade, Surveyor of the Navy from 1755 to 1771, working from Spanish and French warships captured in the 1740s, designed a series of two-decker 74-gun warships that were both manoeuvrable and capable of holding their own in the punishing close-range artillery duels of line-of-battle engagements. The old ship types, with 80, 70 and 60 guns, were abandoned in favour of 74 and 64 gunners (fourteen of the former were in service by 1759), the 50-gun ship was discarded as a ship of the line but retained in limited numbers as a heavy cruiser, the small two-deck cruisers of 44 guns were abandoned in favour of the single-decked 32-gun frigate, and better three-deckers were also designed.

British shipbuilding policy therefore was radically reviewed after 1744, with much more emphasis on large two-decker ships of the line and single-decked frigates. Battery height was the decisive element in this. Small three-deckers were often unable to use their lower cannon in offensive actions from a windward position because the battery came too close to the water. The same problem occurred with small two-deckers, although they were useful as defensive convoy escorts as they had much firepower in relation to their size. Although not as heavily armed as a large three-decker, the 74-gunner was a successful class, considerably cheaper to build and maintain, and able to mount a satisfactory number of 32-pounders.

The new ships were better for both sailing and fighting, manoeuvrable and capable of holding their own in the punishing artillery duels of the line-of-battle engagements that the British preferred to conduct at close-range, in contrast to the French preference for long-range fire.[33] The British preference became more potent as crew were combat-hardened, which tended to happen during the course of wars, while French crews weakened as part of a more general compromising of French naval warmaking. Thus, the French were unable to repair damage sustained in the action off Porto Novo in 1759, so leaving the British in command in Indian waters.

Although far smaller, the French navy managed no worse than the British in 1755–7, but in 1758 it was hit hard by the strains of the war, losing fourteen of the line, mostly to the weather and sea, and with its manpower, supply chain and finances under great pressure. Failure in 1759 was in part a continuation and culmination of the developing situation, but more clearly was due to British success in battle, with 11 of the line lost accordingly.[34]

The crucial mid-century naval victories occurred in 1759. The French prepared a knockout blow, an invasion of Britain by 100,000 troops. Had even only part of the French force landed, it would still have posed serious problems for the British, but the division of the French navy between the ports of Brest and Toulon made it difficult to concentrate the necessary covering force, and the blockading British squadrons sought to maintain the division, while attempts were also made to disrupt invasion preparations especially by blockading the invasion port of Le Havre. Already, in 1756, the Admiralty was reassured that 'the *Fortune* sloop is still on the Gibraltar station so that if the Toulon Fleet or any part of it should pass the Streights, she will be ready to run home with the intelligence agreeable to a standing order her commander had for that purpose'.[35]

In 1759, although the Toulon fleet, under La Clue, managed to leave first the harbour and then the Mediterranean, it was defeated by the pursuing British under Boscawen near Lagos on the Portuguese coast on 18–19 August. Stubborn resistance by the rearmost French warship, the *Centaure*, held off the British while La Clue sailed the rest of his fleet into neutral waters, but, on the following day, Boscawen violated Portuguese neutrality and launched a successful attack. Mortally wounded, La Clue ran his vessel ashore and burnt it to prevent British capture, and the outnumbered French lost a total of five ships, three captured and two destroyed. The remainder of La Clue's fleet was then blockaded in the River Tagus. Portuguese complaints absorbed a lot of diplomatic time, but the verdict was decisive.

Lagos was followed by Quiberon Bay. All possibility of a French invasion of Britain was shattered by these two decisive victories. Quiberon Bay gets all the credit, but the battle of Lagos was a huge relief to politicians and naval officers alike: they knew that the invasion had become that much more difficult. As in 1778 and 1805, it was easier, or at least less difficult, for the British to maintain the blockade of nearby Brest and harder to control more distant French threats and British squadrons. After Hawke's victory, much of the Brest fleet took refuge in the River Vilaine, further up Quiberon Bay. Blockaded, they stayed there until 1761,[36] while political and financial support for the navy ebbed in France.[37] The aftermath resembled that of Barfleur in 1692. 1759 also saw important naval activity in the Caribbean in support of amphibious operations, with a failed attack on Martinique but the capture of Guadeloupe.

Given the size of its navy – 47 ships of the line by 1760 – it is understandable that Spanish neutrality was crucial at this stage. Had the British navy also had to watch Cadiz and Ferrol and to maintain a presence in the Caribbean sufficient to deter or defeat the Havana squadron, then it is difficult to see how it could have concentrated its strength sufficiently to defeat the French. Instead, it is possible that the Mediterranean would have been abandoned and the British would have concentrated on watching Brest, as they did in 1778.

The British, who did not face financial problems comparable to those of France, were left to take the initiative at sea. Thus, although close to Brest, the French navy did not disrupt the eventually successful British attack on the island of Belle Isle off Brittany in 1761 nor the dispatch of troops to Portugal in 1762, despite the fact that both enterprises were vulnerable to naval forces based in Brittany. A squadron under Keppel covered the Belle Isle expedition, while in 1762 a fleet based at Gibraltar under Sir Charles Saunders discouraged a junction between Bourbon naval forces in the Atlantic and the Mediterranean.

More generally, British warships were increasingly successful both in limiting French privateering and in damaging French trade. Insurance rates registered British success. James Mackenzie, crossing France in 1758 on his way to his posting in Turin, reported on

> the great difficulty they labour under in carrying on their foreign trade; they having had in parts of France a very indifferent corn harvest, and a miserable vintage. All these circumstances will undoubtedly add to, rather than diminish, the discontents of the people.

Mackenzie suggested that agricultural and industrial difficulties would make it very hard for the poor to pay their taxes, and he pressed for the interception of grain from Italy, urging the stationing of warships off southern France.[38] Thus, blockade was seen as a means not only to hinder naval and commercial operations, but also to induce collapse through economic and fiscal crises, a form of total war dependent on naval strength, with the impact and measure of the latter not requiring the search for battle.

Such a strategy was made very difficult, first due to the other calls on warships and secondly because of the vexed issue of neutral rights, which made economic warfare hard and limited the possibilities of total war, as did continuing trade between combatants. It was not until Napoleon sought from 1806 to line up most of Europe behind the Continental System, a prohibition of trade with Britain, that a strategy of economic warfare became central, and, if naval blockade had been used beforehand, the effective limiting of the option of neutrality from 1806 made it easier for Britain to mount a naval blockade. The fragile, undercapitalised nature of economies and their dependence on debt made them vulnerable to wartime pressures.

Squadrons were key to local equations of strength, as in 1760, when the French besieged Quebec only for it to be relieved by British warships as soon as the ice on the St Lawrence melted. This situation was to recur in 1776 when the American siege begun the previous year was brought to an end. In 1760, Richard Humphrys of the 28th Foot observed, 'Had a French fleet appeared first in the river the place must certainly have fell.'[39] Yet British naval strength had not prevented the arrival of six French battalions in Canada in 1755, and two each in 1756, 1557 and 1758.

Warships also provided battering power for amphibious operations, 'silencing the batteries by the ships' gunfire' at Martinique in 1762.[40] The seizure of Grenada, St Lucia and St Vincent all rapidly followed.

Spain came onto the French side in 1762, but without altering the progress of the war. The commander-in-chief, Field Marshal John, Lord Ligonier, feared that there were neither troops nor ships enough to prevent an invasion, and that the French and Spanish fleets would overwhelm the British home fleet unless ships were recalled from other squadrons.[41] However, the Spanish navy was not ready to act, while the French had been weakened by defeat and bankruptcy. When in early 1762 Saunders considered an attack on Cadiz to burn the ships in the harbour, he found that the Spaniards had laid them up. In May 1762 Charles, 2nd Earl of Egremont, a Secretary of State, reported that 'multitudes of ships are waiting to sail from Cork with beef and pork, without which the Spanish fleet could not put to sea.'[42]

Nevertheless, the Spanish invasion of Portugal ensured that the *Monitor* was wrong to announce on 1 May 1762,

> A war with Spain is purely maritime. She must submit to the power which commands the ocean. Her strength depends upon her American treasure; and her American colonies are at the mercy of the sovereigns of the seas.

In part because the Spanish navy lacked sailors, and in part due to an unambitious, passive Spanish stance, there was no naval battle to register British success. The difficulties of rapid naval operations were indicated in 1761 when, with Pitt proposing a pre-emptive attack on Spain, Newcastle recorded,

> The King told me, Lord Anson was of opinion that the ships could not be ready in two months and His Majesty says Lord Anson promised him to give this opinion in council, which cuts short, at once, any consideration of immediate operations.[43]

There was no major naval battle to register British success, but, prefiguring comparable American successes in 1898, the capture of Havana and Manila that year provided clear indications of naval power and long-range naval capability. The navy got the expeditions to target and, once there, provided them with crucial support, notably in firepower. The capture of Havana was a major blow to Spanish naval power in the Caribbean. It also helped strengthen British maritime populism, and ensured that the Seven Years War ended in the glow of success.

The force that landed on Cuba was covered by a formidable fleet of 22 ships of the line. Warships supported the bombardment of Morro Castle, which commanded the channel from the sea to the harbour of Havana, but damage from Spanish fire forced the warships to abandon the bombardment. Some of the Spanish sailors served as fortress gunners. The eventual fall of Havana led to the surrender of the squadron in the harbour, with Spain losing ten of the line and three frigates. Bases could well be traps if warships were unable to leave.

Victory at sea, combined with successful amphibious operations which proved a major force-multiplier for an otherwise relatively small army,[44] had altered the strategic situation. Nonetheless, despite the hopes of Pitt, repeated attacks on the French coast had failed to divert French forces from the war in Germany. Indeed, whereas Britain could be threatened by invasion with serious strategic consequences, France was not thus affected. This reflected the greater vulnerability of Britain to amphibious attack and the smaller size of its armed forces, both regulars and militia. Because Britain suffered the disadvantages of seeking to act as a European great power without possessing the requisite large army, it was necessary to be the leading naval power. The numbers of sailors rose from 62,000 in June 1757 to 84,000 in 1762. There were also the problems of operating in the Channel, both on expeditions and for blockade, as Rear-Admiral George Rodney pointed out in 1759 while masking the invasion port of Le Havre.[45]

British naval success was not due to superior weaponry. Neither the ships nor the guns were fundamentally different from those of the Bourbons, although the British had more dry docks and deep-sea sailors. Moreover, in building larger and stronger ships in mid-century, the French built primarily for speed, largely because they adopted a mission-orientated strategy to get to the location as quickly as possible, while the British built for endurance, to stay at sea for as long as possible, and built up a complex support network to sustain them. This enabled them to operate the Western Squadron strategy from 1747 onwards to contain their enemy, which, in turn, enabled them to send ever more expeditions over ever greater distances overseas and sustain them there. From being a European naval power, Britain became the world power. Others had the potential to imitate this, but they failed to build up the sophisticated capacity on the scale and efficiency necessary to do so.

Crucial factors included, first, a level of continuous high commitment and expenditure that helped to ensure that a high rate of both was regarded as normal and necessary and that naval strength never collapsed; secondly, the inculcation of an ethos and policy that combined the strategic and operational offensive with tactical aggression; and, thirdly, within the constraints of naval warfare and technology, an effective use of the warships of the period.[46] British naval commanders generally took the initiative and therefore were best placed to obtain propitious circumstances. At a gut level, the British preferred artillery exchanges at close range, unlike the French, who preferred longer-distance exchanges. The British, then, fought to win and not just to survive for another day. This quality was apparent in the victories that gave them the commanding position in the European world. Regular gun-drills also enabled the British to maintain a heavier and more accurate fire for longer.

Trans-oceanic success was due in part to the policy of establishing naval bases in the Caribbean including Kingston, Jamaica (1655); English Harbour, Antigua (founded 1728); and Port Antonio, Jamaica (1729); as well as Halifax, Nova Scotia (1749). The harbour facilities at Halifax were able to support the overwintering of a substantial squadron in 1758-9, and the growth in naval capability was one factor in the difference between the failure of the 1690 and 1711 expeditions against Quebec and the success of that of 1759.

Naval operations outside Europe, however, especially in the Indian Ocean and the Caribbean, remained greatly dependent on climate and disease. The British expedition sent from Chennai (Madras) in October 1756 to recapture Calcutta from the Nawab of Bengal was hit by the weather, by sickness and by running aground.[47] Yet, it was successful as it was possible to deliver verdicts, and the history of military operations is a matter of difficulties overcome.

Thus, while attacks on Gheria on the west coast of India, a stronghold of the Angrias used for privateering, had failed in 1718 and 1720, there was more success in 1756 when Rear-Admiral Charles Watson, in command of six royal ships and eight from the East India Company, 'began such a fire upon them as I believe they never before saw and soon silenced their batteries, and the fire from their grabs (ships)'. The five-hour bombardment led to the destruction of Tulaji Angria's fleet, with 12 grabs set ablaze. The next day, the warships closed in to bombard the fort at pistol-shot distance in order to make a breach in the wall for storming, and this breach swiftly led to its surrender. British casualties were slight. Watson reported, 'The hulls, masts and rigging of the ships are so little damaged that if there was a necessity we should be able to proceed to sea in twenty four hours.' George Thomas noted, 'We in *Salisbury* fired 120 barrels of powder.' Watson had earlier emphasised the artillery role of his warships: 'If I can come near enough to batter ... I shall make no doubt of success, but if by the shoal water, the large ships cannot come within distance to do execution, it will be doing of nothing.'[48] Water depth was a key problem in coastal operations.

More generally, despite improvements in some spheres, the conditions of service at sea continued to be bleak. Disease led to high mortality from, for example, yellow fever in the British and Spanish fleets in the 1720s, and typhus in the British and Dutch fleets in the 1740s. The situation was exacerbated by cramped living conditions, poor sanitation, and inadequate and inappropriate food; although the salted beef and pork, peas, cheese, oatmeal, raisins and biscuits that were eaten had the advantage of being storable for long periods, while the monotony of diet could be varied in ports, notably by taking on board fresh meat. Unfit food was thrown overboard and charged to the Victualling Board. However, there was a shortage of fresh food, fruit and vegetables, and hence a lack of vitamin C, contributing to scurvy. The cumulative impact was to make naval service unappealing, although it is not clear to how many, and to ensure serious losses among those already in service, especially if away on long voyages. Those who came from service in the merchant marine, however, would have been used to a similar diet. On a more general pattern of group employment in this period, but with the added element of patriotic purpose, male camaraderie, maritime professionalism and naval discipline served to integrate crews. Even so, there remained tensions in part due to impressment, particularly during the first year of service and therefore the early stages of a war.[49]

Conversely, improved conditions, notably the supply of vitamin C, could lead to greater effectiveness. As an instance of the administrative underpinning of such conditions, the British Navy Board, Victualling Board and Ordnance Board were able effectively to direct a formidable re-supply system, including on the far-flung East Indies Station.[50] The navy had operated across the oceans before, but never with this intensity. The financial credits made available for the navy were particularly significant for this range. As revictualling at sea was developed, the use of the blockade against Brest became more effective, which in part turned into an instance of the possibility of controlling particular sea areas, albeit with the limitations of control in this period. Although there were major problems in securing sufficient gunpowder at the outset of the war, the Ordnance Board also proved successful and proactive in arming the navy.[51]

It proved easier to meet wartime expansions of logistical commitments at sea than on land, as shown with British forces in Germany in 1758 and in Portugal in 1762, but there were inevitably problems. Indeed, after Louisbourg fell on 26 July 1758, Brigadier-General James Wolfe wrote from there on 9 August:

> I do not well know what we are doing here – with the harbour full of men of war and transports – and the fine season stealing away ... Our fleet, it seems, wants anchors, and cables, and provisions and pilots, pretty essential articles you will say.[52]

Indeed, naval success stemmed in general not from any new strategy but from the ability to keep a large number of ships at sea and from their fighting skill, determination and motivation.

Effectiveness was challenged by the problems of command and control posed by operations outside Europe, problems related to the difficulties of deploying ships so as to match the moves of opposing fleets and in a context in which intelligence could only move at the speed of the fastest ship. Disease was also a problem. Sailing to India in 1754, Watson thought it prudent to stop at Madagascar for fresh supplies as 170 of the crew on *Kent* were ill with scurvy.[53] Yet, serious as health and supply problems were for long-distance oceanic operations, they did not prevent them. There were improvements, for instance the publication of *A Treatise on the Scurvy* (1754), in which the naval surgeon James Lind correctly advocated eating citrus fruit, although this method of prevention was only widely adopted from the 1790s, and scurvy remained a problem. Serving in African, Caribbean and Mediterranean waters, Lind also worked on cures for malaria and typhus among sailors and on supplying ships with fresh water by distillation. He was a key example of the naval enlightenment, the continual process of applying knowledge that was particularly apparent in the second half of the century, as in the attention devoted to charting inshore waters, establishing a means to measure longitude, improving signalling and introducing the copper sheathing of ships. Furthermore, bad as people think the navy was in its conditions for sailors, its rivals were much worse and had more dire mortality figures.

Naval superiority provided an ability to pick where to direct efforts, and permitted the application of strength to achieve local superiority at a time of choosing at crucial points, for example Louisbourg in 1758. The French empire depended on the maintenance of its major bases, all of which could be approached by water, and unless the French could threaten the British at sea these bases could be isolated and attacked with overwhelming force. They also provided shelter, supply, and refitting and repair possibilities for warships. Indeed, while always important, the growing significance of trans-oceanic bases ensured a need to work through the possibilities and consequences of particular sites.

The resources required for naval primacy – or, for Britain's opponents, just to remain as major powers – were immense, which led in Britain to consideration of placing the navy in the context of a broader national defence in the shape of a strong militia. Charles Jenkinson argued in 1757,

> Either we must establish an internal constitutional force for the defence of our own country, and send forth our fleets for the protection of our colonies, or keep our navy at home for the preservation of the former, and leave the latter an easy prey to the first enemy that shall seize upon them.[54]

This was part of a debate about how best to use the navy, the *Monitor* declaring on 24 December 1757,

> A fleet is our best security; but then it is not to lie by our walls; nor be confined to the navigation of our own coasts. The way to deliver Rome from the rival ships and hostilities of the Carthaginians was to carry fire and sword upon the African coast. Employ the enemy at home, and he will never project hazardous invasions. Our fleets are able to bid defiance to all the maritime forces of Europe. And as the surest and most rational means to humble the ambition of France is to destroy her power by sea, and her trade from America; no service but what is directed towards this salutary object of British politics, can be worthy of the attention of a British ministry.

The resources required were varied as well as immense. Its keel laid in 1759, and the timbers seasoned in frame for six years before the ship was planked up, the *Victory* required the felling of over 2,000 oak trees, while other timbers were also used, notably elm for the keel.[55] Launched in 1764, *Triumph*, a standard 74-gunner, needed 3,028 loads of timber, each 50 cubic feet. The 100-gun *Royal George* required 5,760.

So also with manpower, with large crews required to work the sails and man the guns. Impressment encouraged desertion, and 12,700 men deserted in 1755–7 out of a total of

70,000 recruited, while 143 died in combat and 13,000 were lost through disease and the need to discharge unfit men.⁵⁶ In February 1759, when it was learnt that the French were intending to invade, only 21 of the 41 ships of the line in British waters were properly manned. Alongside the onetime view of the sailor's lot as rum, sodomy and the lash has come the argument that the superior quality of British seamanship was a product of a relatively harmonious nature of maritime life. Officers had to persuade and reward, not least in order to encourage recruitment and limit desertion, respect was the lubricant of obedience, and ratings aware they possessed scarce and valuable skills. Unlike soldiers, the constant exercise of trained initiative in circumstances where they could not be properly supervised was required of sailors, which ruled out any rigid system of control, as did the problem of manning the fleet in a society that would not condone the treatment of sailors like galley slaves.⁵⁷ Far from automata, crew played a key role in British naval victories. They were skilled men living in cramped conditions and maintaining an impressive professionalism. The seamen slept on the lower gun deck in hammocks and also ate there on mess tables, usually at 8 a.m., noon and 4 p.m., with sleep beginning at 8 p.m. The sailors alternated four-hour watches with necessary work on the ship, which required continual maintenance. So also with the skills of the sailors: these required practice.

As a result the pressing of 'landlubbers' served only a limited purpose, as the requirement was for experienced seamen. At times of real difficulty, pressing was extended, but the extent to which that was of dubious value was indicated by the numbers discharged as medically unsuitable. Moreover, whereas volunteers, who were encouraged by bounties, could be expected to offer a natural discipline, that was not necessarily the case with conscripts, which might account for the need to move from discipline to punishment.

With officers, discipline could be patchy, not least as they were officially gentlemen, while they had very varied backgrounds and connections. Linked to that, their financial exigencies and expectations varied greatly. A lack of peacetime service created additional issues for officers.[58]

The Bourbons were still able to launch a massive programme of naval rearmament after the war ended in 1763, but British colonial conquests during the war ensured that the geopolitics and infrastructure of power were different. With Canada conquered from France in 1758–60, and Florida acquired from Spain in 1763, North America now appeared to be securely British. When, in 1770–1, there was the prospect of war with the Bourbons over the Falkland Islands, there was little need for Britain to consider the security of North America; the situation was totally different from that of 1754–6.

There were to be new strategic challenges in the two decades after 1763 – the rebuilding of the Bourbon fleets, a Russian-led League of northern European powers in the Baltic, the combination of France and Mysore in southern India, and, most obviously, rebellion in the Thirteen Colonies in North America from 1775 – but for now the situation appeared promising. Whereas in the 1690s the British had had to rely on Dutch support to achieve a naval edge over the French, and that only with difficulty, in the Seven Years War Britain, alone on the oceans, had defeated France and Spain. A sense of power was offered, *Owen's Weekly Chronicle* on 16 September 1758 giving British naval strength as 274 warships (including sloops) with 12,750 guns, the paper proclaiming 'the naval power of Great Britain has always commanded the ocean, as it does at present, to the terror and destruction of France'.

6

DETERRENCE AND DEFEAT
1764–83

On 12 April 1782, in the most spectacular naval battle of the period covered in this chapter, a British fleet under Admiral George Rodney soundly defeated François de Grasse off the Isles des Saintes. Although there were 36 British ships of the line against 30 French ships, the French ships were larger and the total displacements of the two fleets roughly equal. Indeed, in most fleet actions, the number of ships of the line tends to overestimate British and underestimate French strength as French ships were on average larger than the British. The same applies to number of cannon, as the French pound was heavier than the British, and the larger French ships had 36-pounders against British 32-pounders. However, the British gradually obtained a qualitative advantage in cannon. At the battle off the Saintes, Rodney captured five ships of the line, including the flagship, the *Ville de Paris*, and de Grasse himself. Commissioned in 1764 as a three-decker with 90 guns (30 36-pounders, 32 24-pounders, and 28 12-pounders), the ship had 14 8-pounders added in 1779. De Grasse had sailed with 33 ships, but had to send three back to port, one with battle damage and two due to collisions Helped by a chance change in wind direction, Rodney broke through the French line. Moreover, British cannon fire was especially effective, thanks in part to the innovations of Captain Charles Douglas of the *Formidable*, which increased the ease of serving cannon, of firing them instantaneously and the possible angles at which to train them, along with improvements in flintlocks, tin tubes, flannel cartridges, wedges to absorb recoil, and steel compression springs, British cannon fire was especially effective. Although Rodney was widely blamed, notably by commanders who were to influence Nelson, for a failure to mount an immediate pursuit that would have led to more captures (in the event two fleeing French warships were captured later), the French strategy was wrecked and, thereafter, the Bourbon fleets remained on the defensive in the Caribbean, ending the Franco-Spanish threat to Jamaica.

This, however, was a contrast with the British naval record earlier in the War of American Independence (1775–83), a conflict that was transformed navally when France came in on the side of the American rebels in 1778. Earlier, after the Seven Years War ended in 1763, the French had planned a renewed war, and built up their navy accordingly.[1] British newspapers were soon reporting on French naval preparations, and it was the focus of espionage;[2] in turn, France spied on British naval moves, including by means of an agent in the Admiralty.[3]

British attitudes very much focused on the naval dimension. The navalism of earlier Tories and opposition Whigs had been pushed to the fore during the Seven Years War, which left Britain triumphant and encouraged British commentators to a bold assessment of what Britain could achieve. This was especially true of Tories such as Tobias Smollett who, on a long-established pattern that was based partly on criticism of the Hanoverian connection, wished to emphasise British naval power, and thus the degree to which Britain was not dependent on allies.⁴ Smollett reported of Monaco in his *Travels* that it 'might be laid in ashes by a bomb-ketch [firing mortar shells] in four hours by sea' (Letter 26); while the Gulf of La Spezia was described in terms of 'an admirable station for a British squadron' (Letter 26). For Rome, Smollett wrote with total implausibility:

> The popes will do well to avoid misunderstandings with the maritime protestant states, especially the English, who being masters of the Mediterranean, and in possession of Minorca, have it in their power at all times, to land a body of troops within four leagues of Rome, and to take the city, without opposition ... altogether incapable of defence. (Letter 30)

When in 1766, on the death of 'James III and VIII', the College of Cardinals debated the recognition or non-recognition of Charles Edward Stuart as king in succession to his father, there was indeed the view that the British would retaliate by bombarding the Papal ports of Ancona and Civitavecchia.⁵ Smollett's bold claims for the British navy extended to Antiquity:

> I do believe, in my conscience, that half a dozen English frigates would have been able to defeat both the contending fleets at the famous battle of Actium [31 BCE], which has been so much celebrated in the annals of antiquity, as an event that decided the fate of empire. (Letter 32)

Although rated fifth or sixth class, frigates were not usually line-of-battle warships due to their limited armament. Although the Royal Navy had successfully operated on Mediterranean coasts in the Wars of the Spanish (1702–13) and Austrian (1744–48 for

Britain) Succession, Smollett also offered an unrealistic view of the consequences of British naval power. This power was to be brought low by failure in the War of American Independence, but, dying in 1771, Smollett was unable to comment on that disaster.

Smollett's views were echoed in the press, not least in the recovered memory of the Seven Years War. The *Monitor* on 13 September 1760 declared,

> France cannot maintain a land war when she has lost her trade, and the means to supply her armies, by the riches of her commerce, which are the sinews of war. Hence it is, that France has always attempted to draw the attention of our ministry, from their naval power.

The exaggerated sense of naval capacity was seen in the *St James's Chronicle*, a leading paper, on 29 April 1769 when it claimed,

> Commodore Holmes, at the beginning of the late war [in fact 1758], bombarded Emden, capital of East Friesland, and by that means drove the French out to give possession to the English. It is plain then, that one of the Prussian ports is accessible, in case that monarch should demand our notice.

In fact, the vulnerability of Hanover to Prussian attack was far greater than that of Prussia to the navy, as was to be made obvious in 1772 when a hostile response to the First Partition of Poland by Austria, Prussia and Russia was considered.

More significant was the general failure to place naval power in perspective, in particular in the context of the foreign policy goals that it was designed to serve. The argument should not have been about what squadrons could achieve militarily, concerning which public views were commonly misplaced, but about what political ends the use of naval power could serve. Ministers were aware that naval power was a precarious asset that did not allow them to dictate to other states.

The contentious nature of foreign policy and strategy helped ensure a post-war emphasis on a navalism that could be seen as particularly national in its expenditure[6] and goals. In 1763, Charles, 2nd Earl of Egremont, a Secretary of State, informed the Admiralty that he had been pressed by the East India Company for the maintenance or even reinforcement of the wartime naval establishment in the Indian Ocean if naval intelligence bore out reports that France was sending more warships thither.[7] There was, indeed, a series of disputes with the Bourbons in which there was the possibility of naval action, notably the Falkland Islands crisis of 1770–1, in which there was the possibility of war with France and Spain, instead of with only one of them, as had appeared the case in 1764–9 and would later in 1772–7. A fleet of 55 ships was prepared, and by May 1771 it was three-quarters manned. Spain and its French ally could not match these preparations, and this helped lead them to back down, although this decision owed much to factional politics at the French court. Moreover, the pace of naval confrontation continued: in 1771, four ships of the line were sent to the Indian Ocean to deter a possible French threat to British interests in India. The following year, the threat of action led the Danes to release into exile Caroline Matilda, George III's sister and their adulterous queen.[8]

'Blue water' policies appeared to have been transformed into Britain's destiny. The arts contributed to this impression, including songs, poems, the stage, statuary and artists. 'Hearts of Oak' was written by William Boyce and David Garrick for Garrick's pantomime *Harlequin's Invasion*, which was staged at the Theatre Royal in Drury Lane in December 1759. Thomas Newcomb contributed the more ponderous *Vindicta Britannica: An Ode on the Royal Navy, inscribed to the King* (1759), while Dominic Serres, one of the founding members of the Royal Academy in 1768 and Marine Painter to George III, exhibited 105 works at the Academy.

Meanwhile, given the time taken to mobilise fleets, there was the concern that a rival might get in a first blow. Much like in the Cold War, this concern produced a key issue of trust, as well as a continual stress on the value of naval intelligence for Anglo-French relations. In 1769, Thomas, 3rd Viscount Weymouth, a Secretary of State, referred to French assurances 'that ministers openness in giving an account of the object of any military preparations cannot fail to have salutary effects with regard to that good understanding which is His Majesty's wish to keep up.' In turn, the British ministry felt able to give 'strong assurances'.[9] In 1773, when Russia threatened Sweden, the French Foreign Minister asked the British envoy,

> Could you be satisfied with the most solemn engagements that our fleet shall do nothing but repel the attack upon our ally, and after having done that shall immediately return home without any attack upon Russia, or any other attempt whatever, we would give you every security on that head that you could desire.[10]

The British Secretary of State responded,

> It is not right that the Duke D'Aiguillon should deceive himself by imagining that a British fleet when once out, in such a crisis as this is, can parade about the seas doing nothing, and that His Majesty can long continue without taking a decisive part.

The British envoy in Paris pressed D'Aiguillon on the matter:

> I explained to him in the fullest and clearest manner I could that a French fleet in the Baltic would necessarily and inevitably draw a British one thither too. That it was a step we should be obliged to take, that the honour of the nation and the King's dignity called for it, and that the call must and would be attended to. I added that it was the general opinion of every man I had talked to upon the subject, that it was impossible for Great Britain, to be an indifferent spectator, and see a French fleet in the Baltic ... I am sure that if you could but pass a week in England and see with your own eyes, your conviction would be the same as mine.

British naval strength can be best appreciated when achievements are compared with those of other European states, and considered in the light of systemic operational and strategic difficulties, rather than contrasted with the aspirations of ministers and public opinion. In 1734, Wager, the First Lord of the Admiralty, was able to tell George II 'I thought that we were at present stronger than any nation at sea, perhaps than any two.'[11] After the Seven Years' War, French and Spanish naval construction challenged such hopes, but that war had left a sense of naval destiny, one fortified by success. Thus, threats and a naval mobilisation helped dissuade France from deploying its navy against Russia in the Baltic and the Mediterranean in 1773, a course assisted by Franco-Spanish tensions.

Yet, at the same time, alongside confidence-building statements, there was an emphasis on necessary naval watchfulness:

> You cannot watch their motions more than they will ours. If they see us upon our guard to keep pace with them, or if possible get before them, that may operate more strongly

than any declarations how explicit soever. Of this at least I am persuaded that if they see the smallest backwardness in our preparations, from that backwardness joined to the knowledge they have of the great ability and activity that directs our Board of Admiralty at present, they will conclude that we are not in earnest, act accordingly and go too far to make it possible for them to retreat with honour.[12]

The significance of the navy for the display as well as projection of force was captured in a report to the Admiralty about a voyage to the vulnerable limits of the empire on the River Gambia in West Africa in 1775:

> Upon sending an officer up to James' Fort, I was informed by the commanding officer that the French had spirited the natives up against the English, and that he had been obliged to take a schooner of some force belonging to the traders into the service in order to supply himself with water ... I therefore went up the river in the *Pallas* ... I stayed in the river eight days, during which time we got the king of the country on board.[13]

Very differently, these were also years in which Britain took the leading place in maritime exploration, with the Admiralty adopting the key organisational role and naval officers being the central figures. In 1767, Samuel Wallis on *Dolphin* entered the Pacific through the Straits of Magellan and then, instead of following the route established by the Spaniards, was able to 'discover' many Pacific islands including Tahiti. Wallis had served throughout the Seven Years War from Boscawen's attack on the French in 1755 to the capture of Belle Isle. Philip Carteret in *Swallow* crossed the Pacific further south and 'discovered' a large number of islands and for naming used naval references including Sandwich, Byron and Admiralty. Another veteran of the Seven Years War, Carteret had scant good fortune in his naval career, in part due to a lack of the necessary connections. James Cook in 1769–79 sailed more extensively in the Pacific. Joining the navy in 1755, Cook served a great deal in the Seven Years War, notably at Louisbourg in 1758 and Quebec in 1759. He developed expertise in surveying and cartography. Advances in navigation, hull design and rigging were all important to these voyages, which were to be continued by others, notably George Vancouver in 1791–5.

Yet, these were also years in which Britain, struggling with the debt left by the vastly expensive Seven Years War and keen to keep expenditure and taxes low, lost its edge in naval strength. French and Spanish launchings in the late 1760s were each more numerous than those of Britain, as were those of Spain in the early 1770s. As a result, the Bourbons had a quantitative superiority in tonnage of about 20 per cent by 1775.[14] Nevertheless, the British navy remained the leading one, as well as the largest of any sailing, cannon-armed warship fleet hitherto. Given the major problems of manning the fleet and maintaining ships, the advisability of further construction was limited. Moreover, the Seven Years War and the Falkland Islands crisis both indicated the weakness of Bourbon co-operation. In addition, a full-scale American rebellion appeared improbable until it occurred, as did Dutch alliance with the Bourbons.

Warships were used in the 1760s and early 1770s to try to 'improve' imperial governance, or at least centralise and rationalise it by a variety of means including producing accurate charts and enforcing fiscal and other regulations. The navy was an important tool of colonial governance both in North America and the Caribbean because it was the means to regulate maritime trade and harbours, and because naval officers took the perspective of the imperial government rather than the colonists. But as imperial authority collapsed in North America, the navy was unable to police the entire coastline, lacked sufficient small vessels, and in pursuit of overawing opposition was able to concentrate ships in Boston harbour and along the New England coast in 1774–5 only by abandoning the rest of the coast to virtually unregulated trade.[15]

Rebellion broke out in 1775 and was rapidly successful on land. In contrast, the eastern seaboard of North America was a relatively benign area for British naval operations. Halifax was an important naval base, guarding the mouth of the St Lawrence and enabling the projection of British naval power down the seaboard.[16] About 75 per cent of the population of the Thirteen Colonies lived within 75 miles of the coast. Their vulnerability to sea power was accentuated by the weak state of roads and bridges, which led to an emphasis on coastal traffic, while waterways helped maritime penetration, notably the Chesapeake, the Delaware, Long Island Sound, and the area around Charleston.

The British sought to use this vulnerability. Thus, in January 1779, the movement of some of the Halifax garrison to join the army around New York was approved in part because 'the sea coasts of the New England provinces' were to be attacked, meaning the Americans would be in a poor position for mounting any attack on Halifax.[17] Indeed, the campaigns that led to the British relief of Québec in 1776, and their capture of New York (1776), Philadelphia (1777), Savannah (1778), and Charleston (1780), and to the Franco-American concentration against the British in Yorktown in 1781, each reflected, at least in part, the amphibious capability stemming from naval strength and drawing on a development of relevant doctrine.[18] However, in every case, the exploitation of this capability was dependent on the campaigning on land. More generally, British naval strength could not ensure a decisive victory over the main American field army.[19]

This factor, and the consequences of French entry in 1778, were important to the course of the war; American experimentation with new naval technology in the shape of the submarine, meanwhile, had no effect. The ideas were genuinely revolutionary, but successful execution was a different matter. David Bushnell's *Turtle* was first employed against the *Eagle* in New York harbour on 6 September 1776, but Bushnell encountered serious problems with navigating in the face of the currents and could not attach the explosive charge to the ship. The second attempt, against the *Phoenix* on 5 October, also failed. George Washington pointed out the difficulty of operating the machine satisfactorily, and it is not surprising that Bushnell received scant support from the hard-pressed Patriot government.

More significantly, the Americans had privateers able to operate far afield but lacked a fleet, let alone the amphibious capabilities and strike force to take the war to the British Isles. American privateering hit Bristol in particular, while in 1777 George III wrote to John Robinson, Secretary to the Treasury:

> I trust the different vessels that hover round the island will be put on their guard particularly to protect Liverpool, Whitehaven, the Clyde, and even Bristol, for I do suspect that the rebel vessels which have been assembling at Nantes and Bordeaux mean some strike of that kind which would undoubtedly occasion much discontent among the merchants.[20]

American privateers also attacked elsewhere across the empire including hitting the valuable Newfoundland fishery, which the navy was unable to protect.²¹ At the same time, British economic warfare was more effective. Two months earlier, George had suggested that a few vessels stationed on the coast of Virginia might be able to control the tobacco trade from the Chesapeake. Indeed, leaf prices rose tenfold in Europe.²²

The difficulty posed by British naval power was differently captured in August 1777 when George Washington commented on a British force that had sailed from Staten Island:

> They have stood out to sea again, but how far, or where, they are going remains to be known – From their entire command of the water they derive immense advantages, and distress us much by harassing and marching our troops from post to post – I wish we could fix on their destination – in such case, I should hope we would be prepared to receive them.²³

In 1775–7, the British government focused on the war in America, including its cost, without also bolstering the fleet to cope with the possibility of war with France and Spain. The latter two, in contrast, built up their fleets. French entry into the war in 1778, followed by that of Spain in 1779 and the Dutch in 1780, totally altered the maritime situation, leading to a worldwide naval conflict, at once more extensive and in some spheres, such as the vigorous Anglo-French struggle in the Bay of Bengal, more intensive than previous maritime wars between Western powers. Britain gained control of neither European nor American waters, and therefore was unable to repeat its success in the Seven Years War. Instead, British warships had to be redeployed from 1778 in response to the integration of the American conflict into a wider struggle, in which the naval balance in American waters was interrelated with that in European and, more obviously, Caribbean waters.

The War of American Independence posed serious problems of naval strategy for Britain, France and Spain. Some were new, but they did not result in any revolution in strategy. For Britain, aside from the logistical nightmare posed by supplying the forces on the other side of the Atlantic, the issue of numbers of warships interacted with disputes over strategy. Having failed in the essential strategy of using naval strength as a means to deter France, and thus keep France and the Americans apart, there was still a lack of clarity concerning how best to adapt British navalism.[24] The failure to defeat the French in 1778 before Spain entered the war the following year was a major blow, while the arrival of the French in American waters reflected the inability to keep the French fleet in European waters.

At the same time, French entry into the war led to a fundamental strategic debate as to whether or not to withdraw troops from the Thirteen Colonies and mount an offensive war in the Caribbean and a naval war against American trade and ports, thus bringing them to terms. This idea was supported by John, 4th Earl of Sandwich, the First Lord of the Admiralty in 1748–51, 1763 and from 1771 to 1782, but it met with the response that once the Americans had ports they could attack the West Indies.[25] Less extreme decisions were taken in 1778, first to retain New York but withdraw from Philadelphia, which would not be as important in any naval war, and then to mount an invasion of Georgia which would be easier for the navy to support while also maintaining a presence in and close to the Caribbean.

In European waters, the desirability of blockading French ports, for which there were arguably too few British ships, clashed with Sandwich's prudent argument that naval strength should be concentrated in home waters, not only to deter invasion but also to permit a serious challenge to the main French fleet, which was based nearby at Brest, and thus to gain a position of naval dominance. This goal would be compromised by dispersing much of the fleet among distant stations, where it could support amphibious operations and protect trade, but could not materially affect the struggle for naval dominance. Due to the state of communications technology – a situation that was to be transformed by the telegraph in the nineteenth century but was not to change radically until the use of radio in the early twentieth century – the commanders of those distant stations were difficult to control effectively. These commanders jealously guarded their autonomy and resources, allowing them to deal with local challenges of which only they were well informed, causing an overall inflexibility that was ill suited to the need to react to French initiatives.[26] In theory, a matching squadron could be sent in pursuit of any French or Spanish naval moves, but there was no guarantee that it would arrive in time.[27] The fierce government dispute over strategy[28] was matched by public concern over the level of naval preparedness, not least because there were no victories to ease political tension.

In 1778, the operational paradigm was that of keeping a close eye on Brest but failing to blockade Toulon or block the Straits of Gibraltar. This left the Toulon fleet free to sail to North America, which posed dangers for the British. Sailing on 11 June, d'Estaing was able to reach American waters, leaving the British vulnerable in three respects. First, their forces were based on ports – New York and Newport – and if these were cut off from maritime supplies they might well be forced to surrender. In a later parliamentary hearing, General Sir William Howe, the commander-in-chief of British land forces in North America, was to claim

> that had the French got to Sandy Hook, all the naval force that England could send out, could not have saved the army,

who must have been starved, as the victuallers could not in that case have reached the port of New York.[29]

Secondly, army movements were by water, and in 1778 a number of important moves were made. Some were over short distances, for instance in the last stage of General Sir Henry Clinton's retreat from Philadelphia via the New Jersey shore to New York; others were long-range affairs, like the projected detachments for St Lucia, the Floridas and, eventually, Georgia. Thirdly, if a superior French fleet defeated a smaller British one, it would alter permanently not only the balance of naval advantage in American waters, but also the Anglo-French maritime balance, with possible fatal consequences for the defence of home waters.

In March 1779, proposing a motion of censure on the government for not sending reinforcements to Admiral Lord Howe (brother to Sir William) at New York the previous year, Charles James Fox, the leading opposition figure in the Commons, claimed,

> If Lord Howe had been reinforced, or the Streights of Gibraltar watched, in either event the net effect would be similar: that of securing to Lord Howe the full advantage of the force under his command, or giving him a superiority in case the Toulon squadron was permitted to cross the ocean.[30]

Outnumbered, Howe had prepared in 1778 off New York for one of those frequent occasions in naval history, the battle that did not occur. He anchored his ships so that they would be able to cannonade the French warships as they were obliged to enter the channel individually. The unwelcome nature of their position was compounded by the shallowness of the bar at Sandy Hook covering the approach to the harbour – a bar on which the

French, who lacked adequate pilots and information, might run aground – and the deployment of British troops and cannon. Having understandably failed to attack, d'Estaing finally sailed away on 22 July. A week later, he appeared off Newport, which an American force was preparing to attack.

However, Howe's fleet in turn approached Rhode Island on 9 August, leading d'Estaing to sail to engage. Having manoeuvred to gain the weather gauge, Howe was prevented from attacking by a storm on 11 August that damaged both fleets. The need to repair his ships led d'Estaing to sail from Rhode Island, to the fury of the local American commander who had to abandon the siege of Newport. Due to adverse winds, Howe failed to intercept d'Estaing before he reached Boston. The British used their command of the sea to raid New Bedford and Martha's Vineyard, but Howe rejected Clinton's pressure for an amphibious attack on Boston in order to destroy the French fleet.[31] As with d'Estaing at Sandy Hook, the obvious note was of a reluctance to take chances and risk warships and crew, notably in partly unknown inshore waters; although, in July 1776, the British had run what were supposed to be strong American batteries at the entrance to the Hudson, thus threatening the western flank of the American troops on Manhattan.

The British plan for 1778 in North American waters came to depend on the navy. That August, Clinton was ordered to pursue the strategy outlined in the instructions of 8 March of attacks on New England and a winter expedition to the south,[32] which indeed took Savannah that December. Lord George Germain, the Secretary of State for America, had followed this up in November 1778:

> The rebels will severely feel the effects of a war which will keep their coast in perpetual alarm, and by taking or destroying their ships and stores whilst we prevent their

growing into a maritime power, our own commerce may be freed from the insults of their privateers.³³

Clinton, complaining about the risks of attack by a French and maybe a Spanish fleet, wrote, 'The Admiral tells me that the number of ships which he is to have on this coast will not be above a peace establishment and one half of those are detained in the West Indies.'³⁴

The battles of the period indicated the difficulty of achieving a sweeping naval victory, which, in successive wars, the British were not to gain until 1747, 1759, 1782, 1798 and 1805. Off Ushant, on 27 July 1778, Admiral Augustus Keppel failed to destroy the evasive Brest fleet, with Keppel lacking the naval superiority that would have been provided by the addition of Vice-Admiral John Byron's squadron which had been detached to pursue the Toulon fleet to North America. Blankett's account suggested that the French fought well:

> The French fired first and very effectually destroyed our rigging and sails, and very much damaged our masts and yards; however, the Admiral [Keppel] made the signal to wear and stand towards the enemy; but finding our ships to be so much shattered, he wore again in order to give them an opportunity to repair their damage. The French wore about 3, and stood towards us, in good order, only one of their ships appearing to be disabled; on this the Admiral made the signal to form the line, but as our disabled ships formed very slowly it was evening before our fleet were in any order. The French advanced in a most regular line and in a masterly manner ... The French behaved more like seamen, and more officerlike than was imagined they would be, their ships were in very high order, well

managed, well rigged and ... much more attentive to order than our own. In short, they are truly formidable, nor will I admit the general received opinion of their inferiority in any one point ... their fire was brisk and well directed, nor was there the least appearance of fear ... As our fire was directed low and was well kept up, I have reason to think killed a great number of their men and did them great damage in their hulls.[35]

Blankett also indicated the dependence on wind direction:

The forcing a fleet to action, equal in force, and with the advantage of the wind must always be done with great risk, and our fleet was not equal to that manoeuvre, but chance, which determines many events, put it out of the Admiral's power to choose his disposition ... the truth is, unless two fleets of equal force are equally determined for battle, whoever attacks must do it with infinite risk, but a fleet to leeward attacking one to windward is a dangerous manoeuvre indeed.[36]

The indecisive character of this battle ensured that Britain faced French intervention in the War of American Independence in a difficult situation. Conversely, British victory that day would have limited the possibilities of French attack on the British empire, and would have increased French dependence on Spain.

Ushant was a total failure compared to Quiberon Bay in 1759, leaving the French able to take the initiative in 1779. In response to the Spanish demand for a short war, France and Spain sent a fleet of 66 ships of the line into the Channel. This was an attempt at invasion focused on the British base at

Portsmouth. It was thwarted by disease and poor organisation, rather than British naval action, for the outnumbered Western Squadron under Admiral Charles Hardy failed to mount an effective response. Yet, by keeping to windward off the Scillies, the French were scared of proceeding or being driven by wind up the Channel where they lacked fleet bases from which to replenish or refit, a situation that lasted until they developed Cherbourg as a naval base.

Despite grave strategic and organisational problems, the French were more successful at sea than in the Seven Years War, in part thanks to the British delay in mobilising and in part to determined and effective French leadership.[37] Indeed the role of the latter emerges clearly in the French war effort. There is a ready contrast between the able and energetic Admiral Pierre André Suffren, who proved a persistent, redoubtable and brave opponent to the British in the Bay of Bengal and off Sri Lanka in 1782–3, and Louis, Count d'Orvilliers, the commander of the attempt to invade England in 1779. Criticism led d'Orvilliers to resign as vice-admiral.

There was now an incessant need to assess how best to respond to French moves. In late 1779, Admiral Marriot Arbuthnot, in command of the warships in New York, had to consider how to respond if d'Estaing attacked New York, Newport or Halifax. Preparing to defend New York in October, he positioned his ships at Sandy Hook as Howe had done the previous year, arguing that, unlike Newport, New York was crucial – if it fell, so also would 'all the ships stores, provisions and magazines of all sorts'. However, Arbuthnot wrote to Clinton that if Halifax fell it would be necessary to retain Newport, 'because New York is not a place for large ships', but if Halifax was retained it would not be worth using up troops to hold it. Arbuthnot added,

> The ships of the line cannot winter in the port of New York, much less can they come upon the coast near it, being of all others the most dangerous for large ships ... the line of battle ships will be as soon with you from Halifax and in better order than they could be from any other port on this continent.[38]

Rhode Island was abandoned and the French were able to use it as a base. This, however, freed 5,000 British troops and a number of warships at a time when both were in short supply and when coastal operations in New England were a decreasing priority.

The new emphasis was seen on 26 December 1779 when Arbuthnot and Clinton sailed from Sandy Hook for South Carolina with 7,600 troops. The voyage illustrated the drawbacks for such operations because, on 28 December, a terrible storm struck the fleet off Cape Hatteras. Much of it was dispersed by storm and current, one transport ending up off Cornwall, while most of the horses and much of the supplies, especially ordnance stores and entrenching tools, were lost. John Hayes, an army physician, suffered 'full forty days beating the boisterous ocean'.[39] As a result, the fleet did not anchor off North Edisto Inlet, 30 miles south of Charleston, as intended but instead went to Savannah for recuperation and repair, sailing again on 10 February. This delay shows the questionable nature of claims that Britain could have made a better effort to move forces between America and the West Indies in order to achieve seasonally propitious annual campaigns in both, as such movements entailed risk, not least in terms of predictable timing.

The navy played a major role in the subsequent attack on Charleston. The disruption of the siege train in the storm meant that cannon and artillerymen had to be supplied by the fleet, while Arbuthnot and seven warships forced their way past

American fortifications on the north side of the harbour. A Hessian quartermaster recorded that 'we could see nothing of the ships except the flashes of their guns because of the smoke. The majesty of this sight can hardly be described.'[40] The capture of Charleston entailed the seizure of most of what was left of the Continental (American) navy which had been anchored there and employed only in static defence.

Clinton, however, was worried by his exposure to Franco-Spanish naval action. In comments that Yorktown in 1781 were to show as prescient, he observed, on 4 July 1780, that operations in the Chesapeake depended on 'if the French and Spaniards are kept at home ... if ... a superior enemy's fleet awes this coast I shall be reduced to a strict defensive here [New York] not to say worse, and all our detached corps will be beat en detail'.[41] A week later, a French expeditionary force accompanied by seven ships of the line anchored at Newport. Clinton pressed Arbuthnot, a difficult man with whom his relations were increasingly poor, for a joint attack designed to destroy the French force, but Arbuthnot was unwilling to back an attack during the crucial period before the French could fortify Newport.

The British defensive preparations for repelling invasion in 1779 had indicated a lack of confidence, and this remained an issue. In practice, Bourbon amphibious forces were effective elsewhere, notably in West Florida (1779–81) and Minorca (1782), in each case in the absence of any significant naval opposition. In contrast, there was no invasion of Britain or Ireland. Nor, although there were disturbances in the Channel Fleet at Spithead in 1780, was there anything to match the naval mutinies of 1797.

In both the Caribbean and the Indian Ocean, the French were more successful at sea than in the previous war, in part thanks to determined and effective leadership, as with Suffren in the Indian

Ocean, but other factors also played a role. When Byron attacked d'Estaing off Grenada on 6 July 1779, he was outnumbered and roughly handled. In three engagements in the Caribbean in 1780, Rodney was unable to defeat the Comte de Guichen. Sir Charles Middleton, the Comptroller of the Navy from 1778 to 1790, who had served in the Caribbean during the Seven Years War, notably against French privateers in 1761, pressed its importance on William, 2nd Earl of Shelburne, the Prime Minister, in 1782: 'The West India trade is not only a great nursery for seamen, but, by the immense revenue arising from its produce, a great support of the navy.'

The Caribbean proved formative to the career of Horatio Nelson. Born in 1758, he sailed first to the Caribbean in 1771–2 on a merchantman. After seeing naval service in Indian waters in 1775–6, Nelson was promoted to lieutenant in 1777, and then made several cruises to the Caribbean, being promoted to captain in 1779, a year in which he took American prizes there. A failed attack on a French position in the Turks Islands in 1783 was followed by the capture of French and Spanish prizes, winning prize money. In peacetime, Nelson served in the Caribbean in 1784–7, enforcing the Navigation Acts.

From the Caribbean, French warships could sail north into American waters, where they were able to put pressure on the British, notably in support of amphibious operations. Success could prove elusive, as in the American–French failure to seize Savannah in 1779, but in 1781 there was a crucial French success with Cornwallis' army encircled at Yorktown on the Chesapeake.

De Grasse had been able to leave Brest for Martinique with 20 ships of the line in March 1781, and that August he sailed from Saint-Domingue for the Chesapeake. The previous winter, a British force was sent to the Chesapeake. Leaving Sandy Hook on 20 December 1780, it had been characteristically disrupted by a winter storm, reaching Hampton Roads on 30 December and establishing a base at Portsmouth. This was challenged in January 1781 by three French warships that escaped the blockade of Newport, and, more seriously, two months later, when the entire French squadron was able to sail, because the British blockaders had been badly disrupted by a storm. Fortunately for the British at Portsmouth, the French were engaged by Arbuthnot off the Virginia Capes on 16 March. He was outmanoeuvred and several of his ships badly battered, but the French did not press their advantage to gain control of the Chesapeake. This meant that the American forces in the area could not act effectively against the British.

British commanders were well aware of the dependence of Chesapeake operations on naval command, Clinton informing Cornwallis on 29 May 1781 of 'a circumstance which I am ever aware of in carrying on operations in the Chesapeake, which is, that they can be no longer secure than whilst we are superior at sea ... nor have I any reason to suspect we shall not' remain so. Clinton had pressed Arbuthnot to consider this, 'having repeatedly told him, that should the enemy possess it even for 48 hours your lordship's operations there may be exposed to most imminent danger'. Although more concerned about the situation at Newport, Arbuthnot promised to guard the Chesapeake.[42]

Clinton was concerned about an attack on New York, but

> I am however under no great apprehensions: as Sir George Rodney seems to have the same suspicions of de Grasse's intention that we have and will of course follow him hither. For I think our situation cannot become very critical, unless the enemy by having the command of the Sound should possess themselves of Long Island, which can never be the case, whilst we are superior at sea.[43]

Clinton pressed Rodney to send sufficient ships to counter de Grasse's expected arrival. Meanwhile, the continual British presence in the Chesapeake was increasingly discussed in terms of its acting as a naval base, Clinton writing to Cornwallis,

> I am just returned from having a conference with Rear-Admiral Graves ... we are both clearly of opinion that it is absolutely necessary we should hold a station in the Chesapeake for ships of the line, as well as frigates.[44]

This would entail control of the Williamsburg peninsula, but Cornwallis was more sceptical:

> Desultory expeditions in the Chesapeake may be undertaken from New York with as much ease and more safety, whenever there is reason to suppose, that our naval force is likely to be superior for two or three months.[45]

The quest for a naval base ensured that the British forces in Virginia were to surrender the initiative. Moreover, although Yorktown offered an anchorage suitable for ships of the line, it was a poor defensive position against land attack.

The navy, however, wanted a Chesapeake base. Graves, who had replaced Arbuthnot, did not think that New York or Gardiner's Island at the eastern end of Long Island, from which Newport had been watched, were suitable winter anchorages. As Newport had been lost, the Chesapeake appeared the only alternative to distant Halifax, and Clinton, who did not want the naval base far from New York, informed Cornwallis that he did not think there was any chance of the French 'having a naval superiority in these seas for any length of time, much less for so long a one as two or three months'.[46]

The naval situation was unsettled. De Grasse did not sail directly to America but went first to the West Indies where Tobago was forced to surrender on 2 June. De Barras, the commander of the Newport squadron, did not relish the idea of serving under de Grasse and was only dissuaded with difficulty from sailing to attack Newfoundland. In addition, de Grasse might have been recalled, or Rodney might have defeated or pre-empted him. In the event, an indecisive and ailing Rodney sailed for Britain, escorting prizes back to England. De Grasse got to the Chesapeake before Graves, who did not appreciate the seriousness of the situation.

In marked difference to the battle on 16 March 1781, Graves' failure to defeat the French off the Virginia Capes on 5 September 1782, while also indecisive in terms of the damage and not leading to any shift in naval superiority, was highly significant as it prevented Cornwallis' relief. Thanks to a temporary and localised French superiority, which reflected Rodney's failure to detach a matching number of ships from the Caribbean to North American waters, Graves was outnumbered 24 to 19 in ships of the line. Instead of taking the risky course of ordering a general chase on the French van as it sailed in disordered haste from the Chesapeake, he manoeuvred so as to bring all his ships opposite to the French line of battle, which was given time to form. The engagement lasted for just over two hours, neither side having any ships sunk but both suffering considerable damage.

The French both retained their superiority and still blocked the entrance to the Chesapeake, while Graves did not feel able to engage de Grasse again. He instead decided to sail to New York for repairs first, but before doing so he delayed a week. Clinton promised Cornwallis naval relief, but the repairs took longer than anticipated. New York did not have a naval dockyard, there was a shortage of naval stores and food, and a number of accidents delayed matters. As de Grasse had been strengthened by the Newport squadron but Graves only by three ships of the line from England, the French superiority increased and Graves was worried about the danger of attacking a superior force. This was understandable as the risky plan advocated by Clinton and Hood endangered both the largest British naval force in the western hemisphere and the continued viability of the New York garrison. Graves did not sail until 19 October, but Cornwallis surrendered that day. Clinton blamed the disaster totally on the lack of sufficient warships.[47]

Although the French rejected the American desire to exploit Yorktown by a joint attack on Charleston or Wilmington, North Carolina, the impact on British political opinion ensured that the campaign had a strategic impact. The ministry of Lord North fell, to be replaced by that of Charles, Marquess of Rockingham, which was pledged to negotiate peace. Yet, this fall can only be seen as a result of naval action if it is appreciated that such action could not force this result. Instead, news of the conflict interacted with major political tensions in Britain. In turn, by precluding a French attack, victory at the battle of the Saintes in 1782 helped to keep New York for George III for another year. The Saintes also ensured that the navy ended the war with the appearance of success.

The British navy responded to the pressures of the war by arranging a major programme of construction. This included, to an extent greater than in the two previous years,[48] the use of private shipbuilders to enhance capacity. So, moreover, with dockyards. There were also technological advances. Copper-sheathing reduced the difficulties caused to wooden hulls by barnacles, weeds and the teredo worm, with the consequent loss of speed, and also made refits easier. This sheathing was pressed forward from February 1779 by Middleton, the recently appointed Comptroller of the Navy. In 1780, 42 ships of the line were given copper sheathing. Politicians noted a sense of new potential, Charles, 2nd Marquess of Rockingham claiming in 1781, 'The copper bottoms occasioning our ships to sail so much better enables us either to go and attack if we should see an inferior fleet or to decline the attempt if we should see a superior fleet.'[49] By reducing the need for frequent hull repairs and refits, this substantially increased the size of the operational (in proportion to the nominal) fleets. The value of copper sheathing can be questioned, but the administrative achievement it represented was considerable, and this achievement encouraged the assumption that similar changes should be possible.

The introduction of the carronade was also important. A new, light (for the weight of the shot), short-barrelled gun that was very effective at close quarters and required a relatively small crew, it was adopted by Britain in 1779 and proved potent at the battle of the Saintes in 1782, where copper-sheathing also helped the British; the French, in contrast, had neither. There had been experiments with flintlocks on cannon in mid-century, but they were applied from 1778. Flintlocks were applied to cannon from 1778 as a result of the initiative of the innovative Captain Sir Charles Douglas, who fitted out his ship of the line, *Duke*, with them at his own expense. This led to faster, more reliable and better-controlled fire, and the British benefited at the Saintes.

Increases in the size of warships and also in their width in relation to their length made them far more seaworthy and hence much more able to undertake operations across the oceans. It was thus possible to have so many fleet battles in Caribbean, North American and Indian waters during the War of American Independence; and also to continue operations in European waters into the winter months when, in contrast, the first and second rate ships of the line had had to be laid up in the past.

There was also a great expansion of the naval dockyards at Portsmouth and Plymouth between 1763 and 1790. The 1,095 foot-long ropery opened at Portsmouth in 1776 may have been the largest building in the world. Far greater concern for the health of sailors, including hospital provision, contributed to the improved ability to keep ships and crew at sea, as well as the intensity of naval warfare. As another instance of naval enlightenment, many naval officers showed scientific interest and application, notably in astronomy and mathematics, both of which were necessary for navigation.

The British empire, and with it the navy, was under considerable challenge around the world, a situation that was accentuated when the Dutch were added to Britain's opponents at the close of 1780. Around this time, a key task for the navy became the defensive support of endangered positions. In particular, Gibraltar was besieged from 1779 to 1783,[50] leading to three naval relief expeditions. On the first, a Spanish squadron was defeated off Cape St Vincent on 16 January 1780 when Rodney and 21 of the line chased 11 Spanish ships of the line in a battle conducted on a stormy night. One Spanish warship was destroyed and six captured, including the flagship. The next year, however, saw the British under a range of pressures that prefigured the crisis of 1796–7. There was no sense that Britain controlled the war at sea.

Failure off the Virginia Capes was far from the sole issue. Closer to home, in the summer of 1781, another Franco-Spanish fleet was able to cruise in the Channel approaches without the outnumbered British risking battle. Many merchantmen were lost. In September, the British were concerned about a possible invasion of England or Ireland from Brest and also about the danger that the French fleet there would be employed against Gibraltar. Furthermore, there was pressure in the North Sea as a result of Dutch entry into the war. The Dutch succeeded in keeping a British squadron busy watching them. Vice-Admiral Sir Hyde Parker fought a costly, close-range, indecisive battle with a nearly equal Dutch fleet at Dogger Bank on 5 August. Each fought in a fairly rigid fashion and the British suffered from having several old ships of poor seaworthiness. The result was similar to that of Ushant in 1778, the lack of a victory ensuring that the strategic burden on Britain remained great. Moreover, a naval engagement with the Spaniards off Cape Spartel on 20 October 1782 after the last British naval relief of Gibraltar was indecisive.

A British attempt to capture Cape Town from the Dutch in 1781 was prevented by a French fleet under Suffren. He pressed on into Indian waters to provide support for Haider Ali, the Sultan of Mysore, France's ally against Britain. This deployment led to a series of battles with Vice-Admiral Sir Edward Hughes in the Bay of Bengal and off Sri Lanka from February 1782 until June 1783: those of Sadras, Providien, Negapatam, Trincomalee and Cuddalore. Suffren proved a redoubtable opponent who sought to scatter Hughes' fleet and defeat it piecemeal by concentrating strength against vulnerable sections. At Cuddalore, he attacked the more numerous British at close range and inflicted greater damage than he suffered. Hughes, however, avoided defeat, and the resilience of his command helped ensure that the British did not have a failure in India to match that in America. So also with Gibraltar. Suffren suffered from the lack of a well-equipped local base and had poor relations with some of his captains whom he thought timid and incompetent. There was not the cohesion in command that Nelson was to achieve.

No warships were sunk or captured in the Anglo-French battles in Indian waters, but, as the British force there was built up by reinforcements, this represented a failure for France. The infrastructure of British naval power was improving. By the mid-1770s, Bombay's dry dock could take three third-rate warships and could make repairs.[51] Owned by the East India Company, use of the dry dock by the navy required its permission. Hughes' poor relations with the Company affected naval operations.

The British were more successful in overcoming native naval forces. In 1775, two British warships encountered a Maratha squadron and engaged the largest ship. It was fired on from within pistol range by 'great guns and small arms, some few of both were returned by the enemy, but far short of what might reasonable have been expected from a vessel of her force'. Maratha hopes of boarding a British warship were thwarted by its gunfire, and the Maratha ship blew up with no British casualties. In 1780, Hughes found Haidar Ali's fleet off Mangalore. Covered by gunfire from the warships, and in the face of fire from coastal positions, the ships' boats of the British squadron moved in and successfully boarded the two leading Mysore warships.[52]

Naval intervention against coastal positions had remained crucial on the pattern of the Seven Years War, as in the successful siege of the French base of Pondicherry in 1778 which owed much to support from Sir Edward Vernon's squadron: it both blockaded the town and landed marines and sailors to help the siege. Success in this case owed much to the retreat to Mauritius of the covering French squadron after an indecisive action. So also with the capture of Negapatam (1781) and Trincomalee (1782) by Hughes, and of St Eustatius in the West Indies by Rodney (1781). In 1782, Lieutenant-General Sir Eyre Coote, the Commander-in-Chief of the East India Company forces, wrote from southern India,

> I wish most anxiously for intelligence of the Admiral and the Fleet being again upon the coast, as I should hope thereby to

have it in my power to move to the southward, as a supply of provisions might then be sent by sea without which I could not in the present position of Haidar and the French undertake such an operation to its full extent, at least with that degree of security so necessary to the preservation of our real interests.[53]

The previous year, Lord Macartney, Governor of Madras, had referred to the army as confined to 'the borders of the sea, by which it is now supplied'.[54]

However, such dominance was no longer certain. Indeed, in 1781, the defeated commander of Pensacola, the major base in West Florida, which had fallen to Spanish attack, attributed the defeat 'to the notorious omission or neglect, in affording Pensacola a sufficient naval protection or aid'.[55] In practice, such a force would have been a detachment from the more crucial naval balances elsewhere, while also being vulnerable to Bourbon attack, not least from nearby Havana.

The British lacked enough warships and crew for the many theatres of activity the navy now had to cover, and this helped ensure that the control of the naval war won by the Western Squadron in 1747 and again during the Seven Years War could not be repeated. The failure to keep the French in port in 1778 ensured the need for a greater overseas deployment of the battlefleet, and this was accentuated once Spain entered the war. A large battlefleet had to be assembled in the Leeward Islands every year to prevent a French or Spanish incursion. Moreover, the Western Squadron had to protect the vast supply convoy sent annually to resupply Gibraltar, which had to pass the French bases of Brest and Rochefort and the Spanish ones of Ferrol and Cadiz. Fitting out, taking the round trip and refitting on return took the squadron off station for two months each year, which gave the French the opportunity to launch their fleet. Thus, in 1781, Admiral Darby was ordered on 31 January to provide the escort. It took six weeks to refit and man the fleet and assemble the stores and shipping. Darby sailed on 13 March with 29 of the line, and reached Cork for the victualling ships on 17 March, but then had to wait for ten days while wind and weather prevented them from coming out to join him. He reached the Straits of Gibraltar on 11 April, finally completing the resupply, before sailing on 20 April and reaching Spithead on 21 May. In the meantime, de Grasse, with 20 of the line, had left Brest for the Caribbean, Suffren with five for the East Indies. La Motte Picquet, sent with six to intercept British trade, had captured a homeward-bound West India convoy worth £5 million.[56]

While the British owed much to naval resilience[57] and fighting quality, they were also fortunate that their opponents frequently lacked the necessary naval strength. This was certainly the case with the Americans and with Indian forces. Both did not have the naval strength to support their land operations and to mount a significant challenge at sea. Thus, the Americans lacked naval support for their eventually unsuccessful invasion of Canada in 1775–6, which meant that Quebec could be relieved by the British in 1776. There was also no American naval protection against the British New York (1776) and Philadelphia (1775) campaigns, and in 1778 the British force that had retreated from Philadelphia was able to sail from New Jersey to New York. Once France entered the war and deployed naval forces, it still remained difficult to arrange consistent co-operation with American and Indian allies. Moreover, the French (like the Spaniards) faced serious problems in balancing their naval commitments and sustaining their squadrons, and these affected the operations of particular fleets. There was also scant co-operation between the fleets of France and its allies. By the end of the war, Britain was winning the naval race with France and planning amphibious attacks on the Spanish empire. The performance of the French navy declined as a consequence of the lack of sufficient skilled officers and seamen both to replace losses and to man new ships.

In James Barry's painting during the war for the Society for the Encouragement of Arts, Commerce and Manufactures, the figure of Father Thames was presented as a reborn Neptune, but naval triumphalism was scarcely in order. Indeed, there was a marked contrast with the situation in recent conflicts. Thus, in 1779, John Collet reported from Genoa, 'As we have no squadron in the Mediterranean, all the news I could offer would be the taking of a few merchantmen on either side.'[58]

In part, there were the problems for Britain of the mismatch between resources and goals.[59] Yet, in the end, although this did not save British rule of the Thirteen Colonies, the British proved better able than the French and Spaniards to support their naval strength and ambitions, which was a product both of long-term trends and of the particular circumstances of the war.[60] This respective ability with Britain better able to man and pay for its fleet, helped underline the value of economic warfare to both sides, as well as their vulnerability to it. Indeed, in 1775, Vergennes, the French Foreign Minister, argued the need for more frigates so as to hit British trade.[61]

Britain's survival, albeit at the cost of an important part of its empire, was a success, and to a significant degree for British naval capability as well as more specifically with reference to that of its opponents. The war pushed to the fore the reactive operational stance that repeatedly emerged from naval tasks, notably trade protection and invasion deterrence. These were particularly difficult in this war due to the number of opponents, and that made it hard to match the proactive assumptions of the contemporary conception of British naval power.

Deterrence and Defeat

On a pattern that was widely shared, George III typically saw divine support as well as human action as important. In October 1778, he expressed to North his trust that the navy would be in a state to cope with both France and Spain, adding,

> Lord North must feel as I do the noble conduct of the three fifty gun ships that with so much bravery have driven off separate ships of far superior strength; I doubt not whenever it shall please the Almighty to permit an English fleet fairly to engage any other a most comfortable issue will arise.[62]

Two months later, however, correctly concerned about naval factionalism, George pressed for a new head of the Admiralty Board in place of Sandwich: 'In a war and more so in the present which is a naval one, it is highly advantageous to have in the Cabinet a person able to plan the most effectual manner of conducting it.'[63] There was to be no replacement, however, until the fall of the North ministry in 1782 when Sandwich was succeeded by Augustus, 1st Viscount Keppel, a veteran and Whig dismissed in 1779 in the politicised aftermath of the disappointment of the battle of Ushant. Keppel was at the centre of naval factionalism.

The king's identification with the navy was demonstrated with his third son, William (later William IV), born in 1765, entering naval service in 1779 and in 1780 becoming a midshipman and seeing active service. He was to be the 'Sailor King'. George also visited the fleet in 1778 (both Chatham and Portsmouth) and 1781 (the Nore), paying minute attention to the naval review of 1778, following Keppel's court-martial and pressing for a battle with the combined Franco-Spanish fleet in 1779 even though it was larger.[64]

The sense of national alarm was to leave a humorous aftermath in Richard Brinsley Sheridan's play *The Critic* (1779), a drama that included the rehearsal for a play about the Spanish Armada, clearly now apparently pertinent. However, in practice, there had been a serious shock for Britain, one in which naval weaknesses, indeed failure, appeared even more consequential than at the time of Byng's debacle in 1756. Alongside euphoric relief in the aftermath of the battle of the Saintes in 1782, a sense of vulnerability was to be seen going forward into the post-war world. It was to be demonstrated anew in the naval crisis of 1796–7.

Spanish Armada off English coast, 1588, by Cornelis Claesz. van Wieringen. (Rijksmuseum)

The departure of William of Orange's fleet from Hellevoetsluis on their successful seaborne invasion of England in 1688. (Rijksmuseum)

Above left: Admiral Edward Russell, naval commander-in-chief from December 1690, attacked the French on 29 May 1692 off Barfleur. (Rijksmuseum)

Above right: George Rooke, then a vice-admiral, acquitted himself well at Barfleur. (Rijksmuseum)

The Battle of Barfleur or La Hougue, depicted by Benjamin West. (National Gallery of Art)

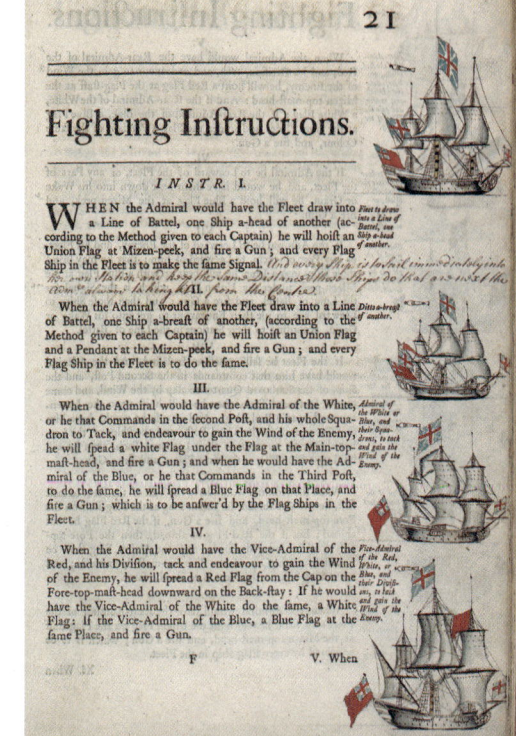

Right: A signal manual from 1711, reflecting the burgeoning influence of this tactical innovation. (Yale Center for British Art)

Below: HMS *Hampton Court*, a 70-gun third-rate ship of the line under the command of Charles Wager, later First Lord of the Admiralty, during the Spanish War of Succession. (Birmingham Museum)

Samuel Scott's painting of the First Battle of Cape Finisterre, which took place on 14 May 1747. In the centre, Anson's flagship *Prince George* can be seen firing a broadside into the French *Invincible*. (Yale Center for British Art)

Above left: George Anson, victor at the First Battle of Cape Finisterre. (Yale Center for British Art)

Above right: Rear-Admiral Edward Hawke would follow Anson's example in a brilliant naval action at the Second Battle of Cape Finisterre in October of the same year. (Yale Center for British Art)

Above left: Admiral Edward Boscawen, a thorn in the side of the French navy through the 1750s. (Yale Center for British Art)

Above right: The unfortunate Admiral John Byng, who on 14 March 1757 was shot as punishment for his failure to hold Minorca. (Rijksmuseum)

Boscawen's victory over the French at the Battle of Lagos in August 1759 was a vital boost shortly before the better-known victory at Quiberon Bay. (Rijksmuseum)

The Battle of Quiberon Bay, which destroyed French invasion hopes in 1759. (Yale Center for British Art)

The Battle of Chesapeake in 1781, where French victory under François de Grasse arguably sealed American victory in the War of Independence. (US Naval History and Heritage Command)

Admiral George Rodney soundly defeated de Grasse in a stunning victory at the Battle of the Saintes in April 1782. (Yale Center for British Art)

Above left: Richard, Earl Howe, victor at the Glorious First of June in 1794. (Cleveland Museum of Art)

Above right: Horatio Nelson, who set such a high standard for naval success in his lifetime. (ASKB Collection, Brown University Library)

The explosion of the French ship *L'Orient* at the spectacular Battle of the Nile in August 1798, where Nelson arguably won a victory more complete than Trafalgar. (Rijksmuseum)

John Christian Schetky's painting of the Battle of Trafalgar, perhaps the best known battle in naval history. The British victory in 1805 settled naval dominance in the West. (Yale Center for British Art)

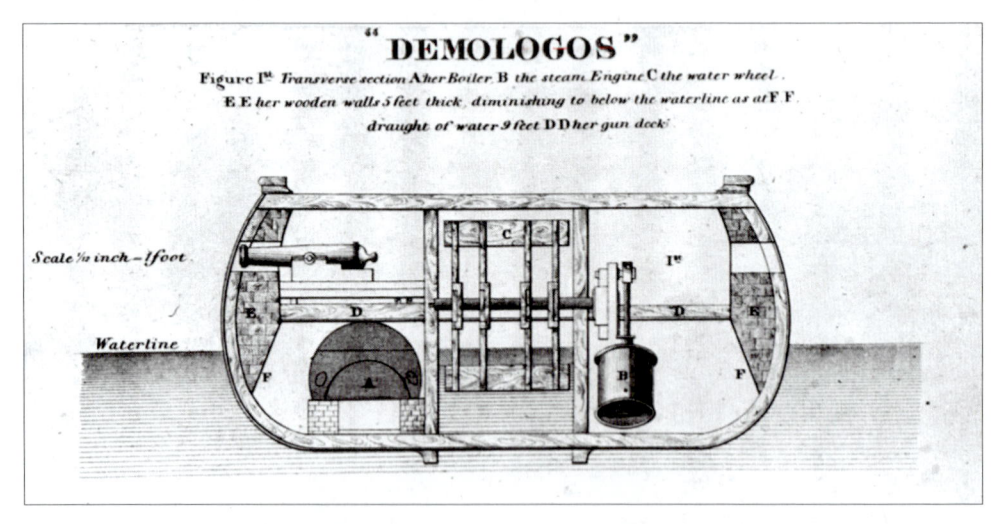

Robert Fulton's paradigm-shifting early nineteenth-century innovations, in the form of submarines and steamboats, were not brought to bear against the British despite his offers to the French and Americans, but such technologies were to play a major role in the development of naval warfare in the years to come. (US Naval History and Heritage Command)

7

BRINKMANSHIP TO THE FORE
1784–92

> Our British tars shall crop your ears
> And drive your Fleets to hell.

The British Tar's Laughing-stock, or The Royal Quixote (1790), a caricature attack on Charles IV of Spain, expressed confidence in the event that the Nootka Sound Crisis over Pacific territories and trade should lead to war. There had been far less confidence in the aftermath of the War of American Independence. Although there was some concern about Dutch naval strength in, and near, the Strait of Malacca,[1] anxiety in 1783–7 overwhelmingly focused on French naval strength and intentions, and as part of French activity both in Europe and further afield. Anxiety about the latter fed through into the perception of French naval moves, and vice versa. At every stage, there was a sense that the French needed to be matched, and yet uncertainty about what the next French moves would be. Thus, in 1786, Thomas, 2nd Lord Walsingham, wrote to William Pitt the Younger, the first minister and a fellow member of the Board of Control for India,

> Look at the naval force in India at this moment of the French and of the Dutch compared with our own ... The Governor General says 2 French frigates could stop all supplies and all communication with Madras, and, he adds, the worst of consequences will follow unless you have a naval force on a rupture equal to your enemies.[2]

Closer to home, there was anxiety that the French development of Cherbourg was intended to provide a better and closer invasion base than Brest. There were reports that it would be able to contain 100 ships of the line.[3] Louis XVI's visit in 1786 helped to focus public concern. Although the French Foreign Minister, Charles, Count of Vergennes, pointed out the difficulty for France of sustaining war on land and at sea,[4] in a case of strategic asymmetry, the French threatened Britain simply by keeping their fleet in being; with this, an invasion by the more numerous French army remained a serious prospect.

The British responded by pursuing intelligence, trying to arrange a mutual reduction of warships in the Indian Ocean (an early disarmament process),[5] and trying to build up their naval strength both beyond and within Europe. This included interest in developing distant naval bases. The vulnerability of the existing British roadsteads in the Bay of Bengal, and concern about the danger that France would establish a naval base in north-west Sumatra, led to interest in the possibilities offered by the Nicobar Islands, or on Rhio off the Kara Isthmus. Admiral Richard, Viscount Howe, 1st Lord of the Admiralty from 1783 until 1788, warned of the Bay of Bengal, however:

> It would require a long time before magazines could be formed for keeping a squadron on that side of India all the year. The settlement would be exposed in the meantime, in

the absence of the squadron, to the attacks of an enemy, before notice could be conveyed for obtaining reasonable assistance from the other British settlements where the squadron might be stationed.[6]

In the event, in response to instructions in 1787 about the need for a base, Commodore William Cornwallis established Port Cornwallis as a base in the Andamans in 1789.

There was a sense of vulnerability elsewhere, and also an emphasis on the navy as the response. Thus, the *Morning Post* of 17 March 1786 noted,

> By the last accounts from Halifax ... we learn ... Capt. Stanhope of the *Mercury* man of war, with four frigates, to cruise on the Banks of Newfoundland, in order to prevent the French from making encroachments on the British fisheries.

In Europe, the navy sought with considerable success to repair the damage of the recent war, a situation that was helped by the shipbuilding in its last stage. Assisted by Middleton's successful administration,[7] naval power played a major role in British foreign policy.[8] In a confrontation with France in 1787 over Dutch politics, the British primarily relied on their ally Prussia by land, but also sent warships to sea. If George III was concerned that a shortage of sailors limited what could be done,[9] the situation was worse for France. Indeed, whereas Britain had about 118,000 skilled trained seamen, the French had only about 55,000 saltwater-trained seamen; the large numbers in addition of those used to river navigation were of limited value at sea. The comparable Dutch and Spanish figures were 45,000 and 35,000. Charles, 3rd Duke of Richmond, Master-General of the

Ordnance, referred in 1787 to consideration of 'the practicality of our taking the Texel and the Helder and stationing a fleet there to cut off all communication by sea with Amsterdam'.[10] When Prussia invaded, British naval preparations were stepped up, with an order for the preparation of 40 of the line, in order to deter the French. John, 3rd Duke of Dorset, the Ambassador in Paris, reported the Brest squadron as only having 12 of the line fit for service.[11] France did not act.

This set a pattern for subsequent crises. Allied now with the Dutch, the fifth-largest naval power, the British were in a better position, not least as the price of naval security was numerical superiority. In September 1788, William Grenville, a member of the Board of Control for India, pressed Pitt on the need for Anglo-Dutch naval superiority over, and British equality with, France in the Indian Ocean, adding a clear economic rationale: Britain should 'never again' be exposed to the danger of losing the homeward-bound East India fleet, whose value, including the China trade, he estimated at £8 million.[12]

In the event, the next serious crisis emerged primarily with Spain and due to rival interests in Pacific trade and territory. Spain remained the third naval power, its fleet was increasing in size, and the naval shipyards in both Spain and at Havana were efficient. Massive 112- and 120-gun three-deckers, as well as 74-gun two-deckers of high quality, were launched in the 1780s, while training and seamanship improvements were begun in 1785, although there were also significant post-war cuts in naval expenditure.[13]

News of the seizure of the British base at Nootka Sound on Vancouver Island in July 1789 reached London on 21 January 1790 and Spanish naval preparations in April encouraged the British government to decide on force as the means to ensure satisfaction. On 1 May, the Admiralty was ordered to fit out a fleet of 40 of the line to be assembled at Spithead as soon as possible, on 3 May a press for sailors was authorised, and on 6 May Pitt asked the Commons for supplies. In response, France, as Spain's ally, decided to arm 14 of the line, although the Dutch armed 10 of the line which were sent to join the British fleet. The British were fully informed of the build-up of the Spanish fleet at Cadiz, but, isolated and intimidated, Spain agreed to back down in July. The promise on 26 August by the French National Assembly to arm 45 of the line raised tensions anew, but there was not the necessary support or funds, whereas by 8 October Howe's fleet at Spithead consisted of 43 of the line. Spain backed down later that month. Convinced that naval superiority had helped him, Alleyne Fitzherbert referred to 'negotiating with 60 sail of the line at one's back'.[14] Had there been war and the Bourbons obliged by offering their fleets for battle, then the British navy would have stood a good chance: though good and underrated, the Spanish navy was smaller, while the French was affected by the internal problems and disorder of the French state.

If no such major actions had taken place, then the prospect was less favourable for Britain. If the Spanish navy stayed in its bases, these would have to be blockaded or closely watched, neither of which was easy. Any concentration of Spanish naval strength would have posed problems, while a large fleet would have had to be kept in the Channel to mask Brest.

The following year brought confrontation with Russia, the fourth naval power, in an attempt to regain conquests from Turkey. The dispatch of a fleet to the Baltic was seen as the guarantor of Prussian support,[15] and bold hopes were advanced, Francis Jackson, Secretary of Legation at Berlin, observing,

> All that is required here is that Russia may not be allowed to employ her naval force against the coasts of Prussia, and

that a declaration should be made at Petersburgh to that purport, and supported, *if necessary*, by the appearance of a fleet in the Baltic; of this, however, the necessity appears very doubtful; as the very idea of such an apparition will probably suffice to frighten the Russians into almost any terms that may accompany it.

The aptly named Francis Drake, envoy in Copenhagen, was convinced that the arrival of a British fleet would ensure Danish support.[16] Moreover, a misleading, not to say false, history was at play. A London item printed in the *Newcastle Courant* of 15 January 1791 claimed that the fleet sent to the Baltic in 1719 had forced Peter the Great to accept British mediation in the conflict with Sweden: 'The ambition of Russia was checked by the power of Great Britain.' This was woefully inaccurate, a classic instance of the rewriting of history to create a myth of easy naval success. In practice, the navy could as little influence the fate of Ochakov in 1791 as that of Livonia and Estonia in 1719–20, or Poland in 1939.

On 22 March 1791, the Cabinet decided to send 39 of the line and a proportionate number of frigates on the supposition that Denmark would provide the use of its ports, while 10 or 12 of the line were to be prepared for the Black Sea. Vice-Admiral Hood was confident that he could evade Danish control of the Sound by sailing through the Belt. Joseph Ewart, the envoy in Berlin, who was present at the Cabinet, was confident that Russia's ships and docks could be destroyed by fireships, and that naval power would permit the landing of Prussians able to take St Petersburg and lead to Sweden joining the alliance.[17] On the 25th, the government offered able seamen £3 to join the navy, ordinary seamen £2 and able landsmen £1. A strong showing in Parliament for the opposition, however, led the government to break down, the opposition on 12 April citing in the debate in the House of Commons the unwillingness of William Pitt the Elder to send a fleet to the Baltic during the Seven Years War. Ministerial speakers, in contrast, emphasised the danger that Russia, once in control of the Black Sea, would become a hostile naval power. On 16 April, the Cabinet sent new instructions. Once the decision had been reached not to send the fleet to the Baltic, there was pressure from Prussia that a squadron still go to the Black Sea. Pitt the Younger's elder brother John, 2nd Earl of Chatham, the First Lord of the Admiralty, offered prudential operational considerations against such a step but focused instead on strategy:

> The undertaking would be rather an arduous one, the navigation being so little known, and the prevalence of particular winds in the summer months, rendering the passage up the canal of Constantinople very precarious, but these obstacles are to be surmounted, and I should see no objection to this step, but on the contrary considerable advantage, were vigorous measures in question, but ... this plan has not been approved here from the consideration that the sailing of a squadron for the Black Sea would be considered as tending to immediate hostility, and would renew all those alarms and discussions which have to a degree subsided, only from the persuasion that the business was in a train of negociation.[18]

That Britain backed down was due in part to a divided cabinet and concern about Prussia, and certainly about far more than the limitations of naval power. Indeed, the latter were not to the fore in the public or government discussion of the crisis. Instead, the image of this power had been strengthened by the king's visit to the fleet at Plymouth in 1789. The king visited the dockyard twice, going on board the *Royal Sovereign*, inspecting the dockyard facilities, and boarding 'the *Southampton* to see the sham fight'. This commitment took four days and, in 1804, George noted that 'viewing the business of dockyards is ever a most pleasing entertainment to him'.[19]

Yet the hopes placed by some British diplomats had been shown to be unrealistic, and others more perceptive, notably William, Lord Auckland, who had observed of Russia, 'Her dominions and her resources are so imperfectly open to our attacks that our menaces are not greatly regarded by her.'[20] Subsequent years were to demonstrate the problems involved in trying to bring naval power to bear on a France that was more successful in Europe than over the recent decades. At the same time, the mobilisations of these years were significant because usually in peacetime there was a process, due to demobilisation, of forgetting lessons learned in the last war – indeed, the entire business of living and fighting at sea – such that there was a fluctuation in effectiveness. This contributed to a situation of ups and downs within a slow trajectory of improvement. The dramatic growth in British trade in these years was also significant, not least because the relationship between trade and naval power was understood. Edward Gibbon wrote in 1788, when Britain was clearly thriving,

> The policy of Venice was marked by the avarice of a trading, and the insolence of a maritime, power; yet her ambition was prudent; nor did she often forget that, if armed gallies were the effect and safeguard, merchant vessels were the cause and supply, of her greatness.[21]

The same year, the political salience of naval power was brought out in the *London Chronicle* of 19 January when it argued that although Britain and France were disarming their navies, it was necessary for the ministry to

> remember well that a fleet at Cadiz or at Ferrol is as much the object of British attention as at Brest or Toulon: and that he who suffers the House of Bourbon to have a superior squadron lying in their ports, deserves not to direct the helm of state.

The background of accountability and partisanship is all too easy to underplay, but it was a constant factor in the strategic and operational dimensions.

In power from December 1783, William Pitt the Younger's ministry was determined to undo the situation that had caused Britain so much difficulty in the American War of Independence. Once that was over, there was no stop in the building programme, while a more effective maintenance schedule brought the fleet to a high state of readiness. This was helped by successive mobilisations, the first of which brought the Dutch into the British camp, the second of which followed up by further hitting the anti-British alliance of the recent war, and the third of which helped bring the fleet to a high state of readiness, although being unsuccessful in ensuring a different source and route for naval stores than dependence upon Russia. The lesson had been learned. When war broke out in France in 1793, the navy was in a better state of readiness than it had been in 1778.

8

TO CONFRONT A REVOLUTION
1793–1802

'So now my brave countrymen be not in fear of an invasion for the Lord will prosper your island': John Jup, an ordinary seaman serving on the *Orion*, was in no doubt that God was behind Horatio Nelson's victory at the Nile, one in which the explosion of *L'Orient* 'made a whole element shake and was a most glorious scene'.[1] Egypt was a new sphere for British naval power, but Nelson was able on 1 August 1798 to win a spectacular victory that indicated the possibility of total victory at sea. While Nelson was driven away by a strong northerly gale, the Toulon fleet had left for Egypt on 19 May, taking Napoleon and his army to fulfil plans for the general's aggrandisement. A long and unsuccessful search was finally ended when Nelson found the French fleet anchored in Aboukir Bay. As with the British victory at La Hougue in 1692, and that of the Russians over the Turks at Cesmé in 1770, an attacked fleet in an inshore position was especially vulnerable.

Nelson unexpectedly attacked the French on both sides: on the shallow inshore side of their line, where the French were not prepared to resist, as well as simultaneously on the other side. This manoeuvre was not without risks. *Culloden* ran aground and was unable to take part. In a battle fought at night, without reliance on the signal book but rather with reliance on a decentralised method of command and control that Nelson felt would help him release merited Providential support, in which the British fired at very close range, the French lost 11 of their 13 ships of the line present; the other two fled, as did the frigates. The nature of the French position was such that Nelson was able to achieve a battle of annihilation, first defeating the ships in the French van and then pressing on to attack those moored behind, which had been unable to provide assistance. Nelson had ably prepared his captains to act vigorously and in co-operation in all possible eventualities, and had fully explained his tactics to them. British seamanship was superior, and the well-drilled gun crews outshot the French, who were not only surprised and poorly deployed but also failed to respond adequately to the British attack.

The Battle of the Nile was the most dramatic of the naval struggles in the French Revolutionary War. Albeit on a smaller scale, it was a victory more complete than Trafalgar, the most dramatic of the battles in the Napoleonic War. Although Napoleon's army had already been landed, the victory in 1798 was also important in that it was the culminating naval success in recovering from a serious crisis in 1795–7, one that had brought to a head the difficulties in winning naval supremacy against a background of a radically deteriorating position on the Continent. Opposing fleets were repeatedly shown in 1797–8 to lack the fighting quality and organisational strength of the British navy, although there was nothing inevitable in their defeat. Yet, the example of the naval crises of 1778–81 was to the fore in the 1790s and, indeed until Trafalgar.

As relations with France had deteriorated in the winter of 1792–3, the British government had anxiously sought reports on French naval preparations, while simultaneously considering how best to use British naval power. On 27 December 1792, when the two powers were still at peace, the Cabinet decided to send warships to Flushing in order to help the threatened Dutch against any French attack on their territory or ships.[2] However, intervention further afield faced difficulties. In particular, Britain only had a small squadron in Italian waters and that was outnumbered by a French fleet which successfully put pressure on Italian states. Separately, the naval situation was to the fore in what was the last British government attempt to keep the peace, with Britain promising not to commit hostilities while hopes of peace remained,

> unless such measures should be adopted on the part of France in the interval as would leave His Majesty no alternative. Among these must unquestionably be reckoned the plan said to be now in agitation in France, of sending immediately to the West Indies a squadron of ships of war, some of them of great force, together with a very considerable body of land forces. Even in time of the most profound peace, and with the utmost confidence that could be entertained in the good dispositions of France, such a measure would place His Majesty's colonies in that quarter in a situation of the greatest uneasiness. In the present moment … it is impossible that he should forego the advantage of his naval superiority in these seas, and suffer a large force to proceed on a destination eventually so injurious to the security of his own dominions, and to the property and interests of his subjects.[3]

In the event, the declaration of war was not followed by fleet engagements in 1793, in part because the French fleet, in desperately poor condition with the collapse of the officer corps since 1790 and turmoil in the ports,[4] was unprepared. Meanwhile, the policy of open, rather than close, blockade limited British opportunities for combat. At any rate, the leadership and administration of the French fleet was badly affected by the collapse of royal authority in the French Revolution and the resulting political and administrative disruption. Aside from a breakdown in relations between officers and men, there was factionalism within the officer corps and the contrary demands of politicians in Paris and the ports. Disaffection within the French navy proved more serious than its British counterpart during the naval mutinies of 1797.

In 1793, the British were invited into Toulon by French Royalists, before being driven out again by Revolutionary forces benefiting from the well-sited cannon of Napoleon, then a young artillery officer. France lost 13 ships of the line as a result of the rising in Toulon. France was in a particularly vulnerable situation not only due to acute internal instability but also because Spain was an opponent from 1793 to 1795. British ministers used their naval strength to pursue a policy of Caribbean gains, which was seen as a way to weaken French finances, trade and ability to sustain naval power. The issues of campaigning there, however, notably disease, helped make this very difficult.[5]

In 1794, the British, whose fleet had been greatly strengthened over the previous decade, got their opportunity. At the Glorious First of June, Richard, now Earl Howe, with 25 ships of the line, attacked a French fleet of 26 of the line under Louis Thomas Villaret-Joyeuse sent to escort a grain convoy from America into Brest. Howe, who had gained the weather gauge as a result of skilful seamanship, was unable fully to execute his plan for all his ships to cut the French line so that each passed under the stern of a French ship and engaged it from leeward, but, with fleet seamanship operating effectively, sufficient ships succeeded and British gunnery was superior enough and at close range for long enough to cost the French seven warships (six captured and one sunk) and 5,000 casualties, crucial given the difficulties of obtaining skilled manpower. The French fleet was affected by the revolutionary churn, which left captains inexperienced, and in some cases insubordinate, while there was no practice in acting like a fleet.

Success indicated the broad-based nature of command ability on the eve of Nelson's triumphs. George III had hastened to Portsmouth to congratulate his commanders, giving Howe a diamond-hilted sword on the deck of the *Queen Charlotte* and presenting the admirals involved with gold medals. The Glorious First of June saw the superior force win as a result of its skill, experience and tactical nous, but the damage to the British ships in breaking through the French line, followed by the French ability to reform their fleet, ensured that the exploitation was limited. Conversely, the Brest fleet thereafter tended to avoid the risk of battle,[6] although that winter the fleet went to sea to attack British commerce and to stop British support for the Vendée rebels, and lost five more ships to the elements in consequence.

Service at the Glorious First of June was used by Admiral Sir Allan Gardner in his successful contest for a parliamentary seat for Westminster in 1796.[7] Whereas in the first four years in the Anglo-French stage of the War of American Independence France had only lost four ships of the line, in the first three years of the new war France lost 33 of the line, and, aside from providing the British with additions for their fleet, these losses affected the number of sailors available. The pressure on its navy was intense, and France in the 1790s suffered a fall in the number of warships greater than Spain and the Dutch. Britain was again winning the naval arms race, helped also by the loss to opponents of talented, trained seamen, which made the skilled handling of warships increasingly difficult for Britain's rivals.

In 1794, however, the vital convoy reached France. Moreover, the victory did not affect the conflict in the Low Countries where the war very much went France's way. So also with British naval success over the French in 1795, off the Ile de Groix (23 June) and the Ile de Hyères (13 July). In the former, a larger British fleet hit the French Brest fleet in its mismanaged fighting retreat and the three slowest French ships of the line were captured. The Brest fleet had suffered from detaching its six fastest ships to the Toulon fleet. In the latter, the French were outnumbered by 23 to 17 warships, but the French only lost one warship in an engagement that infuriated Nelson. The caution of Vice-Admiral William Hotham led to a failure to push home the British advantage, but was in part justified by the limited support facilities Britain then had in the Mediterranean. He and Nelson had notions of duty in command that differed, just as with Nelson and Calder in 1805. The need for battle and initiative was a given, but within strategic, operational and tactical contexts that varied in the implications drawn from them. Formal doctrine did not exist to bridge the divide, which was just as well as it could not have done so given the multiple uncertainties of naval conflict, not least the unpredictability of opposing moves.

Successes were of little value compared to the collapse of the anti-French alliance as France overran the United Provinces in 1795, and pushed Spain first to peace (1795) and then into alliance (1796), thus restoring the formidable anti-British alliance of the American war. The potential loss of the Dutch to France was the key factor that had led Britain to act in 1787 and 1793, and from 1795 it forced Britain to act against the Dutch fleet and Dutch colonies.

War with Spain provided the British with the opportunity to cut Spain's colonial links. There was now the need to blockade Spanish ports and a threat that Britain's opponents, who enjoyed a numerical superiority when combined, would be able to cover an invasion. As a result, the British, prioritising anew, withdrew their navy from the Mediterranean in early 1797, instead using Lisbon as their base. In consequence, the British garrisons on Corsica and Elba were withdrawn and the British could not mount a response when the French seized Venice's navy and its bases in the Ionian Islands, notably Corfu. Moreover, affected by long service, the fleet was now increasingly in a poor position, which greatly increased the pressure on the dockyards. It was scarcely surprising that Britain sought peace, albeit unsuccessfully. In addition, the French were able to land some troops in Wales in 1797, and to threaten to land more in Ireland. Having failed earlier due to storms blocking a landing in Bantry Bay in December 1796, however, that did not occur until 1798.

There were also the issues posed by serious mutinies in the British fleet in 1797. These occurred against a background of lengthy and arduous service, and of the acute need for manning that had led to the Quota Acts of 1795 and 1796 and the Navy Act of 1795, which were intended to co-opt local government into the recruitment process. Moreover, aside from the burdens of naval service and, far more, impressment, there were the uncertainties created by the variations in shipboard discipline, and by naval pay and pensions, not least as government finances tottered.[8] Drawing on the strong occupational identity of sailors, their role as wage earners, their strong contractual view of naval service, and tradition of collective action, including in pressing for change,[9] the mutiny initially was a mass protest in April about conditions, especially a failure to raise wages (since 1632) in the face of inflation, the lessening of leave as a result of the coppering of ships, the operation of the bounty system, food supply and the treatment of the injured; and there was scant violence in what were essentially conservative affairs aiming, like popular riots throughout the century, to restore a supposedly just system and moral economy that had formerly existed.[10] The more frequent transfer of sailors between ships in the 1790s, a rate that reflected the exigencies of wartime pressures on the Admiralty, may have harmed relations between captains and men, as well as affecting the standard method of leaving unhappy ships for what were believed to be better ones, a classic instance of rational choice by sailors and of the role of information and rumour.

The mutineers were ready to sail if the French left Brest, and emphasised their loyalty, which helped reduce tension. George III wanted 'any neglect that may have given reason' for discontent remedied, but was also keen on the enforcement of 'due subordination',[11] and was worried:

> The spirit seems to be of a most dangerous kind, as at the same time that the mutiny is conducted with a degree of coolness it is not void of method; how this could break out at once without any suspicion before arising seems unaccountable ... it must require a cruise and much time before any reliance can be placed on a restoration of discipline.[12]

The original mutiny ended when many of the demands were accepted and a royal pardon was granted, but in May there were renewed disturbances reflecting the failure to fulfil governmental promises, George noting the unfortunate consequences of Parliament's delay in increasingly naval pay. Vice-Admiral John

Colpoys mishandled the situation on *London*, sealing the crew below decks, refusing to talk with them and then ordering the marines and officers to fire on sailors climbing out through the hatches. He was then obliged to surrender. The episode led to the verse:

> The murdering Colpoys, Vice-Admiral of the Blue,
> Gave order to fire on the *London*'s crew.

Once again, the mutiny ended when the mutineers' complaints were met with higher pay and more rations for all sailors in the navy and not just the mutineers. There was then another mutiny, on the ships in the Nore anchorage off Sheerness who were masking the Dutch. Dissatisfaction over conditions provided a fertile basis for political discontent. The Board of Admiralty was opposed to further concessions, and the supply of fresh water to the ships was stopped, while, as the mutiny became more extreme, it lost support and collapsed in early June. There was also trouble in the British fleet off Cadiz. French and Irish nationalist agents played a smaller role in the mutinies than the government, faced by the anxieties of a revolutionary age, believed; these agents were in fact to be more apparent in 1798.[13]

Later mutinies were on a smaller scale and more specific in their grievances. Thus, a conditional nature of naval service was suggested by the unpopularity of the brutal and unpredictable Captain Hugh Pigot of the *Hermione* which led to a mutiny and the killing of Pigot and nine other officers in September 1797. Encouraged by George, who was concerned about 'the discipline of the navy', much effort was devoted to trying to hunt down the mutineers.[14] In December 1801, the crew of some of the ships ordered to sail for the Caribbean mutinied. The mutiny was crushed and the ringleaders executed. Not all captains and admirals sought to punish mutineers harshly. In 1797, after a mutiny in Rainier's squadron, several sailors were sentenced to death, but Rainier was loath to execute them, and when news of Camperdown came through, he took the opportunity to pardon them and send them back to their ships.

More positively, although the exact percentage of volunteers will never be known because of the navy's accounting system, a majority of sailors were volunteers,[15] the food provided (as in the later world wars) was plentiful and of reasonably high quality, and efforts were made to limit sickness, which made it easier to maintain missions including blockades. During the War of American Independence, Rodney had taken great care of the health of his fleet in the Caribbean, supporting the efforts of the fleet's doctor, Gilbert Blane, who emphasised the use of fresh fruit to deal with scurvy and the importance of sanitation. The routine use of lemon juice from 1796 ensured that deaths due to scurvy fell dramatically. In addition, paternalism was a factor and George could praise the 'humanity' of naval officers.[16]

However inherently unfair and affected by irregularities it might have been, the distribution of prize money helped maintain morale. In 1793–1815, the yield averaged £1 million per annum, a formidable sum that provided an attraction and underlined the disadvantages of peace. The set division ranged from an eighth for the commander-in-chief (bringing great wealth, for example, to Admiral Lord Keith) and a quarter for the captain, to a quarter for the seamen and marines combined; but, in 1808, the share of the first two fell to one-twelfth and one-sixth, while that of petty officers and able seamen improved.

Moreover, most officers were careful of their crew, respecting their professionalism and feeling committed toward them. This was particularly shown among the growing number of officers who were Evangelicals,[17] but was also the case with most. There was a move to regularise punishment, which helped make it less arbitrary. 'Starting' or pursuing men to their work with a cane or rope's end was prohibited by the Admiralty in 1809 while the collection of punishment data that followed two years later was designed to rein in harsh captains. Flogging was regarded as necessary, but not to be used without due cause. Promotion, especially to petty and warrant officers, was another way to maintain morale, as was a growing willingness to provide leave, for the lack of that was a major grievance and cause of desertion.

George also took an approach that reflected his social values and the prevalence of patronage, but a patronage in which merit played a major role. That offered a way to address tensions between social and official rank. Thus, after the capture of a French frigate in 1795, George applauded the promotion of the captain and the first lieutenant, adding,

> As the Second Lieutenant, Mr Maitland, conducted himself very well, I trust he will soon meet with the same favour, being a man of good family will I hope also be of advantage in the consideration, as it is certainly wise as much as possible to give encouragement if they personally deserve it to gentlemen.[18]

Frederick Maitland, the grandson of an earl, was indeed a brave officer and was to have a distinguished naval career, including being Napoleon's captor in 1815.

Throughout, and for officers and seamen at all ranks, there was danger, in war and peace, and in port and at sea. Thus, *Jackson's Oxford Journal* of 3 July 1790 recorded of the *Saturn*, preparing at Spithead:

> The sailors, by accident, let a boom slip from the maintop, which struck Mr Chalmers, the Second Lieutenant, on the

head, and knocked him overboard, so that he never rose again. It is supposed the blow killed him. He was a good man, and an able officer.

Ill discipline was a particular issue in 1797 due to the crisis of British naval power and the threat to Ireland. George felt it necessary to affirm his 'confidence in naval skill and British valour to supply want of numbers. I am too true an Englishman to have ever adopted the more modern and ignoble mode of expecting equal numbers on all occasions.'[19] In the event, battles enabled the British to transform the situation that year. On 14 February off Cape St Vincent, Rear-Admiral Sir John Jervis and 15 of the line attacked a superior and far more heavily gunned Spanish fleet of 27 of the line under Don José de Cordova, using tactics similar to those of Napoleon on land, to operate on interior lines and concentrate his strength on attacking one section of the Spanish fleet. On his own initiative, and copied by others, Nelson kept the two sections separated, while British warships took advantage of the melee Nelson created and of their superior rate of fire to win a number of individual ship encounters. The Spaniards lost four ships of the line captured, including two 112-gunners, and had ten more ships badly damaged. Their fleet fell back into Cadiz, ending the plan for them to repeat 1779 and join the French at Brest.[20] British skill thus helped exploit the difficulties in achieving co-operation and co-ordination between the French, Dutch and Spanish fleets, and self-confidence increased.

Nelson very much looked to the example of action. Referring back to the early 1780s, he was to write to William Cornwallis in 1804:

I imbibed from you certain sentiments which have greatly assisted me in my naval career – That we could always beat a

Frenchman if we fought him long enough; that the difficulty of getting at them was oftentimes more people's own fancy than from the difficulty of the undertaking; that people did not know what they could do until they tried, and that it was always to err on the right side to fight.[21]

The victory off Cape St Vincent was followed by the naval mutinies, but they, in turn, did not prevent victory over the Dutch in the North Sea at the battle of Camperdown on 11 October 1797. Two advancing lines of warships broke the Dutch, also 16 of the line, into three sections. The battle developed, with Admiral Adam Duncan reliant on his captains and not pursuing a rigid order, into ship-to-ship engagements. In this, both sides deployed effective cannonry, Dutch gunnery skill being such that British killed and wounded were proportionately closer to that of their opponent than in any other fleet action of the period. However, superior British fire helped ensure that the Dutch lost seven of the line as well as two 50-gunners.

The battle was celebrated in the arts, notably in a painting by Philip James de Loutherbourg. In December 1797, George III took the leading role in the Naval Thanksgiving held in St Paul's Cathedral after he had processed in state through the thronged streets of London, while captured flags were paraded through the streets by sailors and then deposited in the cathedral. That year saw a particular peak in victory sermons, many of which were printed, notably those by George Pretyman, Martin Benson and the naval chaplain Laurence Hynes Halloran, the latter a one-time midshipman imprisoned for killing a fellow midshipman. Transported to Australia for forgery in 1818, he was a bigamist who falsely claimed to be ordained.

The victories of 1797 were an important background to the battles with France in 1798, as the British were able to use fewer warships to mask the Dutch and Spaniards. There was both the battle of the Nile, as a result of which five of the line were added to the British navy, and the defeat of a French squadron off the Irish coast on 11 October by a larger British force. By the end of the year, France had lost 49 ships of the line.

The British remained able to deploy widely:

	Line of Battle	64 gunners	50 gunners	Frigates	Total
Channel	28	3	3	33	67
North Sea	3	11	1	7	22
Ireland	4	-	-	13	17
Mediterranean	24	-	1	14	39
America	1	2	1	6	10
Newfoundland	-	1	-	4	5
Leeward Islands	4	-	1	15	20
Jamaica	6	1	1	14	22
Africa	-	-	-	3	3
Cape and East Indies	4	4	3	13	24
Detached	-	1	1	5	7
Preparing for Commission	11	-	1	9	21
Totals	85	23	13	136	257

British naval forces in February 1798: numbers and global range.

The numerous ships below frigate size were not shown in the table,[22] but the large number of frigates reflected their importance, not least for commerce protection and the unsuitable nature of large warships for many tasks, especially because their substantial crew had to be supported.

Subsequently, the British maintained the pressure on their opponents, helping ensure that the ratio of ships of the line moved in their favour. In particular, although the invasion of Holland in 1799 brought no lasting advantage on land, the Dutch fleet was captured when the entry of British warships into the Zuider Zee was combined with a mutiny on the fleet. Furthermore, in 1801, in a night battle near Cadiz, Rear-Admiral Sir James Saumarez with only four of the line defeated a Franco-Spanish fleet of eight of the line, capturing or destroying three.

In the meantime, in a series of small engagements that it is too easy to overlook if the focus is on large-scale battles, French warships and frigates were destroyed or captured. In part, this was matter of squadron engagements that played a major role in affirming and sustaining British dominance in the Channel and the Western Approaches. Frigate squadrons were ordered to cruise off Brittany and to destroy French forces preying on British trade. In 1794, a squadron under Warren twice destroyed French frigate squadrons, while another under Pellew captured the frigate *Révolutionnaire* off Ushant and it was added to the fleet. In 1795, George pressed for vigour:

> The necessity of keeping constantly detached squadrons to keep the Channel, the Bay of Biscay, and the North Sea clear of the enemy's ships; had that measure been uniformly adopted by the Admiralty I am certain by this time the trade of France would have been totally annihilated.[23]

A frigate squadron under Richard Strachan greatly harassed coastal trade on the Norman and Breton coasts while, in 1796, another under Pellew captured two French frigates. The number of French and Dutch frigates fell dramatically between 1795 and 1800. There were individual engagements, as in 1795 when the

Nymphe frigate under Pellew captured the *Cléopâtre* frigate in the Channel, and the *Crescent* frigate under Saumarez captured the *Réunion* frigate which had been using Cherbourg as a base to attack British trade.

Such success helped to reduce the losses of British trade, which was important as losses ensured higher insurance premiums, danger money for sailors, and the need to resort to convoys and other defensive measures that pushed up the cost and inflexibility of trade, both overseas and coastal. Success also maintained the sense of British naval power. It was not surprising that when that sense was challenged in 1797 as a result of the naval mutinies, French privateering revived. Moreover, the protection of trade took the navy far afield, as in 1795 when Samuel Hood led a squadron into the Aegean to protect trade against French frigates based in Smyrna (Izmir).

The pursuit of commerce raiders was not restricted to European waters. In April 1797, boats from a frigate squadron attacked the town of Jean-Rabel on the northern coast of Saint-Domingue, recapturing nine merchantmen seized by the privateers based there and inflicting damage and deterrence to help protect the northern Caribbean sea lanes. Earlier that month, a French frigate had been destroyed nearby. In 1798–9, in command of the *Surprise* frigate, a captured French ship, Edward Hamilton took numerous French and Spanish privateers in the Caribbean.

Nelson's victory at the Nile delighted the public, set a new standard for fighting determination and leadership capability, and transformed the strategic situation, notably so in the Mediterranean. The dangerous commitment made by the dispatch of this fleet, not least the weakening of the fleet in home waters, was justified by victory. Now cut off, the French army in Egypt was to be defeated by an invading British force in 1801. Meanwhile, the navy blockaded French-held Malta, captured Livorno and Minorca (1798) and, the following year, provided naval support to the Turks in their successful resistance to Napoleon's siege of Acre. Sent by sea, his siege artillery was captured by British warships. Moreover in 1799, Captain Thomas Troubridge used naval power to make an important contribution to the struggle with the French in southern Italy, capturing Ischia, Procida and Capri, blockading the Bay of Naples, and playing a major role in the successful sieges of coastal positions, notably Civitàvecchia and Gaeta. In 1800, the 80-gunner *Guillaume Tell*, the last surviving French warship that had escaped the battle of the Nile, was engaged at night off Malta by the 36-gun *Penelope* and delayed until two British ships of the line could come up and capture her. Malta was captured that year and the starving French were temporarily driven from Genoa by blockade and bombardment. By 1800, the navy had a clear numerical advantage over France, particularly in the frigates crucial for trade protection.

This was scarcely an easy process, and many ships were lost, not least through going aground, as with the frigate *Jason* that was wrecked when pursuing a convoy near Brest in 1796 and the frigate *Artois* while chasing a frigate off La Rochelle in 1797. The *Amazon* was wrecked in Audierne Bay in 1797 when the *Droits de l'Homme* was driven inshore, while the *Hannibal* ran aground and was forced to surrender in Saumarez's attack on French warships moored off Algeciras in Spain in 1801. That year, nearly 400 men drowned when the *Invincible* ran aground near Great Yarmouth, while the *Queen Charlotte*, flagship of the Mediterranean fleet, was destroyed by fire off Livorno in 1800 with the loss of nearly 700 men. Fire was a great challenge not only due to the inflammable nature of warships and their contents, especially the risks of gunpowder exploding, but also because they did not carry lifeboats or safety equipment, and most sailors could not swim.

Combat could be brutal, as in 1798 when the *Hercule*, a newly launched 74-gunner en route from Lorient, was attacked by the 74-gun *Mars*, part of the blockade of Brest. The two ships came alongside, the bow anchors hooked and the ships exchanged fire while touching, with many of the guns fired from in-board. The British won the hour-long gunnery exchange, the *Hercule* surrendering, but the heavy casualties of such engagements, including both captains in this instance, demonstrated that naval warfare was far from limited, indeed potentially devastating.

Nor, despite repeated success, was there any security for British power. Just as the Toulon squadron had sailed out for Egypt thanks to the British blockaders being driven off station in 1798, so in April 1799, covered by fog, had sailed the 26-strong Brest fleet, leaving the British unsure whether the French would head for Ireland or the Mediterranean. Concern about the safety of Minorca, then under British control, handicapped the subsequent British pursuit in the Mediterranean, freeing the French to sail to Toulon and thence relieve besieged Savona, and eventually return to Brest, without being intercepted.[24] They returned with 15 Spanish of the line, ensuring that Brest posed a major challenge and that its blockade had to be strengthened.

It was generally possible for a lookout to see only about 15 miles from the top of the main mast in fine weather. However, fleets used a series of frigates stationed just over the horizon, and they signalled using their sails, which were much bigger than flags and could be seen at some distance over the horizon. This relay system was particularly important for blockading British fleets: there would be an inshore squadron of highly manoeuvrable ships (which were unlikely to get caught against the dangerous lee shore toward which the wind was blowing) that physically watched the French in Brest and Toulon, and they then signalled using a relay of frigates to the main fleet which was located a few miles off in greater safety. Surveillance capability was surprisingly sophisticated: by simply 'looking' at a ship, its nationality, strength, skill, manpower, capability and performance could all be determined.

More generally, operational limitations were tested by skill and developments, as with signalling, and thereby the use of the signal book to direct command and control, which lessened the role of Fighting Instructions. Howe's 1776 signal book was followed by his improved version in 1790. This helped in tactical flexibility. As another instance of change lessening limitations, specialised sailing ships, in particular bomb ketches, were designed with coastal operations in shallow waters foremost in mind. There were examples of successful campaigns in precisely such waters, for example the Chesapeake campaign of 1814.

Having seized power in France in late 1799, Napoleon focused on his land war with Austria, which was forced to peace in 1801. Britain's war goals toward France did not change, but in 1801 the British expanded their commitments by taking action against the threatening Armed Neutrality of the North, a Russian-founded confederacy of Baltic powers launched in 1800 that was seen as a way to defend neutral shipping in order to stop the British naval blockade of France. Denmark rejected an ultimatum to leave the Confederacy. The British fleet sailed through the Sound between Denmark and Sweden on 30 March, but then faced forts, warships and shoals before Copenhagen. Nelson was allocated the ships with the shallower draft and on 2 April moved forward amid the shoals, although three warships ran aground. Brought into position, Nelson's warships opened a long-range exchange of fire with the Danes. Heavy Danish fire led Nelson's commander, Sir Hyde Parker, to order him to 'discontinue the action' if he felt it appropriate, but Nelson continued the bombardment. Eventually, superior British fire prevailed. Three Danish ships were destroyed and 12 captured. Denmark left the Confederacy, which, due to the assassination of Tsar Paul, collapsed. Nelson had sailed on to Russian waters, but this collapse prevented further hostilities.

Nelson's reputation rose greatly as a result of the Battle of Copenhagen, *Bonner and Middleton's Bristol Journal* of 25 April reporting, 'The zeal, spirit, and enterprise of Lord Nelson were never more completely developed than upon this great and memorable occasion, and they happily diffused their influence through the whole of the squadron under his immediate command.' Then appointed to command the squadron assembled to repel the French invasion force believed to be assembling, Nelson attacked the boats in Boulogne harbour in August 1801 although heavy fire from the shore limited his impact.

The strategic threat remained. Britain and France negotiated the Peace of Amiens in March 1802, but an armed truce was all that pertained, with France still in control of the Dutch fleet and continuing an active programme of naval construction. Naval officers were divided over the peace, a division that reached to the naval MPs in the House of Commons, with George Berkeley joining attacks on the Addington ministry and its Admiralty.[25] A resumption of war seemed very likely, and the navy readied itself accordingly.

Malta was a key element in contention and helped lead to an outbreak of conflict anew in 1803. Then, due to the strategic assumptions bound up in a Mediterranean fleet, both as a force enabler and as a facilitator of alliances, a large force was deployed to the Mediterranean in 1803. With France and Spain allied, Britain was in a very difficult position.

9

DEFEATING AN EMPEROR AND FIGHTING A REPUBLIC
1803–15

Trafalgar saw what was to be the culminating great battle of the Age of Fighting Sail. This was not the last major battle, which was Cape Navarino in 1827, the Anglo-Franco-Russian defeat of the Turkish–Egyptian fleet off Greece. However, Trafalgar settled naval dominance in the West. In this, it was the apotheosis of the naval strength of Britain and an achievement that had to be sustained over the following decade. Both these points can serve to lessen the significance of Trafalgar, but were also in part anchored and given significance by it. Trafalgar brought to a close a period of particular crisis in which the navy offset the combination of Franco-Spanish warship numbers and confidence in invasion plans.

At Trafalgar (21 October 1805), George III's belief that the British could defeat larger opposing fleets and his reference to 'the bulwark of the nation, the wooden walls of Great Britain'[1] were justified. Nelson's objective was to force battle on his opponents by engaging the larger Franco-Spanish fleet (33 of the line to the British 27) as rapidly as possible, attacking in two lines in order to split his opponents into smaller groups that could be attacked in strength, with his opponents' van left redundant. By using his windward position to attack the Franco-Spanish rear and centre, Nelson achieved numerical superiority as his opponent's foremost ships could not intervene effectively, albeit with a weak wind that dramatically slowed the opening moves. Such slowness inhibited both the dressing of lines, not least to avoid gaps, and manoeuvres. Yet, at Trafalgar, this slowness did not prevent the build-up of British pressure as more ships joined in and as seamanship led to advantageous manoeuvring during the battle. At the same time, the French ships were unable to bring the numerous soldiers they carried into effective use for boarding.

The line was penetrated as planned, making it difficult for Pierre Villeneuve to retreat or regroup. The Franco-Spanish ships were raked from the stern, and, unlike the Nile and Copenhagen in which the British had fought in line, the battle saw an abandonment of detailed control over the development of the combat and became a series of small struggles between individual ships or groups of ships in which British gunnery and seamanship prevailed, albeit at the cost of heavy casualties in the close combat that such engagements entailed. This was particularly so in the centre with *Victory* and *Temeraire* defeating *Bucentaure*, Villeneuve's flagship, and *Redoutable*; and again with *Tonnant*, a French ship captured in 1798, defeating the French *Algésiras* and the Spanish *Monarca*. Close-quarter fighting led to the decimation of boarding crew on *Redoutable* and *Algésiras* by British cannon, particularly cannonades, while ships were entangled, notably *Algésiras* and *Tonnant*, the former set alight by enflamed wads from *Tonnant*'s cannon. *Mars* had less success with the French *Pluton*. The number of cannon was over nine times and the weight of fire more than 30 times those at Waterloo, where, instead, muskets were much more important. Showing inspiring leadership in all respects, by being exposed in the warship at the head of the key line of attack, Nelson was mortally wounded by a French sharpshooter firing from the rigging of the *Redoutable*. Wellington was also exposed to fire at Waterloo, but not fire from such close range.

The risk of such an attack was justified. One French ship blew up and 18 French and Spanish ships of the line were captured, including the *Santisima Trinidad*, the largest eighteenth-century warship, a four-decker carrying 136 guns, although she, like many of the prizes, sank in a strong storm that followed the battle. Villeneuve was captured. The losses of sailors, including prisoners, in the combined fleet was serious, amounting to about 14,000 whereas British dead and wounded totalled 1,690. Four of the French ships of the line that escaped Trafalgar were attacked off Cape Finisterre on 4 November in the battle of Cape Ortegal by a squadron of four of the line and four frigates under Captain Sir Richard Strachan. After inflicting much damage, with his ships of the line firing from one side on the French line and his frigates from the other, Strachan captured them all and they were commissioned into the Royal Navy.

Unlike Barfleur (1692) and Quiberon Bay (1759), Trafalgar was not the consequence of an attempt to invade Britain. Instead, Villeneuve was dispatched to help in the invasion of Naples. Yet, that was the aftermath of the failure of a plan to invade Britain, a failure that was the consequence of British naval power, albeit without a major battle. Trafalgar was the opportunity to secure this, and, had the Franco-Spanish fleet not been engaged then, it would have remained as a possible force for an attempt directed against Britain or Ireland, as on the pattern of the indecisive 1778 battle of Ushant and the 1779 invasion attempt. However, the strategic direction and operational command of the French navy did not match that of the Dutch in 1652–88, and this helped provide Nelson with his opportunity.

Napoleon had prepared an invasion of England for which he required naval superiority in the Channel and this seemed a prospect when Spain joined France. French squadrons successfully escaped from Toulon and Rochefort, threatening a concentration of strength to cover an invasion. He planned for his squadrons to join at Martinique and then to return as a united force able to defeat the British. Napoleon required superiority in the Channel for four days in order for his troops to cross, planned to land in or near Pegwell Bay in Kent, and intended to overrun London within a week before dictating peace.

The failure of the naval plan ensured that the detailed preparations for the landing proved fruitless. The Rochefort squadron arrived first in the Caribbean and captured Dominica, but it returned to Europe when no other squadron arrived within the prescribed time. Villeneuve and the Toulon squadron were able to join a Spanish squadron at Cadiz in April, the outnumbered blockading squadron under the cantankerous and prickly Vice-Admiral Sir John Orde falling back to the Channel. Envious of Nelson, who had been promoted past him, Orde failed to coordinate with him in the sense of information sharing, a failure in which the Admiralty's creation of unnecessary and avoidable seams in the command structure played a significant role, while the tension between the two men was exacerbated by the frequently difficult issue of distributing prize money.

Villeneuve reached Martinique on 14 May, a passage of 35 days, but he was pursued by Nelson, who reached Barbados on 4 June, a passage of only 26 days, albeit one delayed by Orde's failure to provide intelligence. Nelson understood much of the French strategy and was determined to dislocate it.[2] Evading the pursuit, Villeneuve set sail for Ferrol on 11 June, but was unable also to join the Brest fleet thanks to the British close blockade under Admiral Cornwallis. This highlighted the longstanding French difficulty of coordinating fleets, one that was greatly accentuated rather than eased by the idea of adding in a voyage to the Caribbean. The significance of British blockading capacity emerged clearly in this instance.

Villeneuve fought a British fleet under Vice-Admiral Sir Robert Calder west of Cape Finisterre on 22 July. Although outnumbered by 15 to 20 ships of the line, Calder engaged Villeneuve in the fog and captured two Spanish warships. Villeneuve failed to renew the battle over the next two days, and put in successively to Vigo, Ferrol and Corunna. Looked at differently, Calder had not inflicted serious damage on Villeneuve in terms of ship numbers. The outnumbered Calder fell back to join the British fleet off Brest, although he was to be reprimanded by a court martial for failing to renew the battle: the emphasis of the age was on an aggressive spirit and an opportunity to weaken Villeneuve had been lost.[3]

On 25 August, Cornwallis drove the emerging Brest fleet back into harbour. This was not only a key element in the campaign but also a means to the establishment of the navy's 'moral ascendancy' and one that helped lead Napoleon to demobilise his invasion flotilla on 31 August.[4] The increasingly hesitant Villeneuve had sailed again on 15 August, but, instead of trying to fight his way into the Channel, made for Cadiz, taking advantage of discretionary orders from Napoleon, who responded with fury to the news of his admiral's caution. Nelson took command of the fleet assembled to blockade the well-fortified port where Villeneuve could refit his fleet.

Napoleon marched, instead, against Austria. This accorded with the wishes of Spain which did not back the invasion plan. When the Franco-Spanish fleet set sail on 19–20 October, it was for Italian waters to act primarily against Naples. Intercepted and defeated off Cape Trafalgar, a fleet of this size was never again sent to sea by Napoleon. At the same time, Trafalgar displayed on the British side a wide variety in command competence which in part reflected the lack of a structured and rigorous system of officer training in command skills.[5] The Ayshford Trafalgar Roll indicates that of the seamen whose source of service can be gauged, 9,113 were volunteers, 3,932 unknown and 1,837 pressed. 53 per cent were from England and 21 per cent from Ireland, which reflected the general trend. Of the 18,425 who fought on the British side –ranging in age from eight-year-old William Wilcott, boy third class, to the 67-year-old William Burke, a purser – 432 were killed and 110 died of wounds. Casualties varied greatly, *Victory* losing 57 killed and 102 wounded but others very few, in part reflecting delays in coming into action. The impact of the victory was shown across society and in some unexpected forms. Mary Hardy, the Methodist wife of a 'middling order' Norfolk farmer and brewer, rarely used adjectives in her diary except when considering the weather, but Trafalgar was 'A Great Victory'.

After Trafalgar

After Trafalgar,[6] there was no aftermath comparable to that after the Spanish Armada. The British enjoyed a clear superiority in ships of the line, although continuing to suffer the serious shortage of sailors that had much vexed the Admiralty during that campaign.[7] The army received far more of the annual cohort reaching military age, and at about 250,000 strong was larger than the navy,[8] as well as being able to call on allied forces. Napoleon subsequently sought, with some success, to rebuild his fleet, contributing to a continued intensity in the naval war. By 1809, the Toulon fleet was nearly as large as the British blockaders. However, French naval strength had been badly battered by losses of sailors in successive defeats, while his attempt to translate his far-flung territorial control into naval strength was unsuccessful. Due to the Peninsular War, Napoleon lost the Spanish navy, while the six French ships of the line sheltering in Cadiz and Vigo surrendered to the Spaniards in 1808. The Portuguese and Danish fleets were kept out of French hands, the former by persuasion and the latter by British military action in 1807, while Russia's Black Sea fleet, then in the Tagus, was blockaded until the British were able to seize it.

By 1810, Britain had 50 per cent of the ships of the line in the world, up from 29 per cent in 1790. These ships of the line were on average bigger than those of the eighteenth century and able to carry heavier guns. Whereas the average ship of the line in 1720 had 60 guns and was armed with 12- and 24-pounders, that of 1815 had 74 guns, with 32- or, in the French case, 36-pounders on the lower deck.

Nevertheless, this increase in firepower, which began earlier, did not lead to dramatic changes in naval warfare. More mundanely, but also as part of a general process of improvement, there were developments in fittings such as new patterns of anchors and the first chain cable, as well as iron water tanks in place of wooden casks. However, although there were experiments in the 1800s with the use of diagonal bracing, in order to strengthen hulls, prevent the arching of keels and permit longer two-deckers, the first ship built entirely on this principle, *Howe*, was not launched until 1815. Britain's proportion of world mercantile shipping also increased: effective convoying ensured that ships could be constructed with reference to the goods to be carried, rather than their military effectiveness. The profits from trade enabled Britain to make loans and grants to European allies.

The navy had numerous tasks in European waters after Trafalgar. Some were defensive, notably commerce protection and also, linked to this, blockade of hostile ports. The latter was arduous. The exposure of warships to the constant battering of wind and wave placed a major strain on an increasingly ageing fleet. Thus, the Channel Fleet was dispersed by a strong gale on 3 January 1804 and the blockade of Le Havre lifted, although that of Brest was swiftly resumed. The prevalent westerly and southwesterly winds created major problems for the blockaders off Brest.

More generally, the majority of warships lost fell victim to wreck or foundering and not to enemy action: the weather and rocks combined to be of particular danger. On Christmas Day 1811, while escorting 120 merchantmen from the Baltic to England, the *St George*, a 98-gunner, and *Defence*, a 74-gunner, were driven onto the Danish coast in a storm with the loss of all bar 17 of the combined crew of about 1,400. Tropical storms could be especially hazardous; in 1807, Rear-Admiral Sir Thomas Troubridge and the *Blenheim* disappeared in one off Madagascar. Fog could accentuate problems. The *Venerable*, part of the squadron covering Brest, sank on the Devon coast in 1804 after running ashore in a thick fog. Moreover, fog continued to help in the evasion of blockade. In January 1808, the Rochefort squadron evaded British blockaders in bad weather and poor visibility, and sailed to Toulon.

The very presence of British blockading squadrons was crucial. Blockade was designed to prevent French squadrons from sailing out in order to mount attacks. It also served both to prevent the squadrons from uniting and becoming a more serious threat, and to limit the supplies that they could receive. The threat posed by the united Franco-Spanish fleet in Cadiz in 1805 was a salutary reminder of the need to keep French squadrons separated.

The places that had to be blockaded changed, notably with Cadiz held against Napoleon from 1808, but the spread of French power in Continental Europe 1805–12 created greater responsibilities, not least as the entire North Sea coast was brought under French control. There were also significant changes in the region already in French control prior to Trafalgar, notably the development of shipbuilding in Antwerp and Venice. The former was a particular challenge to British control of the North Sea, and thus of trading routes to the Baltic and Norway, which were important for the economy as a whole and, more significantly, for the supply of both naval stores and grain. Antwerp did not pose the challenge to Britain's trans-oceanic position or, indeed, control of Ireland offered by Brest and other Atlantic ports, but it was also harder to mask than the latter, not least by a 'Western Squadron' able to act both as a blockade and as a strategic reserve capable of supporting British goals and detached naval forces elsewhere, notably in the Mediterranean and the Caribbean. The build-up of Antwerp put pressure on the navy, and thus on the warships available elsewhere, as well as encouraging the unsuccessful 1809 Walcheren expedition and operations in 1814.

There was also concern in negotiations with allies in 1813–14 about a possible peace with Napoleon that France would be allowed to retain Antwerp, not least as Austria wanted French power as a balance to Britain. Fortunately for Britain, Napoleon rejected the deals on offer and lost Antwerp, which, in the subsequent peace negotiations at Vienna, Britain had allocated to its ally the Netherlands as part of a Belgium that provided a buffer against France. Wellington at Waterloo was defending this outcome. Another aspect of the naval response to French expansion was provided by the British seizure from Denmark in 1807 of the Heligoland archipelago, a cession affirmed by treaty in 1814.

The need for the fleet and the pressures on its condition forced the government to maintain an expensive programme of repair, refitting and new construction. Aside from the expense, this programme faced serious deficiencies in the dockyards and in supplies, especially of timber. A rapid rise in the demand for timber led to the use of inferior (even unseasoned) stock, and thus to warships rotting rapidly. Part of the strain was met by adding captured warships to the fleet, which was a key instance of the attritional aspect of naval warfare, but more by building ships in private shipyards to an unprecedented extent. This applied particularly to the ships of the line, which neither France nor Spain had a willingness or capacity to build in private yards. Aside from the wear on the ships, the shortage of sailors also ensured that blockade posed a major burden. Close-in blockades of the scale and for the duration maintained by Britain were formidable organisational, operational and technical achievements.

Blockading skills changed over time. They were really very good off Brest by the end of the war, although ships could still escape even then. A key goal was to stop food and naval stores from getting to Brest, which was more easily achieved. Thus, blockade was as much to do with preventing goods from getting in as much as stopping ships leaving. This was especially important for Brest because of its atrocious landward communications: everything had to come by sea.

After Trafalgar, the British presence off Spain and in the Mediterranean was maintained by Vice-Admiral Cuthbert Collingwood, who had received a peerage for his role as second in command at Trafalgar. In 1805–7, Collingwood blockaded Cadiz, but he then moved into the Mediterranean where his main concern was the French fleet based in Toulon. Threatening Sicily, this fleet forced the British to adopt a defensive strategy.

At least after Trafalgar, this strategy was based on clear maritime dominance. In 1808, Collingwood failed to intercept Ganteaume when he relieved the French garrison on Corfu, largely because he only received belated news of French moves and responded in an overly cautious fashion. The blockade of Toulon was more successful the following year, and on 26 October two ships of the line attempting to carry supplies to the French garrison at Barcelona were driven ashore and destroyed.

Nevertheless, concern about the Toulon fleet persisted. At times, the British fleet seemed particularly stretched. In 1810, as the French continued to increase their fleet, concern about the situation in the Mediterranean reached a post-Trafalgar peak. Stretching over 2,000 miles, the command was critically short of frigates. In January 1811, there were fears that the Toulon squadron would be able to escape and attack Wellington's position at Lisbon,[9] which was certainly exposed to naval attack, although any French expedition thither would have been more so. British concern with Lisbon in part arose from a determination to prevent France from controlling this key anchorage.[10]

Despite a range of problems, there was no repeat of the retreat from the Mediterranean in 1796, and a sortie from Toulon was turned back in 1812. Two years earlier, writing about Greece, George, 4th Earl of Aberdeen observed that a 'French connection, from the absence of naval intercourse and protection, is much less desired than the friendship of this country'.[11] Somewhat differently, Napoleon was to remark while on *Bellerophon* in 1815, 'If it had not been for you English, I should have been Emperor of the East. But wherever there is water to float a ship, we are sure to find you in our way.'[12]

Everywhere, despite the size of the navy, and the crucial combination of both battlefleet and smaller warships, there were too few ships and sailors for the myriad tasks expected of the navy, and the situation could become hazardous if the French or their allies acted in strength. At the same time, successive battles and other clashes wore down opposing strength. None was as dramatic as Trafalgar, but, as the naval war continued, they produced a cumulative impact. The dislocation of the French and Spanish (until Spain turned to civil war as a result of the 1808 French invasion) imperial systems was a key task. Thus, on 25 September 1805, Samuel Hood and the blockading squadron off Rochefort attacked a French frigate squadron bound for the West Indies with reinforcements. Four of the five frigates were captured, although Hood had to have his arm amputated after his elbow was smashed by a musket shot. On 6 February 1806, Duckworth and seven of the line engaged off Santo Domingo a French squadron of five of the line that had escaped from Rochefort. Superior British gunnery brought Vice-Admiral Sir John Duckworth a complete victory: three of the French ships were captured and two driven ashore and destroyed. During the battle, a portrait of Nelson was displayed aboard the *Superb*. On 13 March 1806, Rear-Admiral Sir John Borlase Warren captured two warships sailing back from the East Indies as they neared France. The battle in the Basque Roads on 11–12 April 1809 put paid to a French attempt to reinforce the Caribbean, with four warships destroyed, although a failure to press home the attack led to recriminations. Guadeloupe fell the following February. In 1809, when the French in Santo Domingo surrendered, Captain William Cumby wrote of

> the unremitting perseverance with which the vessels maintained the stations assigned to them, through all the variety of weather incident to the season, on a steep and dangerous shore, where no anchorage was to be obtained, as well as to the vigilance and alacrity of those officers and men

who were employed in the night guard-boats, by whose united exertions the enemy's accustomed supply by sea was entirely cut off, and the surrender of the city greatly accelerated.

British commanders sought to combine the fighting quality of individual ships with a bold command culture that emphasised manoeuvre and seizing the initiative in order to close with the opposing fleet and defeat it in detail, as recommended in the influential *Essay on Naval Tactics* by the Scottish merchant John Clerk of Eldin (1728–1812), a work published in 1790 that greatly impressed Nelson. This was an aspect of the consideration of tactical innovation that had gathered pace from the Seven Years War, as was also seen on land.

Any list of successes can lead to a failure to note the difficulty of these tasks, difficulties underlined by the failure in the battle of Grand Port of 23–27 August 1810 of an attempt to capture Mauritius, an important French base for warships and privateers and a threat to the British naval position in Indian waters. Two frigates of Samuel Pym's squadron ran aground and were set on fire and abandoned, and two others were captured by the French, indicating the danger of overconfident British forces in the face of French squadrons enjoying a local superiority. Pym's bold leadership proved rash in the face of the fighting quality of the more heavily gunned French force. Yet, naval reinforcements helped ensure the capture of Mauritius later in the year, with the navy blocking Port Louis and providing 2,000 sailors for the operations on land.[13] The successive capture of French overseas bases lessened their ability to challenge the British, and by the end of 1810 there had been a clean sweep, the British pressing on to conquer the Dutch East Indies (Indonesia) from that year, with Batavia (Djakarta) falling in 1811. None of these many expeditions could have been achieved without naval superiority, organisation and active participation. The navy was a main actor in amphibious operations.

In Europe, the situation proved more difficult. Duckworth's attempt to obtain the surrender of the Turkish fleet in 1807 was unsuccessful, Duckworth destroying a squadron of Turkish frigates but obtaining no surrender and encountering a heavy bombardment when he returned through the Dardanelles. He suffered from indecision, unfavourable winds, and French assistance for the Turks.

More success was obtained later that year when concern about Danish intentions led to an attack on Copenhagen that yielded its surrender and the seizure of the entire Danish fleet. John Oldershaw Hewes (1789–1811) recorded British frigates engaging Danish mortar boats, as well as casualties, for example:

> On the 31st the enemy hove a shell in the Charles tender and she blew up and wounded nineteen men belonging to us besides took of one of our Lieutenant's legs, broke his collar bone, cut him very bad on the head and almost knocked one of his eyes out ... It killed a young man about my own age, my most particular acquaintance a masters mate and killed two sailors besides what belonged to the vessel. On the 1st of September I went on shore with 15 sailors to make a battery close under the enemy's walls. We were obliged to go when it was dark ... We could hear them talking and playing a fiddle. It rained excessively all night and I was almost perished with wet and cold.[14]

Hewes drowned off West Africa in 1811.

There was also British naval action in the Baltic. In 1808–9, Britain helped Sweden against Russian attack, but although this helped lessen the possibility of a Russian invasion of Sweden itself, it could not prevent the conquest from Sweden of Finland. Thereafter, as Sweden was forced into the French camp, steps were taken to protect British trade and, crucially, naval stores: much of the timber, tallow, pitch, tar, iron and hemp required for the navy came from the Baltic.[15]

The prime task, however, remained combating France. Its blockaded navy was no longer a force that was combat-ready as the longer it remained in harbour the more its efficiency declined: officers and crews had less operational experience. It remained difficult to predict French moves when at sea, but the French were less able than hitherto to gain the initiative. British fleet commanders had to blockade French ports and respond to the possibility of sorties, but a more aggressive note could be struck by frigate commanders, notably William Hoste, one of Nelson's protégés, in the Adriatic which he kept in awe. On 13 March 1811, in command of four frigates, he engaged a squadron of six that was approaching the island of Lissa. Hoisting the signal 'remember Nelson' to the cheers of his crew, and helped by superior seamanship and gunnery, Hoste defeated the French, who attacked in two columns on the Trafalgar model only to lose three frigates to British gunnery. Hoste also attacked French trade as well as coastal positions, notably in Calabria (1806) and Croatia (1814), helping ensure the surrender of Cattaro and Dubrovnik.

As captain of the frigate *Pallas* in the Bay of Biscay, Cochrane harried French trade and destroyed corvettes, while in 1808, as captain of the frigate *Impérieuse*, he attacked semaphore stations, fortifications, lighthouses, batteries and bridges on the coasts of southern France and Catalonia. Flexibility and all-round military skills were shown by operating successfully on land. In 1810, Murray Maxwell and the frigate *Alceste* stormed a battery near Fréjus on the Riviera. As a strategic response, Napoleon built, from 1800, the Sempione arterial road from France to Italy so as to bypass the British coastal blockade, but the route itself was attacked.

Intervention was not always successful. In 1808, Cochrane delayed the fall of the Catalan castle of Rosas for a fortnight when he took over its defence but only so much could be achieved against superior French forces. Yet British naval activities harassed the French and forced them to deploy considerable forces to garrison their coasts, providing a counterpart to the commercial challenge posed by British contraband. Attacks on coastal shipping and positions required less military effort and resources than amphibious operations.

In the Channel, there were far fewer opportunities for operations against coastal positions, but, as in the Mediterranean, there were many small-ship actions, not least in an attempt to stop French commerce raiding. Captain John Loring of the *Niobe* was a particularly active frigate commander, acting both on his own, for example in the capture of the brig *Néarque* in 1806 and of the privateer *Loup Marin* off Le Havre in 1811, and in co-operation with other warships, as in the destruction of two frigates off the Cherbourg peninsula in the winter of 1810–11. As commander of first the *Loire* frigate and then the *Emerald*, Captain Frederick Maitland attacked French privateers and coastal batteries around the Bay of Biscay. Furthermore, effective convoying ensured that ships could be constructed with reference to the goods to be carried rather than their military effectiveness.

Thomas Fray of the *Elephant* captured the tedium of blockade when describing his patrol off Flushing and the Texel in the winter of 1812, noting of the Dutch ships in Flushing,

> They have not thought it prudent to venture out as yet though I suppose they will be looking at us in the summer. If

they should we shall do our best to give you a good account of them as we are all heartily tired of this station.

He added that July, when back in Spithead, 'A wife is a very useless piece of furniture for a Man of Wars man.'[16]

The navy also played a major role in making possible the British presence in the Peninsular War[17] and, more specifically, in supporting operations, for example by means of the landing in Portugal and the withdrawal from Corunna, both in 1808, and of successful amphibious attacks on the north coast of Spain in 1812. Ultimately, the navy was the guarantor of the British presence, Wellington observing in 1813, 'If anyone wishes to know the history of this war, I will tell them that it is our maritime superiority that gives me the power of maintaining my army while the enemy is unable to do so.' Aside from the navy guaranteeing British supplies, it prevented France from moving the same by sea, and thus pushed them to rely completely upon Spain's terrible roads. More generally, the sea provided Britain with a power projection that France lacked. Foreign commentators, notably Clausewitz, were apt to underrate naval warfare because they did not really understand it.

The War of 1812

Similarly, the naval component was crucial to the British role in the War of 1812, a conflict between two very different naval powers, which is a pattern that is far more common in naval history than tends to be appreciated. Aside from contrasts in their strength, they used their navies for very different purposes. Because there were no large-scale naval clashes on the high seas – a marked contrast with the situation between Britain and America on the inland lakes (at least in so far as the available forces made possible) – it is all too easy to underrate the crucial strategic dimensions of naval power and its importance for the character and development of the war.

The American mercantile marine had grown rapidly in size after the War of Independence, and its range had greatly increased. However, there was no comparable expansion in American naval power, because the new state, whose navy had not done well during the War of Independence, did not seek command of the sea nor trans-oceanic commercial or political dominion. Indeed, the last American warship was sold in 1785.

The American navy, however, was revived in the mid-1790s, with work on three frigates begun in 1793, initially in order to fight the privateering Barbary States of North Africa (Algiers, Tripoli and Tunis), but then in response to French pressure in the 'Quasi War': war was not declared, despite a number of clashes between warships from the summer of 1798, the majority of which were successes for the Americans, but in that year the military character of the American state was ratcheted up with the establishment of the Department of the Navy. There was also a significant reliance on free enterprise as it was necessary to commission privateers to act against the French at sea.

Napoleon's seizure of power in 1799 led to a change in French priorities, allowing America to settle the 'Quasi War' the following year. The government then stopped the annual payments of tribute to the Barbary States, designed to prevent their privateering attacks on American commerce. It was felt that paying tribute was humiliating and expensive, that operations in the Mediterranean would help train the navy, and that it would cost little more than to retain it in home waters. In 1801, Jefferson sent Commodore Richard Dale, with three frigates and a schooner, to the Mediterranean, while the Bashaw of Tripoli declared war. The blockade of Tripoli, however, proved difficult and in 1803 led to the loss of the frigate *Philadelphia* which had run aground on a reef. Nevertheless, in 1805, peace was negotiated with no annual tribute stipulated.

Although the contexts and issues were very different, maritime rights were also at issue with Britain. Impressment and the capture of neutral American ships largely resulted from the British blockade of Napoleonic Europe, which was vital from the British perspective but oppressive from that of America.

The American navy had experience, but it was on a totally different scale to the British. Although the Americans had an abundance of trained seamen to man their fleet, and the most powerful frigates of the age, which they were adept at handling in ship-to-ship actions, they had no ships of the line, and their total navy at the outset comprised only seventeen ships. They thus lacked the capacity for fleet action, which reflected the force structure and doctrine developed under Jefferson's agrarian republicanism, each of which, in turn, was a product of an urgent political debate. It was very different in its military results from the large fleets developed by the mercantile republics of the United Provinces and English Commonwealth in the seventeenth century. In part, concerns about the cost and likely effectiveness of such a fleet had encouraged opposition within America to its creation, but there was also political backing for a focus on an overland attack on Canada.

Initially, the American plan in 1812 had been for a quick land offensive against Lower Canada up the Champlain Valley, which led to limited interest in a strategic role for the navy. At the outbreak of the war, however, the Americans found it easier to act at sea than to strike on land where there were problems with mobilisation.[18] The need to protect trade was also a key issue. Concern about safeguarding incoming merchantmen, with the key liquidity they offered, for both merchants and customs revenues, helped ensure a shift in attitude. As a result, ships were to be sent to sea not only in order to convoy merchantmen but also to destroy the British warships that might attack them.

A naval emphasis accorded with the politics of those who saw the purpose of the war not as conquering Canada but as putting pressure on Britain in order to end hostile commercial policies, although naval action was also regarded as a possible way to put pressure on the British in Canada. Indeed, there was a common naval focus, because Canada was seen as a key source of the naval resources, especially timber, needed by the British navy, and President James Madison was convinced that Napoleon would succeed in limiting British access to its other major source of naval stores, the Baltic, which would focus greater attention on Canada.[19] Had Napoleon been successful in Russia, then Madison would have been proved correct.

In 1812, the Americans were to capture three 18-pounder British frigates: *Guerrière*, *Macedonian* and *Java* respectively fell victim to the *Constitution*,[20] the *United States* and the *Constitution*, frigates ably designed by Joshua Humphreys, which, with 24-pounder cannon, were more heavily gunned. These successes provided an initially valuable boost to American morale. Indeed, the Americans did better at sea than had been anticipated; and, conversely, did worse on land, which made the victories at sea particularly worthwhile. These victories also helped cover the return of American merchantmen, and their cargoes and customs revenues contributed to the financing of the war.

At sea, the British initially suffered from overconfidence, inaccurate gunnery (reflecting poor gun drill) and ships that were simply less powerful and less well prepared than those of their opponents. Better gunners and heavier guns helped the Americans greatly, as with Stephen Decatur's capture of the *Macedonian*. It was only in June 1813, when the *Chesapeake* found the *Shannon*, that two frigates of equal strength fought, and on that occasion the British were victorious. Moreover, most of the British navy was involved in operations against France.

The American successes in the 1812 frigate clashes caused a furore in Britain, with much soul-searching about fighting quality. The perception of a dominant omnipresence that had become significant to British public discussion was hit hard.[21] In an indication of the continuing need to create a sense of success, John Croker, the Secretary to the Admiralty, felt it necessary to publish the *Letter on the Subject of the Naval War with America* (1813) in defence of the government. In response to a sense of crisis, the Admiralty decided to issue an order that it had not felt obliged to issue in the case of conflict with the French, Croker informing the station commanders-in-chief that the Admiralty in July 1813 did

> not conceive that any of His Majesty's frigates should attempt to engage, single handed, the large class of American ships; which though they may be called frigates, are of a size, complement and weight of metal much beyond that class, and more resembling line of battle ships. In the event of one of His Majesty's frigates under your orders falling in with one of these ships, her captain should endeavour, in the first instance, to secure the retreat of His Majesty's ship, but if he finds that he has advantage in sailing, he should endeavour to manoeuvre, and keep company with her, without coming to action, in the hope of falling in with some other of His Majesty's ships with whose assistance the enemy might be attacked with a reasonable hope of success.[22]

Aside from the three frigates, the other British losses were all of smaller vessels, such as the 20-gun sloop *Alert*, captured by the 32-gun *Essex* in 1812. In this clash, the British guns were

18-pounders, the Americans 32-pounders. A sense of the scale of the task led Admiral Sir John Borlase Warren, the head of the North American Station, to press for reinforcements in 1813. His argument that these were necessary for defensive purposes captured a feeling that American potential and plans were unclear and therefore worrying:

> In consequence of the enemy's privateers becoming daily more numerous and the assembling of a force of three thousand men at Eastport on the frontiers of New Brunswick and menacing that province with attacks ... the very many and serious applications made upon me for aid, and protection for the coasts of British America and the West Indies.[23]

However, aside from the fact that there was to be no American invasion of New Brunswick, American successes in individual clashes did not prevent the implementation of a British blockade, which was seen as the way to deal with American privateering, as well as trade, and to lessen American options. Indeed, Croker wrote to Warren:

> As it is of the highest importance to the character and interests of the country that the naval force of the enemy, should be quickly and completely disposed of, my Lords [of the Admiralty] have thought themselves justified at this moment in withdrawing ships from other important services for the purpose of placing under your orders a force with which you cannot fail to bring the naval war to a termination, either by the capture of the American national vessels, or by strictly blockading them in their own waters.[24]

In March 1813, Warren was ordered to blockade New York City, Charleston, Port Royal, Savannah and New Orleans. Robert, 2nd Viscount Melville, the First Lord of the Admiralty, wrote to him:

> We do not intend this as a mere *paper* blockade, but as a complete stop to all trade and intercourse by sea with those ports, as far as the wind and weather, and the continual presence of a sufficient armed force, will permit and ensure. If you find that this cannot be done without abandoning for a time the interruption which you appear to be giving to the internal navigation of the Chesapeake, the latter object must be given up, and you must be content with blockading its entrance and sending in occasionally your cruisers for the purpose of harassing and annoyance.[25]

Thus, blockade was seen as more important than raiding the Chesapeake, an instructive indication of the importance of economic warfare, and one that is important to bear in mind when considering British operations. In November, the blockade was strengthened, with an attempt to stop trade from Long Island Sound southwards; but doing so put pressure on the finite number of ships and crew.[26] Warren noted the following month that the blockade of the Chesapeake was not fully effective:

> Several large clipper schooner of from two to three hundred tons, strongly manned and armed have run through the blockade in the Chesapeake, in spite of every endeavour and of the most vigilant attention of our ships to prevent their getting out, nor can anything stop these vessels escaping to sea in dark nights and strong winds.[27]

In January 1815, the *Hornet* was able to evade the British blockade of New London.

There were also serious limitations in the surveillance, and command and control capabilities of British naval power. These made it very difficult to 'see' or control in any strategic sense, and certainly limited the value of any blockade. However, the operational and tactical constraints on naval power were tested by skill and improvements, the 1814 Chesapeake campaign showing an ability to operate successfully in shallow waters.

British naval effectiveness improved during the war, both in Atlantic waters and on the Great Lakes. In 1813, Decatur was forced to surrender the *President* to superior force when he tried to run the British blockade of New York. Larger British naval forces were also effective against individual ships further afield. In the *Essex*, David Porter had successfully attacked British commerce in the South Atlantic and the South Pacific, capturing 12 whalers and their valuable cargo off the Galapagos Islands in 1813. This was part of a major extension in American trade warfare, but Porter was forced to surrender by two British warships off Valparaiso in Chile in 1814 after they cannonaded the disabled ship from a distance. Although the British suffered far more casualties when they attacked the privateer *General Armstrong* in 1814, the Americans eventually scuttled and burned the ship.

In addition, the British were successful in conflicts between individual ships. In June 1813, the *Shannon* beat the *Chesapeake* off Boston in a clash fought at close range in which a lack of preparedness on the part of the American commander was a key element.[28] On 14 August 1813, the *Argus* was captured off Wales by the similarly gunned *Pelican* after the British gunners proved superior.[29] By 1814, there were very few American warships able to operate for any length of time. The *Decatur*, the largest privateer to sail from Charleston, was captured by the British frigate *Le Rhin* in 1814. In January 1815, the *President* was seized by a British squadron several hours after it had sailed from New York.

Newspapers frequently reported desperate struggles on the high seas. Thus, Plymouth and Falmouth items in *Trewman's Exeter Flying-Post* of 14 July 1814 detailed clashes with American ships. The former noted the capture of the British brig *Reindeer* by the American sloop *Wasp*:

> The *Reindeer* immediately laid the enemy alongside, and in the most gallant style attempted to carry her opponent by boarding; but after a most desperate and sanguinary battle, which lasted about half an hour, she was overpowered by superior numbers, and obliged to strike.

Both were 18-gunners. In September, the *Wasp* sunk the *Avon*, another 18-gun brig, but she was lost at sea with all hands the following month. As an unwilling testimony to British success, over 5,000 American prisoners from the naval war were sent to Dartmoor Prison on the bleak granite moorland of Devon, joining the numerous French prisoners already there. The food was reasonable, but the prison was old and damp. As more generally in the period, crowded sites ensured a vulnerability to infection, a situation true of both warships and prisons.

Overall, American privateers and small warships had an impact on the British merchant marine across the world, affecting the practice and profitability of trade.[30] According to Lloyd's, the British lost 1,175 merchantmen, of which only 373 were recaptured, and insurance rates rose in some particular trades; although overall marine insurance rates were no higher and the British were able to take counter-measures, including increasing both convoy escorts and the number of warships on the North American coast.³¹ If, by strengthening their blockade, the British lessened the inroads of American privateers and warships, nevertheless the Americans thought it worthwhile pushing ahead with naval construction.

The Americans had also shown an important ability to develop naval capability on the Great Lakes, which provided an important attack component as well as a major cover for the defence. In February 1813, Madison instructed Dearborn on the need to outbuild the British on the Great Lakes:

> If they build two ships, we should build four. If they build 30 or 40 gun ships, we should build them of 50 or 60 guns. The command of those waters is the hinge on which the war will essentially turn according to the probable course of it.³²

A powerful presence was established on Lakes Erie and Ontario. In 1814, however, the British were able to construct the *St Lawrence*, a 102-gun three-decker ship at Kingston on Lake Ontario,³³ while the Americans worked on a ship of the line, the *New Orleans*, at Sacket's Harbor. In practice, there would have been major problems with manning such ships. The naval forces deployed on the Great Lakes rose greatly, from 12 American and six British ships in 1812, to 34 and 17 in 1813, and 30 and 28 in 1814. The number of cannon increased from 84 American and 78 British in 1812, to 221 and 144 in 1813, and 347 and 417 in 1814. The benefit gained from these ships has to be set, however, against the formidable logistical challenge posed by the requirements of building up these forces. This limited the prospects for land operations at the same time that success on the Great Lakes made them a more likely prospect.

Aside from amphibious capability and logistical flexibility, this success forced opponents to rely on the slower prospect of movement by land. Indeed, Wellington, whose command in the Peninsular War had given him experience of combined operations and the benefits of command of the sea, advised the Prime Minister in November 1814 that, without dominating the Lakes, 'it is impossible ... to keep the enemy out of the whole frontier, much less to make conquest'.[34] Mahan was to argue that 'the victories on Lake Erie and Lake Champlain do illustrate, in a distinguished manner, his principal thesis, the controlling influence upon events of naval power, even when transferred to an inland body of fresh water'.[35] British superiority on the Great Lakes provided a key opportunity in the first campaign of the war, but was countered by the Americans in 1813. At the same time, such superiority, while important around the Lakes, did not provide more than an advantage further afield.

Deep-sea naval capability gave the British crucial advantages in the Atlantic. Blockade, to which America was more vulnerable than Napoleonic Europe, greatly harmed the American economy,[36] and it became more effective from 1813, restricting American raids as well as trade. Thus, from that spring, the blockade was tight across the Chesapeake, hindering both trade and privateering. The American navy was not in a position to break the blockade. When the British navy moved into the Chesapeake in force in 1814, the blockade there was transformed, with American ships trapped in harbours, such as Baltimore and Norfolk, or tributaries such as the Patuxent. Privateering also made major inroads on American trade, as well as bringing prosperity to the British possessions of Nova Scotia, New Brunswick and Bermuda, where privateers were based.[37] It was also possible for Britain, as a major aspect of convoy protection, to send reinforcements to Canada.[38]

Raids on the American coast were launched from the start of the war, and the Americans had no control over whether they could escalate into large-scale amphibious attacks, to which they were vulnerable. In 1812, America's ports lacked adequately integrated defences, and there was also a widespread absence of planning for such attacks.[39] Concern about amphibious attacks led, in July 1813, to the creation of a Corps of Sea Fencibles for the 'defense of ports and harbors of the United States'. They were to play a role in the defence of Fort McHenry against the British in 1814.

British amphibious capability was retained to the end, Cochrane capturing Fort Bowyer, which protected Mobile, in February 1815. When hostilities ceased, the capture of Savannah and then Charleston was planned, and both were already blockaded. This was seen as a way to benefit from Cockburn's operations in the region. Having landed on Cumberland Island, Georgia on 1 January, he had captured St Mary's and Brunswick, seizing supplies and recruiting slaves, before menacing Savannah.[40] Indeed, Cockburn was threatening to attack New York City.[41]

In contrast, the American plan in May 1813 and May 1814 for a small squadron to cruise off Nova Scotia and the St Lawrence to intercept British supply ships failed, and in large part due to the blockade of American ports. The Americans built ships of the line, but they were not ready for any battle, which was just as well in light of British numerical superiority.

As an augury of the future, the American Robert Fulton, who had already successfully experimented with underwater warfare, especially mines, tried to make major advances during the War of 1812, not least with submarines, spar torpedoes, underwater guns and steam vessels, especially the proposed *Fulton I*. Elijah Mix experimented with torpedoes, but failed to sink *Plantagenet* in 1813. Fulton was only successful, and then after peace was signed, with steam vessels, but even had he been more so there were serious limits to what the Americans could have achieved with their economic capability. Fulton had argued in 1806 that 'it does not require much depth of thought to trace that science by discovering gunpowder changed the whole art of war by land and sea; and by future combination may sweep military marines from the ocean'.[42] As yet, however, this was not an option.

The War of 1812 was not a success for America as a naval power but it was a triumph for its naval reputation. The ability to win naval duels in 1812 created a lasting impression and helped make the navy more popular than the army. The navy had been more successful in this light than in the War of Independence. On the other hand, emphasising this point detracts from the realist perspective that, on the high seas, American power remained dependent on British acceptance. Britain had had 152 ships of the line and 183 frigates in 1810. The loss of several frigates was humiliating, but represented no real reduction of British maritime power.

The 1815 Campaign

The last was very much in evidence in 1815. Napoleon's very surrender to *Bellerophon* on 15 July and his dispatch on *Northumberland* to the remote South Atlantic island colony of St Helena, and his inability to escape from there, were clear indications of the role of the navy. So was the ability to deploy troops directly from Halifax and New Orleans to Belgium. The inevitable dominance of Britain's navy led Napoleon to recruit sailors into his army.

Re-established with the resumption of conflict, the blockade made it impossible for him to leave France by sea after Waterloo. The navy was always in the way. Britain sought to prevent him from taking refuge in America, and Rear-Admiral Sir Henry Hotham was instructed to 'keep the most vigilant lookout for the purpose of intercepting him'.[43] Unlike the Spanish American revolutionary Simón Bolívar, Napoleon found no foreign bolthole and was denied the final strategic option of his own freedom.

His regime was also put under pressure by British naval demonstrations off French ports, and the navy played a major role in the restoration of Bourbon authority in Marseille, Toulon and Bordeaux. The navy also played a key role in the overthrow of pro-Napoleonic forces on Guadeloupe and Martinique, and that of Joachim Murat in Naples: a small squadron entered the Bay of Naples and threatened to bombard the city unless the Neapolitan navy surrendered within 48 hours, which duly occurred. Marines were landed soon after to help in the occupation of the city. Other warships were present off Ancona and Gaeta.

The Foundations of Naval Strength

British naval strength rested on a sophisticated and well-financed administrative structure, a large fleet drawing on the manpower resources of a substantial mercantile marine (although there were never enough sailors), and an ability to win engagements that reflected widely diffused qualities of seamanship and gunnery, a skilled and determined corps of captains, and able leadership. This was true not only of command at sea, as with Nelson's innovative tactics and ability to inspire his captains, his 'band of brothers'. Progress in British metallurgy improved gunnery towards the end of the century, and the impact of British naval gunfire on enemy hulls and crews markedly increased during the period 1793–1815 when enemy ships were reduced to wrecks in a comparatively short time. Britain had an advantage in technology and, more particularly, industrial capability. In terms of new weapons, the British used ship-mounted rockets designed by William Congreve. Operating on the Biscayan coast in 1812, Commodore Sir Home Popham pressed for these 'admirable' rockets.[44] Congreve also developed a lighter long gun, somewhat resembling the cannonade, which was used by the navy.

Thanks to her naval resources, Britain was able to turn tactical triumphs to operational value and strategic advantage. As on land, mobility, firepower and determination were crucial in battle, although at sea these were always most readily applied in the offensive. Successive victories, especially Trafalgar, conditioned British and foreign expectations, and the latter were crucial as French naval strategy was framed accordingly. Confidence is a vital military resource, and victory both brought it to Britain and denied it to France.

Overall economic capability and institutional experience gave the British a considerable advantage. Aside from being the largest industrial enterprise in the country and a source of industrial development, the navy was an important trading system and source of economic activity. By 1813, the victualling system of the navy was feeding 147,000 men daily, and it was possible to mount a formidable effort in North America and to direct a formidable resupply system on the far-flung East Indies Station. In August 1795, Commodore Peter Rainier sought for the 694-man complement of *Suffolk* 39,000 lbs of bread, 1,400 gallons of arrach, 2,000 lbs of flour, 1,500 lbs of raisins, 6,400 lbs of pease, 10,000 lbs of rice, 3,200 lbs of sugar and 200 gallons of vinegar.[45] This was expected to sustain them for three months.

Effective leadership of the navy as an institution was also important, although there were significant policy issues. For example, Jervis, created Earl St Vincent after his great victory, was an energetic First Lord of the Admiralty in 1801–4, but his hostility to naval contractors and his campaign for economy in the naval dockyards limited the rate of construction and repair, placing the navy in a difficult position in 1804. The reversal of this policy ensured that by the end of 1808 the commissioned fleet totalled 113 of the line and 596 other ships. In 1805, the Commission of Naval Inquiry that St Vincent had set up while First Lord produced charges against his successor, Melville, over his alleged corruption when formerly Treasurer of the Navy, and the Commons' decision for his impeachment led to his being driven from office, which ended his idea for a national register of seamen and selection for the navy by ballot. The impeachment failed, but it led to the criminal prosecution of a minister George III had considered effective. Middleton, created Lord Barham in 1805, proved an effective First Lord in 1805–6. He played an important role both in developing organisational efficiency and in providing able and effective leadership during the Trafalgar campaign.

Able administrators, such as Samuel Bentham and John Payne, did much to develop the organisational infrastructure of the navy. Naval efficiency increased from the 1790s with the introduction of more effective attitudes and practices of financial and administrative control, reflecting a more general openness to new thinking and a readiness to consult those with expert knowledge.[46] The navy was the sole government department that issued its own bonds, which was necessary in order to deal with the shortage of specie. Under Bentham there was a rationalisation of work in the naval dockyards, a key centre of efficiency and its frictions. Improved processes came with unpopular vigilance.[47] The navy's Victualling Board and the Board of Ordnance each proved effective. The Victualling Board was far more experienced and efficient, and less corrupt, than the Army Commissariat, and improvements in provisioning permitted longer-term deployment, which was key both for blockading French ports and for expeditionary warfare. The Transport Board skilfully recruited merchantmen for amphibious operations.[48]

Resources permitted and administrative systems supported the maintenance both of the largest battlefleet in the world and of a crucially large number of smaller warships. There was not much point in building very large warships at the end of the war, since there were no significant enemy warships at sea, but Britain was building small warships for trade protection right up to the close of the conflict. It was the shortage of skilled seamen that was the real issue, and naval commanders could have done with more men.[49]

Moreover, the infrastructure improved and became more far-flung. New naval facilities were developed, including at Barbados, Bermuda, Cape Town, Chennai (Madras), Malta, Mumbai (Bombay) and Trincomalee. Two new deep docks were created at Portsmouth in 1796–1800 and the basin was deepened in order to enable the docking of ships without unloading guns and equipment, although the facility was only occasionally used and then only for frigates requiring attention. Frigates and third-rates were built for the navy at Mumbai.

Signalling at sea, crucial to operational effectiveness, communications and co-ordinated action, improved from the 1780s, and a quick and flexible numerical system of signals was developed and used from the 1790s, with the first official Admiralty signal book issued in 1799. This increased the control admirals had over their squadrons and helped in the shift toward the tactic of 'breaking the line'. However, smoke and poor weather at sea meant that flags were not always effective as signals. On land, the Admiralty was linked to Portsmouth by semaphore stations, but their visibility was also affected by the weather. Furthermore, the Admiralty Hydrographic Office was founded in 1795.

Despite its difficulties, British naval power permitted a great increase in maritime strength, and this was important to the global protection and expansion of her commerce. For example, British commercial penetration of South and South-East Asia and the Far East was aided by naval strength: occupation, as of Java in 1811–16, was important. More generally, her dominant maritime position served to ensure that Britain took the leading role in exploration, trade and the assembling of knowledge about the world. This left its mark on the imperial capital, where there was a major expansion in shipping and docks: the London was excavated in 1801, followed by the West India Docks in 1802, the East India Docks in 1805, and the start of work on the Surrey Commercial Docks in 1807, all of which were important developments in the commercial infrastructure of the empire.

More generally, the war led to an expansion of shipbuilding, both for the navy and for trade. Naval power was a condition as well as a product of economic growth. As the Industrial Revolution was crucial to British and, subsequently, global modernisation,[50] so the ability of the British navy to operate effectively, within existing constraints, in order to foster trade was central. This industrial revolution was to have fundamental implications for the ability, in the nineteenth century, to develop and sustain new-model navies with totally different tactical, operational and, eventually, strategic capabilities to those hitherto.

This provides a way to consider the issues of military revolution, modernisation, modernity and total warfare. Nationalism was also crucial. Although the image of naval warfare was defined in different ways and contested politically,[51] the idea of naval strength was crucial to national identity. Naval power was put in an historical context, notably with Thomas Mante's *Naval and Military History of the Wars of England* (1795–1807).

Jane Austen's Navy

The cultural importance of the navy for British culture and character, as well as the complexity but generally positive contemporary account of the navy, could be found in the work of Jane Austen, two of whose brothers followed naval careers. In April 1805, she wrote to Charles 'in consequence of my Mother's having seen in the papers that the *Urania* was waiting at Portsmouth for the convoy for Halifax'. Ann Barrett later recalled Jane's 'enthusiasm for the Navy'.[52] Charles distinguished himself in the defeat of the Dutch fleet at Camperdown in 1797, and Francis, who escorted the expedition to the West Indies in 1795 and pursued the French thither in 1805, did well in the successful action off Santo Domingo in 1806, while, in *Persuasion*, the fictional Frederick Wentworth is made commander as a result of his role there. Charles and Francis eventually both became admirals, Francis adding a knighthood. Edmund Bertram refers to the navy as 'a noble profession', but, in contrast, Sir Walter Elliot and Mary Crawford are placed as negative characters by their condescension toward naval officers.[53] Indeed, the navy was crucial to patriotic ideas of the nation,[54] and the response to it therefore fixed the nature of character. This was seen in part with the use of sailors as a means to present national identity, sailors rather than officers, as in *John Bull Peeping into Brest* (1803), a caricature by George Woodward, in which a large sailor in a large rowboat saying, 'Upon my word – a very pretty light breakfast' looks at a small Napoleon on his small fleet, with Napoleon remarking, 'Mercy on us what a monster: - he'll swallow all my ships at a mouthful. I hope he don't see me.' However, very few letters from seamen survive.[55]

Yet, Sir Walter and Mary were also capturing the extent to which it was indeed unclear how best to place naval officers socially. In practice, most officers were from the 'middling orders',[56] and an aspect of the social complexities of professionalisation also seen, as Jane repeatedly shows, with the clergy, the law and medicine. Thus, in what was in practical terms the most important arm of the state, naval lieutenants were expected to demonstrate a high level of technical training; and this was very different to the purchase system employed in the army. The navy therefore did not require candidates to have money for them to gain appointment or promotion; and patronage, as with William Price in *Mansfield Park*, was largely a matter of recognising and recommending talent. This was linked to the idea that the talent justified the gentility of the status, and not wealth. Thus, 'politeness' had a particular echo in the navy, a life where there was not the great wealth of much of society unless through the merited means of prize money. This 'politeness' required that naval officers should behave and dress as gentlemen. As Jane showed, they should also be treated as such. Martial values were increasingly part of both English masculinity and gentlemanlike behaviour.[57] This behaviour was more important than the ownership of land in the definition of gentlemen, but clearly not to some of Jane's characters. A sampling of nearly 1,000 commissioned and warrant officers for the period 1775 to 1815 indicates that 72 per cent were English, and 40 per cent had entered the navy between the ages of 12 and 15. There was a major over-supply of qualified lieutenants, although that varied depending on the international situation. Warrant officers had a similar social background to commissioned officers. Some of the technical skills of the officer corps were similar to those found in the Ordnance, but the latter had no comparable need for seamanship and navigation.[58]

Jane's pride in her brothers' naval careers preceded the wars. In her *History of England*, written in 1791, she compared the 17-year-old Francis Austen to Sir Francis Drake: 'I cannot help foreseeing that he will be equalled in this or the next century by one who though now but young, already promises to answer all the ardent and sanguine expectations of his relatives and friends.'[59] So also with her pride in British naval achievements. In her marginalia on Oliver Goldsmith's *History of England*, Jane shows such pride in her comments on Anson's attack on the Spaniards in the Pacific during the War of the Austrian Succession.[60] Jane was an instance of the family links affected by naval service, links very much varying by individual, but also affected by the prevalent notions of appropriate behaviour, by family and other networks, and by the images of national need and religious duty.[61]

Yet, Captain Wentworth offers criticism of the Admiralty that presumably derived from Jane's brothers:

> The admiralty entertain themselves now and then, with sending a few hundred men to sea, in a ship not fit to be employed. But they have a great many to provide for; and among the thousands that may just as well go to the bottom as not, it is impossible for them to distinguish the very set who may be least missed.[62]

The navy also provides Jane with a point of departure for what is a more extended critique of the whole process of socially constrained courtship that she repeatedly anatomises. On leave visiting Fanny Price at Mansfield Park, William Price, faced by the undoubted challenges of being a midshipman,[63] admits that he has had enough of Portsmouth:

> The Portsmouth girls turn up their noses at anybody who has not a commission. One might as well be nothing as a midshipman. One *is* nothing indeed. You remember the

Gregorys; they are grown up amazing fine girls, but they will hardly speak to me because Lucy is courted by a lieutenant.

This earns a heartfelt response from his sister:

'Oh! shame, shame! – But never mind it, William' (her own cheeks in a glow of indignation as she spoke). 'It is not worth minding. It is no reflection on you; it is no more than what the greatest admirals have all experienced, more or less, in their time. You must think of that; you must try to make up your mind to it as one of the hardships which fall to every sailor's share – like bad weather and hard living – only with this advantage, that there will be an end to it, that there will come a time when you will have nothing of that sort to endure. When you are a lieutenant!'

William responds that he doubts he will be,[64] and he is only proved wrong by the exercise of patronage. There is a different, unfair, indeed ridiculous, criticism of the navy in Mary Crawford thinking that 'vile sea-breezes are the ruin of beauty and health'.[65] When William is promoted, this enables Jane both to chart patronage and to show how absurd it is. Indeed, this portrayal is in line with the criticism of the Admiralty given to Captain Wentworth, and that of senior naval officers provided by Joseph Harris, in his 'Naval Characters', published in the *Morning Herald* from 1786 to 1788 and then republished as *The Naval Atlantis* (1788). In order to ingratiate himself with Fanny, Henry Crawford introduces William to his uncle, an Admiral, and persuades the Admiral to help him. This assistance leads to the letters Henry gives Fanny:

The first was from the Admiral to inform his nephew, in a few words, of his having succeeded in the object he had undertaken, the promotion of young Price, and inclosing two more, one from the Secretary of the First Lord to a friend, whom the Admiral had set to work in the business, the other was from that friend to himself, by which it appeared that his Lordship had the very great happiness of attending to the recommendation of Sir Charles, that Sir Charles was much delighted in having such an opportunity of proving his regard for Admiral Crawford, and that the circumstance of Mr William Price's commission as second Lieutenant of H.M. sloop Thrush, being made out, was spreading general joy through a wide circle of great people.[66]

Patronage played a key role in naval life, and notably because the navy contained far more officers than could be employed at sea,[67] although the ratio was not as ridiculous as it is in the modern navy. Patrons were important at every level, including in obtaining command, and of good warships, and favourable assignments, such as the independent cruises that provided the opportunities for gaining distinction and prize money, as well as helping protégés. Yet, this was in the cause of competence as well as connection. Thus, John Wilson Croker, First Secretary at the Admiralty from 1809 to 1830, expected efficiency from the recipients of his patronage.[68] This was more generally the case, and was indeed how patronage not only was supposed to work but indeed generally did. Patronage was designed to select and advance on merit and quality, and the reliability supposedly guaranteed by patronage was part of the equation. This was seen not only with the patronage formally exercised by the Board of Admiralty, commanding admirals and captains, but also of the informal process by which senior officers developed and maintained a cascading system of followers. Patronage helped ensure the appointment of talent while relatively young.

At the same time, merit in terms respectively of social rank, honour and duty was not coterminous, and this caused frequent problems, not least when politics also played a factor in difference and partisanship. Promotion and command were the key foci of disputes, but, in turn, these were lessened by the pressures of war which centred on the obligations of duty and the need for competence. As with any military, there was a wide variety of experience, from the level of admirals to that of midshipmen. The latter were frequently presented in an heroic light in a new periodical, *The Naval Chronicle*, a work that moved the emphasis away from admirals.[69] This move owed something to Evangelicalism, but also to the responsibilities arising from the place of midshipmen in smaller warships where command roles were less structured and there were proportionately fewer commissioned officers.

In *Mansfield Park*, a very positive account is offered of William Price when he meets his sister en route to going to sea, while Edmund Bertram 'tells her such charming things of what William was to do, and be hereafter, in consequence of his profession, as made her gradually admit that the separation might have some use'.[70] It is possible to imagine Jane likewise being reassured about her brothers. The generally quiet Fanny Price, unusually, is 'animated in speaking of his profession, and the foreign stations he had been on, but she could not mention the number of years that he had been absent without tears in her eyes'. On his return from sea seven years later, William, probably modelled on Charles Austen, is an impressive young man.[71] Six years' sea service was required to qualify for a lieutenant, which encouraged embarking on a naval career quickly, although such an early start was common more generally in society. Those seeking to be officers were expected to be able to tackle navigational issues, which meant that shipboard education was important. In part this was provided in 'maritime schools' or the Royal Naval Academy at Portsmouth, although the latter was too small to cope with requirements. Physical resilience was a prime requirement for naval service, and this included those who became officers.

Persuasion was set in 1814 and referred to the homecomings of sailors. Army officers also feature, but, in accordance with the general theme in the long eighteenth century – although not in the aftermath of Waterloo the following year – the navy dominates, not least the deleterious consequence of peace for individual prospects and income: there would be no more prize money. The novel closes with an affirmation of the 'national importance' of the navy. Admiral Croft in *Persuasion* is far more benign than General Tilney in *Northanger Abbey*.[72]

Conclusions

Thanks to the navy, exports could rise from £20.4 million in 1793 to £70.3 million in 1814. This was important due to the continued salience of financial factors in naval capability. A pamphleteer in 1719 had already claimed,

> No superiority in the field could be a match for their superiority of treasure; for money being the basis of the war, in the modern way of carrying such things on in the world, it has long since been a received maxim in the case of war, that the longest purse, not the longest sword, would be sure to conquer at last.[73]

Yet money was not all. The psychological boost from naval power, the sense of national self-confidence and of providential exceptionalism, was not some add-on but a crucial constituent. However successful, the army found it difficult to match these factors. This was not only due to historically based constitutional and political factors, but also to the role of the army as a coalition force in which allied units played a key part in major victories, notably Salamanca (1812), Vitoria (1813) and Waterloo (1815). Moreover, whereas during the French Revolutionary and Napoleonic Wars there was a pattern of naval success, and nothing to match such indecisive battles as Toulon (1744) and Ushant (1778) or failures as Minorca (1756) and Virginia Capes (1781), the situation was very different for the army. Aside from repeated failures in the 1790s and 1800s, including on amphibious operations, and spectacularly so at Buenos Aires (1807), the army went on scoring up defeats into the early 1810s, including at Bergen-op-Zoom as late as March 1814.

Had a French invading force been defeated in England then the situation might have been different, but, for a society that required victories and heroes, these were primarily provided by the navy. There was no repetition of Trafalgar, but only because the rebuilt French navy did not sail forth on such a scale. However, there was a series of smaller-scale battles up to Lissa (1811) to provide glory, as well as the excitement of ship-to-ship engagements for which there was no army equivalent. Moreover, although the navy could be engaged in the cause of allies as in the Adriatic, it was generally realistic to emphasise national interests, and notably so in trade protection, when discussing its role. The navy was closely intertwined with patriotism and nationalism, and at a time when both were central to identity.

The French Revolutionary and Napoleonic Wars saw a very considerable body of naval historical and biographical publication, notably John Charnock's *Biographia Navalis* (1794–8), which left the public and sailors in no doubt what the navy was for, what it had done and what it could do in the future. All were vital for ensuring that the navy remained better financed than its rivals and also entrenching a clear naval doctrine for officers and sailors to imitate. This material was read within a context of musical propaganda for the navy, including Arne's 'Rule Britannia' (1740), Garrick's 'Hearts of Oak' (1759) and the many popular maritime ballads by Charles Dibdin, notably 'Tom Bowling' (1780s).[74] The centrality of the navy to national identity was clearly expressed.

10

CONCLUSIONS

> The very situation of our country, which is surrounded with rocks and seas, seems to point out to us our natural strength.

In its issue of 13 July 1728, the *Craftsman*, the leading opposition newspaper, drew on a strong sense of the naturalness of Britain being a naval power. Still, the navy came even more to play a key role in patriotism. The Armada had long been a staple in the socio-cultural history of naval commemoration and national identity, and the political character of the last helped make its ready role in patriotic discussion and image-making of particular significance. Victory was a key enabler of the varied naval images of appropriate conduct and affirmation, ranging from particular admirals to, by the end of our period, midshipmen heroes.[1]

This sense was consistently important in British strategic culture, and provided the context for the more prudential commitment to naval strength. Until the age of air power and space, fleets were the most complex and costly public artifact of Western societies. For Britain, this capability rested on the strong public finances that stemmed from a central role in world trade, as well as from public confidence in government. Political support was important not only to the number of warships, but also for other aspects of naval operation, including the impressment of sailors. Although not without many difficulties, manpower in large measure kept up with the rise in the number of warships. It drew on the major growth in the mercantile marine, including from 280,000 tonnes in 1695 to 609,000 in 1760, and of the economy and trading system as a whole. In 1744, 'all the ropers at Poole' were making cordage for the navy.[2] The ever-increasing size of British merchant trade and shipping, and its expansion beyond its rivals, both caused and profited from British naval power. It provided the money, men and material to expand the British fleet beyond its rivals, providing more seamen than any other country at a time when the size of ships was constantly increasing and requiring more men to sail and also man bigger guns. Thus, the French navy required 48,000 for its 256 ships (95 of the line) in 1692 and 72,000 for 264 (78 of the line) in 1779.

However, systemic advantages had to be translated into operational advantages and within the parameters of the strategic circumstances of the international situation and the resulting threats to Britain and tasks for its naval power, not least the need to delegate operational discretion to the men on the spot. Successes can be transient and fragile, even providential, and command and control in a sailing navy was always a challenge; but for the British that transience and fragility diminished over time. In consequence, they increased for Britain's enemies. Britain's training, combat discipline and readiness all improved and to a high standard, as did fighting spirit and leadership for the most part.

Diplomatic developments created a major challenge to Britain in the period 1689–1815, ensuring that a powerful navy was a key aspect of the solution, thus providing a valuable instance of the challenge-and-response nature of military power; otherwise described in terms of a stress on tasking. In the sixteenth and seventeenth centuries, England/Britain had benefited from the ability to fight sequentially rather than simultaneously, a key goal for any power, major or minor. Thus, in the sixteenth century, conflict had been with France or Spain, and in the seventeenth century, with France, Spain or the Dutch. A combination between opponents was unusual. In the late 1530s, the Habsburg Emperor, Charles V, and Francis I of France had allied against Henry VIII, and there had been grave concerns in England about the possibility of an invasion. These, indeed, had led to the construction of coastal fortifications, as well as to an effort to build up Henry VIII's navy. In the event, however, the alliance did not last, and, instead, Henry was able to join with Charles against Francis. In the 1620s, England had been at war with both France and Spain, but the two had not been allied.

The system throughout reflected a public-private co-operation that drew on the strengths of society. Thus, although the naval dockyards were state concerns, much shipbuilding and repair was contracted out to private shipbuilders. The private sector played a key role in the provision of stores for naval construction, foodstuffs to the Victualling Board, and the movement of troops and supplies by Transport Board. Contractors understood the market better than bureaucrats and were less constrained by politics. Overseas bases relied on local producers and contractors operating at long range, as well as the ability of credit networks to move funds and to finance the purchase of supplies, privateers played a key role in commerce-raiding, and press gangs relied on the availability of manpower from the merchant fleet. Co-operation with merchants included the navy acting against pirates and entrusting the movement of bullion to warships.

The East India Company ran a navy as well as bases, notably at Bombay (Mumbai), Portsmouth, Blackwall and St Helena.

There was also co-operation in the case of armies, but navies had an earlier requirement for technical specialisation, professionalisation and the development of a military-financial combination, and to needs for bureaucratic regularity and a more general literacy. The professional administration of the navy through the Navy Board and the Admiralty was highly impressive, and replicated at lower levels. The consequences of social hierarchy and political factionalism were present in the navy as well as the army. Yet, on balance, there were significant social, economic, governmental, political and cultural differences.

This situation of sequential conflict helped England in its warfare with the leading European naval powers, whether Spain in the late sixteenth century, the Dutch in the three Anglo-Dutch Wars of 1652–74 or the French in the early stages of the Nine Years War (1689–97). In most cases, moreover, the English were allied to, or co-operating with, other naval powers, notably with the Dutch against Spain in 1585–1604, with Louis XIV against the Dutch in the Third Anglo-Dutch War (1672–4), and with the Dutch (and Spain) against Louis XIV in the Nine Years War. The value of this co-operation helped explain the problems created by the threat of co-operation between France and the Dutch at the time of the Second Anglo-Dutch War.

The navy surpassed the French navy in size in the 1690s, but this achievement did not lead the other states to ally in an anti-hegemonic alliance, although the rhetoric of such an alliance was to play a role in French propaganda over the following century and was also to be employed by Napoleon. Indeed, indicating the extent to which talk of threats was rhetoric as much as analysis, the British employed it when criticising Spanish attempts in 1738–9 to exclude them from trade with the Spanish New

Conclusions

World. *The Citizen or, The Weekly Conversation of a Society of London Merchants on Trade, and other Public Affairs*, in its issue of 9 February 1739, noted that 'the just Balance of Power amongst the European nations might as eventually be broken and destroyed, by an unjust and partial monopoly of the medium of commerce, as by any particular state engrossing to itself too large an extent of dominion, and other branches of power'.

Instead of uniting against England, and thus prefiguring the situation in both the early 1780s and the late 1790s, the Dutch and Spain joined England in the 1690s in co-operating against France. The situation changed, however, during the War of the Spanish Succession, in which England was engaged from 1702 to 1713; but this change occurred as a result of dynastic factors and not due to opposition to Britain's naval position. The accession of Louis's grandson Philip, Duke of Anjou to the Spanish throne as Philip V in 1700 led to an alliance of France and Spain opposed to that of England, the Dutch and Austria. However, after the war, this alliance disintegrated and, in the War of the Quadruple Alliance (1718–20), Britain, France, Austria and the Dutch were united against Spain. Thus, the British were able to defeat a Spanish fleet off Sicily in 1718 (the battle of Cape Passaro) and to mount a successful amphibious attack on the Spanish port of Vigo in 1719 without having to fear the opposition of France.

The same was true of British naval operations, and planned operations, against Spain in 1725–9: France was allied with Britain and the Dutch, as part of the Alliance of Hanover. Therefore, it was possible for Britain to blockade the Spanish ports of Cadiz and Porto Bello without fear of French military action, and that despite major French investment in the cargoes due to be brought back from the Americas in the blockaded ships.

However, this situation changed in the 1730s with the collapse of the Anglo-French alliance in 1731 and the replacement, in

1733, of Anglo-Spanish co-operation by that between France and Spain. The basis of this alliance was dynastic, the first of three Family Compacts between the Bourbon rulers of France and Spain; and this alliance established the diplomatic core of the challenge facing the British navy. Allowing for periods of diplomatic co-operation between Britain and Spain, notably in the early 1750s, when Ferdinand VI of Spain was unwilling to heed French pressure for joint action, and of Anglo-Spanish military co-operation against Revolutionary France in 1793–5, this alignment of France and Spain provided a basic naval challenge to Britain that lasted until Napoleon tried to take over Spain in 1808. The combination of French and Spanish warships at Trafalgar in 1805 demonstrated this challenge, and also how it survived changes in regime, as such co-operation had been seen in the battle of Toulon in 1744, and also when Spanish warships joined the French at Brest in preparing for the unsuccessful invasion of England in 1779.

The impact of this Franco-Spanish challenge was exacerbated by the extent to which Anglo-Dutch naval co-operation became less significant from the 1710s and, indeed, ceased from 1748. This change transformed the naval situation in the English Channel, the North Sea and the Indian Ocean; and, thus, more generally for Britain. Instead, the two powers became enemies, fighting an Anglo-Dutch War in 1780–4, and again, after alliance in 1788–95, once the French overran the Netherlands in 1795, during the French Revolutionary War.

These shifts posed the key problem for the navy, as well as the individual challenges of specific conjunctures, but they did not exhaust the diplomatic difficulties it confronted. In addition, two rising naval powers were opposed to Britain in key periods, although only one actually brought a fight to the navy. Russia became a key regional naval power under Peter the Great (r.

Conclusions

1689–1725), and came close to conflict with Britain in the early 1720s, both during the last stage of the Great Northern War (1700–21) and subsequently. Yet, war was avoided then, as it also was in 1791 during the Ochakov Crisis, and in the 1800s when Russia had periods of alliance with France, notably under Paul I in 1800–1 and after Napoleon and Alexander I signed the Treaty of Tilsit in 1807. By then, Russia was a wide-ranging naval power. Indeed, its fleet had been deployed to the Mediterranean against the Turks from 1769, albeit then with logistical support from Britain. In 1813, an improvement in relations with Russia, followed by the transfer of Russian warships to the North Sea, as well as the contrary requirements of the War of 1812 ensured that the British felt able to deploy fewer warships in the North Sea.

The British relationship with America, in contrast, had become more hostile. Aside from the War of Independence in 1775–83, the two powers waged the War of 1812 in 1812–15, and this conflict posed a challenge to British naval resources, not least as they struggled to develop a blockade of America's ports and to overcome American privateering while also fighting France. The loss of the support of the one-time Thirteen Colonies was not significant in terms of the arithmetic of ships of the line. However, this loss was important for the manpower that had been contributed to the navy, both directly and indirectly through the role of the merchant marine of the American colonies in British imperial trade, notably of the West Indies. Indeed, manpower issues helped lead to the outbreak of the War of 1812. In impressing sailors from American shipping, the British were not interested in claims that these sailors were no longer British subjects because they had become American nationals. Statistical measures of naval power in terms of numbers of warships need to be complemented by analysis of the manpower situation and, separately, by an appreciation of the regional dynamics of naval power, not least if these dynamics related to far-flung empires.

At the same time, there was significant naval co-operation between the two powers in 1798–1800 when the French attacked American merchantmen in response to their part in maintaining British trade routes. Britain provided the Americans with cannon and co-operation, Charles, 1st Earl of Liverpool writing,

> They must depend on our fleet for the general protection of their commerce, and this circumstance will tend, I think to unite the two countries in a closer bond of union: their armed vessels however will afford us a considerable degree of assistance in destroying the small French privateers.[3]

Such an argument looked toward the language used about German submarines prior to America's entry into war against Germany in 1917 and 1941.

If mention of America from 1775 does not exhaust the list of challenges facing the navy, it does provide an indication of their scale and range. The diplomatic dimension underlines the degree to which the navy had to cope with a situation shot through with unpredictability. With reference to a false report of naval preparations at Toulon in 1774, Viscount Stormont noted,

> In the present situation of things, in the present strange disjointed state of Europe, it is equally difficult and necessary to find a just medium between that blind security which might prove fatal, and that anxious jealousy which catches every alarm and in the end often creates the evil it fears.[4]

Stormont's complaint, which referred further to the difficulty of securing reliable information in France, is as valid a qualification to the general habit of discussing international relations in terms of purposeful, coherent and consistent policies, with naval strategy set accordingly, as the remarks of many naval officers about their difficulties are an apt rejoinder to any discussion of their actions in terms of grand strategic conceptions. Both, in turn, interacted with efforts to create, define or destroy images and perceptions of British naval power and capabilities.

Indeed, this effort was a key element in the peacetime British naval strategy, for the prospect of war, as in 1733–5 (when Britain was neutral in the War of the Polish Succession despite its Austrian alliance and, in 1735, sent a fleet to the Tagus when Spain threatened Portugal), might mean war with France or Spain, or both. In reacting to this situation of inherent uncertainty, the British therefore had to rely on diplomacy in order to lessen the build-up of an opposing coalition, intelligence in order to ascertain what their opponents would do, and a strong navy. The three were linked, and it would be misleading to treat them separately.

The navy itself responded within existing technological and institutional constraints. There were significant improvements in both, but no transformative change in either in this period, a point that serves as a reminder about the danger of assuming that hegemonic military strength necessarily reflects the availability of particular technological and institutional advantages. Indeed, there were periods of unnecessary conservatism in ship design, notably from 1714 to 1744, which led to serious complaints about the ships,[5] and then again from 1763 to 1780.

The navy had some comparative advantages, notably access to a greater pool of skilled manpower than anyone else, but within the context of a system in which variations, while important, were not necessarily crucial. Britain's dockyard system was more effective, with more stone dry docks than any other nation, and considerably more dry docks than France, which enabled quicker repair and refit, and hence faster throughput to keep its ships at sea. French warships tended to be better-built in the mid-eighteenth century, while the British subsequently benefited from carronades and copper-bottoming, but neither advantage was decisive. Instead, British fire discipline was a key element, one shown to devastating effect during the French Revolutionary and Napoleonic wars. This fire discipline arose from training and experience, and not from technological advantage.

Challenges played a role in enhancing the British development of the capabilities they possessed. Thus, the need to respond to the Seven Years War (1756–63) helped ensure the emulation of French shipbuilding techniques, while copper-bottoming and carronades were pushed forward due to the War of American Independence (1775–83), which, from 1778, was also an Anglo-French war; and with Spain and the Dutch participating from 1779 and 1780 respectively. Fire-discipline benefited from the experience of frequent conflict.

Opponents who lacked naval experience responded to their weaker position by seeking to build up strength, especially through a diffusion of the technology and personnel from the leading power or powers. Thus, for example, Russia recruited British captains, sailors and shipwrights. It is notable that, in contrast, there was scant interest in the type of paradigm-shifting challenge presented by initiatives in mines and submarines. The latter were associated in particular with Robert Fulton, and he offered threats to British hegemony, pressing both France and America to take his inventions as an opportunity to overcome the British position. Despite the fact that France was at war with Britain, this route was not taken, which was probably an appropriate response to the possibility of effectively manufacturing any new system, but the net effect was to ensure that the navy was not challenged by any radically new system.

Producing a submarine in 1797, Fulton found neither Britain and France greatly interested in its acquisition. His experiments for the French in 1800–1 included the testing of a system of compressed air in a portable container, and the successful destruction of a vessel by an underwater explosion. Fulton also proposed the use of steamships for an invasion of England, but in 1803 the French Academy of Sciences rejected the idea. During 1804–6 he worked on mines in Britain, which were used to little effect in an attack on French shipping in Boulogne in 1804, but trials in 1805 saw him become the first to sink a large ship with a mine. In 1806, he argued that 'it does not require much depth of thought to trace that science by discovering gunpowder changed the whole art of war by land and sea; and by future combination may sweep military marines from the ocean'.[6] British interest declined after Trafalgar, when Britain's naval position seemed safe; Fulton, meanwhile, was held back in his experiments with torpedoes from 1807 by his failure to devise an effective firing device.[7]

During the War of 1812, Fulton found support for naval steam power in his native America, but his work did not threaten the British position any more than David Bushnell's successful effort to create a workable submarine had done during the War of American Independence. Its dependence on human energy for movement, and on staying partially above the surface for oxygen, made it only an intimation of the submarine of the future.

Nor was the British navy confronted with any significant development in the tactical, operational or strategic spheres. Indeed, in contrast to the development in the seventeenth century of professional navies, specialised fighting ships (neither, of course, began in that century) and line-ahead tactics, there was remarkably little change in the eighteenth century nor the first half of the nineteenth. There is scant sign of novelty being seen as the solution for problems, which helps explain the emphasis placed by the British on command skills and character. Indeed, command was regarded as the key element, alongside the efforts of the crews, opening the question whether there were any particular efforts to teach command. In practice, most education was 'on the job', which underlined the significance of serving under appropriate captains, and there was no systematic teaching of naval operational art, let alone strategy.

More generally with the navy, there was an incremental response to possibilities, and this response accorded with the cultural norms of the period. Indeed, such a response can also be seen in governance and the army, although a different emphasis can be presented if the stress is on the 'Financial Revolution' of the 1690s. Britain has been seen as the setting for agricultural, industrial, financial, transport and political revolutions in the period 1689–1815, but not as one for a naval revolution, although the navy benefited from these other revolutions, notably in finance, victualling, and the use of industrial power and method, including steam power at Portsmouth. The relevance of this point for the wider field of military change in this period is also suggestive. There is a tendency to argue that a military revolution arose from the French Revolution and that, in combination with the supposed military revolution of 1560–1660, such military revolutions were possible, desirable, and the route to enhanced capability and success. These arguments, however, tell us more about contemporary and (later) scholarly discourses concerning military power and development than they do concerning the far more complex processes involved. In particular, change tended to be incremental; the gaps in capability between navies (and armies) were smaller, and more contingent to circumstances, than are generally appreciated; and the nature of improvement was not always clear.

These points can be underlined by drawing attention to the variety of tasks that navies were expected to discharge. In particular, there was no one task, and thus no single measure of effectiveness. Britain's navy had the prime strategic requirement of protecting the homeland (as well as the colonies) from invasion, a task also seen with the Dutch navy during the Third Anglo-Dutch War. This was not a goal shared by the navies of France, Spain, Russia or America, the last of which relied against invasion on the militia, on coastal fortifications and on the vast extent of the country.

Again with the exception of the Dutch, the British navy had a role in preventing the interruption of trade routes that was not matched elsewhere. Such interruption posed a fundamental problem for the operation of the French and, to a lesser extent, Spanish economic systems; but there was nothing to match the British dependence – that of the economy, of credit and public finances – on overseas trade. This situation again posed an essential challenge to the British navy, because trade protection, like the sea denial involved in invasion prevention, was fundamentally reactive. It was necessary to block or react to the sailing of hostile warships and privateers; and that within a context in which intelligence (especially prior intelligence) was limited, and communications about any such sailing slow and not readily subject to confirmation. Toward the close of the period, there was a degree of improvement in the shape of the introduction of semaphores, but their impact was restricted. More serious was the extent to which balloons did not offer the capacity for tactical let alone operational aerial surveillance that later developments in powered flight were to provide.

Thus, the navy was trapped by a set of tasks that forced it into a reactive operational stance. That is not the picture that generally emerges from popular accounts of naval battles, but the latter devote insufficient attention to the strain involved in more commonplace blockading. That, in fact, many battles arose as a result of aspects of blockade, and thus of the reactive strategy that was central to the use of British naval power, can be readily established by a consideration of the battles, and, not least, of their location. However, the contemporary conception of British naval power was very different. It was proactive, not reactive and that assumption posed a different form of challenge, one moreover that was accentuated by the nature of British public politics. Indeed, the wider politics of naval tasking arose from the placing of naval requirements within British public culture and government.

As an instance of the challenges posed by the latter, the Glorious Revolution of 1688–9 led to the replacement of a monarch, James II, with a deep personal commitment to the navy, but one who was politically highly problematic given his Catholicism and authoritarianism.[8] His replacement, William III (r. 1689–1702), was the first in a series without any such commitment: although William came to Britain by sea, he was very much a general, although he had a strong sense of the workings of naval power, supporting the development of Plymouth, urging the fleet to operate down-Channel to blockade Brest, and backing the support of a fleet to the Mediterranean. An army preference was even more true of George I (r. 1714–27) and George II (r. 1727–60), although George III was a strong supporter of the navy.

As young men, George I and George II had gained important military experience, but on land and not at sea. Moreover, both men had a powerful commitment to their native Electorate of

Hanover, which was not a naval power and did not become one. George I, however, had a good idea about how British naval power could assist Hanoverian goals.

This attitude on the part of the Crown was taken further by the powerful and longstanding commitment to the army of royal princes, notably William, Duke of Cumberland and Frederick, Duke of York, the favourite sons of George II and George III respectively. In contrast, although George II had considered reviving the office of Lord High Admiral for Cumberland in 1736, and for a year the latter's studies and travels were directed toward the navy, this scheme was dropped, and there was no such politically charged commitment to the navy. William IV, as Duke of Clarence, followed a naval career, but it proved abortive and lacked weight.

Royal attitudes were not central to the political position of the navy, which was largely autonomous from the Crown and its patronage, but these attitudes were an element in the complex circumstances within which it had to operate. Yet compared to the army, the navy had more of a parliamentary flavour. It was economical and accountable to parliamentary norms. Aside from its key role in voting funds, Parliament proved more intrusive than the Crown, not least in the shape of pressure when things went wrong, as they tended to in the early stages of most wars. The resulting controversies were in part an aspect of the problems stemming from an assumption of success. This assumption became more insistent because the Wars of the Spanish Succession (1702–13) and Quadruple Alliance (1718–20) did not leave any legacy of perceived failure and that set political problems for the succeeding period, a situation that was to recur after the Seven Years War. As a result, the concerns of 1744–6, 1756, 1759 and 1779, about projected or possible French invasions, seemed unacceptable and the product of political and/or naval neglect. This situation underlined the political, and thus strategic, problems stemming from a reactive operational stance. The need to plan for acting against attempted invasion was not necessarily a result of failure, however much that might seem to be the case to elements in British public politics.

If the operational and political issues posed by invasion threats provided a key strategic problem, it was not one that changed greatly during the period. There were anxieties about invasion for most of the period, although the extent to which any invasion was seen as likely to enjoy domestic support varied greatly. The last, indeed, constituted a key element in the political challenge to naval power; anxiety about domestic backing for invaders, whether from Jacobites or Irish rebels, created greater pressure for naval security and for an appearance of assured mastery.

This situation lasted until the Irish risings of 1798 and, far less seriously, 1803; but, after that, the French naval threat was not seen in terms of exacerbating domestic disaffection. Thus, in 1805, the French naval threat was, first, of an invasion of Britain and then of intervening in the Mediterranean; but the domestic British response was even more hostile than to France on some previous occasions.

This last point serves as a reminder of the degree to which the (varied) response to the problems faced by British naval power in successive conflicts helped mould the politics of the following years. Success in the Seven Years War lessened the political pressure thereafter, so that in 1765 Edward Sedgwick, an under secretary, expressed his surprise when, in the Commons debate over the number of seamen and marines, the opposition 'contrary to the practice of former oppositions, concluded that small numbers of seamen and marines would be sufficient'.[9] In turn, the Napoleonic Wars provided an appearance of British naval dominance not seen in the American Independence or

French Revolutionary wars. There was no repetition of the large-scale indecisive battles of the former (Ushant, 1778; Virginia Capes 1781); nor of the naval mutinies (1797) and strategic problems of the latter: withdrawal from the Mediterranean in 1796 and failure to prevent French forces landing in Ireland in 1798. Instead, the arduous nature of the Mediterranean naval commitment after Trafalgar, especially of the difficult blockade of Toulon, was overlooked in the post-war glow of remembered glory. So also was the anxiety about France building up its navy after Trafalgar, which focused on the dockyards of Antwerp. This anxiety led to the Walcheren expedition of 1809, as well as to later concern to ensure that any subsequent peace did not leave France in control of the port, which indeed had been the intention of Count Metternich, Chancellor of Austria.

A key element of the politics and strategy of naval power related to bases, and thus to the military operations, planning priorities and international negotiations bound up with their capture from opponents. In the 1750s, the British got to grips with the needs of amphibious warfare and turned it into a worldwide decisive weapon, even publishing a manual, Thomas More Molyneux's *Conjunct Expeditions: or Expeditions that have been carried on jointly by the fleet and army, with a commentary on a littoral war* (1759). Molyneux was an army officer and MP.

There was the related question of the expansion, at home and even more abroad, of the system of naval bases that, in turn, saw the interplay of naval criteria with imperial and domestic policy and politics; the latter, for example, was seen in the bitter debate of 1786 over naval fortifications. The House of Commons narrowly rejected the plan for fortifying Plymouth and Portsmouth, a measure seen as necessary by the government not only to protect the key bases for a Western Squadron but also to free the fleet for wartime offensive operations. This episode, in which the measure was in part perceived as a political job, indicated the range of factors involved in naval politics and strategy, and also the danger of seeing results as a product of plans without noting the powerful mediation of these factors.

This emphasis on politics also directs attention to the degree to which naval power was the product of co-operation between interest groups, notably those that controlled and could finance warships. There were major variations on this head within Europe, and on the world scale, so that naval strength had a dynamic that was not simply located in the realm of competition between naval powers. Instead, intentionality was linked to a structural assessment of the societies and political cultures of these powers.

This insight is a crucial one for understanding the challenges and responses of British naval power, as it locates this power in a different pattern of response to that affecting Britain's rivals. In particular, governmental support for the navy elsewhere could be extensive but tended to lack the political, social and institutional grounding seen in Britain. As a consequence, there could be a mismatch between governmental decisions to expand resources and build up naval strength, and, on the other hand, an achievement in terms of the delivery of effective naval power, a point clearly seen with Russia under Peter the Great. The French financial system lacked the institutional strength and stability of its British counterpart, and this badly affected French naval finances, notably in 1759. The French also lacked an effective chain of naval command, and trade was less important to their government and political culture than in the case of Britain. There was a sociological dimension that deserves attention. In particular, French and Spanish naval officer corps were more dominated by aristocratic patronage, privilege and ethos than the British and

Conclusions

Dutch, both of whom were more clearly professional in their meritocratic ethos and related factionalism. This situation owed much to the sociological impact of a particular politico-religious development.[10]

Relating naval power and strategy to politics is appropriate. A key element in eighteenth-century Britain was the lack of any unpacking of strategy and policy, reflecting the absence of any institutional body specifically for strategic planning and execution, and also the tendency, in politics, government and political discussion, to see strategy and policy as one, and necessarily so. Institutional practices and political assumptions rested on important configurations reflecting linked constituencies of support. Britain's ability to respond to the challenges facing its naval power can in large part be explained by this situation.

At the same time, public expectations posed serious problems. Under the byline of a coffeehouse near the Admiralty, the *Universal Spectator* of 5 June 1742 argued that it would be possible to 'prove the British navy can still maintain the balance' of Europe. However comforting, this statement was a marked exaggeration of what the navy could do, but one that arose from a more general unwillingness to assess the limitations of naval power other than in terms of blame. This unwillingness was related to attacks on naval strategy and operations,[11] although, in response, wartime problems could lead to more realistic assessments, for example the piece by 'Nauticus' in the *True Briton* of 18 March 1797 that drew attention to the severe problems of winter operations. Parliamentary debates saw discussion of naval power and history, as with Pitt's contribution to the debate on the Address in 1755.[12]

In contrast to public hopes, the navy encountered significant problems in being a decisive instrument of power, although being decisive was a political construction. Moreover, in the crucial sphere of home waters, the navy could attempt such decisiveness. The alarm that greeted significant deployments of French naval forces in and near the Channel in 1690, 1744 and 1779 was profound and affected naval strategy, not least as it was impossible to guarantee total security. Invasion plans were based on a perception of a vulnerability, and counter-invasion plans on a prudent assumption of it. Yet, there was sufficient naval superiority to help prevent invasion after 1688. Moreover, the swift and successful naval mobilisations in 1726–31 and 1734–5 made Jacobite proposals for invasions of Britain appear ridiculous. Although France could send support to the Jacobites in 1745–6, an invasion was thwarted in part because of naval strength and moves. So also with the defeat of longer-prepared and larger-scale French plans in 1759 and 1805.

Superiority in home waters was not just a matter of preventing invasion but also enabled British troops to participate in Continental campaigns by allowing their easy movement in both directions. The contrast with Spanish deployments to Italy was apparent, as they were heavily dependent on naval allowance by Britain. Indeed, the refusal of Britain to send a fleet to the Mediterranean in 1733–5 helped Spain to conquer Naples and Sicily from Austria.

Oceanic naval power depended on a maritime economy to supply resources in depth; demand from governments alone would not generate sustainable maritime infrastructure. It required both a strong state infrastructure and a strong maritime economy,[13] and that was not only quite rare but could also be put under great pressure in war, as France repeatedly discovered in conflict with Britain. Britain was able to increase the size of its navy to 193 ships of the line in 1809, at a time when the average size of such ships was considerably greater than earlier in the century. Consistently, unlike the army, whose political support was essentially based on the idea of unfortunate necessity, the navy was seen as the national force. This reflected one of the intersections of naval power, with another being that of chronology. Although the term military revolution is itself problematic, the significant military developments in the 'early modern' period occurred not so much in the classic period thus defined, 1560–1660, but, in the cases of the Austrian, French, Prussian and Russian armies, and the British, French, Russian and Spanish navies, over the following century. Britain was the dominant naval power to an extent that no other single state was on land.

Postscript

ROUTES TO MODERNITY?

Epithets, analyses and descriptions pile up to proclaim Britain's navy not just the largest in the world but also the most modern, the product of a symbiotic congruence of mercantile resource, technological achievement, financial support, organisational sophistication and social grounding. In contrast, other navies emerge as weaker, both due to the lack of this congruence and in terms of actual capability. Thus, Benjamin Keene, the experienced envoy in Spain, captured in 1737 the large gap between aspiration and reality when reporting to the Duke of Newcastle:

> They reckon they have about 50 ships, out of which I believe they can choose 30 both large and well built, but their store houses being unfurnished, it will cost them very considerable sums before they are put in a tolerable order, and the finances are but in a bad state to succour that of the marine.[1]

So also with the availability of sailors in the Spanish navy.

Yet, there were also issues with the British navy, not only concerning the gap between goal and achievement in both capability and activity, but also in the systemic factors given above. Thus, alongside what might appear modern, there were a host of factors that can be seen as anything but, including the nature of strategic planning and the character of patronage. In its edition for 9 February 1745, *Old England*, a leading London opposition newspaper, attacked the government for 'breaking down all regard for personal merit or experience in military offices, either by land or sea, and in making a parliamentary interest the only step by which the bravest, the oldest, and the ablest of our soldiers and seamen could rise to the common justice, which was due to their rank and services'.

Yet, this approach again may be unhelpful, as the assumption of modernity, modernisation and the modern in terms of the perfect operation of a bureaucratic model, one in particular that is not dependent on misguided or irrational domestic political and public pressures, or in part insulated from them, is not an accurate description of the present day. Moreover, such an account is not necessarily an appropriate paradigm for the past. Rather than assuming such an approach, it is better to note the complexities of tasking and capability and, with them, the salience of strategic requirements and fighting quality. Decisiveness, from days to decades, required success, not only with bureaucratic and other structures but also with both strategic understanding and the ability and determination to fight and win.

For much of the world, however, British naval mastery in the nineteenth century was a context for modernisation. This mastery was a consequence of the period covered in this book. Without its foundation of naval success, Britain could not have sustained imperial and economic growth.

SELECTED FURTHER READING

Aldridge, David, *Admiral Sir John Norris and the British Naval Expeditions to the Baltic Sea, 1715–1727* (2009).

Bromley, John, *Corsairs and Navies, 1660–1760* (1987).

Callo, Joseph, *Nelson in the Caribbean, 1784–1787* (2002).

Cannadine, David (ed.), *Admiral Lord Nelson: Context and Legacy* (2005).

Cannadine, David (ed.), *Trafalgar in History: A Battle and its Afterlife* (2006).

Cavell, Samantha, *Midshipmen and Quarterdeck Boys in the British Navy, 1771–1831* (2012).

Colville, Quintin and James Davey (eds), *A New Naval History* (2018).

Crewe, D. G., *Yellow Jack and the Worm: British Naval Administration in the West Indies, 1739–1748* (1993).

Davey, James, *The Transformation of British Naval Strategy: Seapower and Supply in Northern Europe, 1808–1812* (2012).

Davey James, *In Nelson's Wake: The Navy and the Napoleonic Wars* (2015).

Selected Further Reading

Duffy, Michael (ed.), *Parameters of British Naval Power, 1650–1850* (1992).

Dull, Jonathan, *The Age of the Ship of the Line: The British and French Navies, 1650–1815* (2009).

Gardiner, Robert and Brian Lavery (eds), *The Line of Battle: The Sailing Warship, 1650–1840* (1992).

Gill, Ellen, *Naval Families, War and Duty in Britain, 1740–1820* (2016).

Glete, Jan, *Navies and Nations: Warships, Navies, and State-Building in Europe and America, 1500–1860* (1993).

Gwyn, Julian, *An Admiral for America: Sir Peter Warren* (2004).

Harding, Richard, *Amphibious Warfare in the Eighteenth Century: The British Expedition to the West Indies, 1740–1742* (1991).

Harding, Richard, *Seapower and Naval Warfare, 1650–1830* (1999).

Harding, Richard, *The Emergence of Britain's Global Naval Supremacy: The War of 1739–1748* (2010).

Knight, Roger, *The Pursuit of Victory. The Life and Achievement of Horatio Nelson* (2005).

Knight, Roger and Martin Wilcox, *Sustaining the Fleet, 1793–1815: War, the British Navy and the Contractor State* (2010).

Knight, Roger, *Britain against Napoleon: the Organisation of Victory, 1793–1815* (2013).

Land, Isaac, *War, Nationalism, and the British Sailor, 1750–1850* (2009).

Lincoln, Margarette, *Representing the Royal Navy: British Sea Power, 1750–1815* (2002).

Lincoln, Margarette, *Naval Wives and Mistresses* (2007).

MacDougall, Phillip, *Naval Resistance to Britain's Growing Power in India 1660–1800* (2014).

Mackay, Ruddock and Michael Duffy, *Hawke, Nelson and British Naval Leadership, 1747–1805* (2009).

Malcolmson, Thomas, *Order and Disorder in the British Navy, 1793–1815: Control, Resistance, Flogging and Hanging* (2016).

Morgan-Owen, David and Louis Halewood (eds), *Economic Warfare and the Sea: Grand Strategies for Maritime Power, 1650–1945* (2020).

Morriss, Roger, *Naval Power and British Culture, 1760–1850: Public Trust and Government Ideology* (2004).

Morriss, Roger, *The Foundations of British Maritime Ascendancy: Resources, Logistics and the State, 1755–1815* (2011).

Petley, Christer and John McAleer, *The Royal Navy and the British Atlantic World, c. 1750–1820* (2016).

Robson, Martin, *A History of the Royal Navy. The Seven Years' War* (2016).

Rodger, Nicholas, *The Insatiable Earl: A Life of John Montagu, Fourth Earl of Sandwich, 1718–1792* (1993).

Rodger, Nicholas, *The Command of the Ocean* (2004).

Rogers, Nicholas, *The Press Gang: Naval Impressment and Its Opponents in Georgian Britain* (2007).

Starkey, David, E. S. van Eyck van Hesling, and J. A. de Moor (eds), *Pirates and Privateers: New Perspectives on the War on Trade in the Eighteenth and Nineteenth Centuries* (1997).

Syrett, David, *The Royal Navy in American Waters, 1775–1783* (1989).

Syrett, David, *Shipping and Military Power in the Seven Year War: The Sails of Victory* (2008).

Taylor, Stephen, *Sons of the Waves: The Common Seaman in the Heroic Age of Sail* (2020).

Tracy, Nicholas, *Navies, Deterrence, and American Independence: Britain and Seapower in the 1760s and 1770s* (Vancouver, 1988).

Tunstall, Brian, *Naval Warfare in the Age of Sail: The Evolution of Fighting Tactics, 1650–1815* (1990).

Willis, Sam, *In the Hour of Victory: The Royal Navy in the Age of Nelson* (2014).

Wilkinson, Clive, *The British Navy and the State in the Eighteenth Century* (2004).

Wilson, David, *Suppressing Piracy in the Early Eighteenth Century: Pirates, Merchants and British Imperial Authority in the Atlantic and Indian Oceans* (2021).

Wilson, Evan, *A Social History of British Naval Officers, 1775–1815* (2016).

NOTES

Abbreviations

Add.	Additional Manuscripts
ADM	Admiralty Papers
AE	Paris, Archives du Ministère des Affaires Etrangères
AM	Paris, Archives de la Marine
AN	Paris, Archives Nationales
Ang	Angleterre
AST	Turin, Archivio di Stato
BB	Bland Burges papers
Beinecke	Beinecke Library, New Haven, Connecticut
BL	London, British Library, Department of Manuscripts
Bod	Oxford, Bodleian Library, Department of Manuscripts
Cobbett	*Parliamentary History of England*
CP	Correspondance Politique
CRO	County Record Office

Cumb. P.	Papers of William, Duke of Cumberland
Farmington	Farmington, Connecticut, Lewis Walpole Library
FO	Foreign Office papers
HHStA	Vienna, Haus-, Hof-, und Staatsarchiv
HL	San Marino, California, Huntington Library
Ing	Inghilterra
IO	India Office Papers
LM	Lettere Ministri
Lo	Loudoun Papers
MD	Mémoires et Documents
MM	*Mariner's Mirror*
NA	London, National Archives
RA	Windsor Castle, Royal Archives
SP	State Papers
UL	University Library
WO	War Office Papers

1 From the Armada to the Glorious Revolution, 1588–1688

1. BL. Add. 23822 f. 47.
2. Eleanor Hubbard, *Englishmen at Sea. Labor and the Nation at the Dawn of Empire, 1570–1630* (2021), p. 276.
3. Kenneth Andrews, *Ships, Money and Politics: Seafaring and Naval Enterprise in the Reign of Charles I* (1991).
4. Bernard Capp, *Cromwell's Navy: The Fleet and the English Revolution* (1989).
5. J. S. Wheeler, 'Navy Finances, 1649–1660,' *Historical Journal*, 39 (1996), pp. 457–66.
6. Michael Palmer, 'The Military Revolution Afloat: the era of the Anglo-Dutch Wars,' *War in History*, 4 (1997), pp. 123–49, and '"The Soul's Right Hand": Command and Control in the Age of Fighting Sail, 1652–1827,' *Journal of Military History*, 61 (1997), pp. 679–706.

7. William Maltby, 'Politics, Professionalism and the Evolution of Sailing Ships Tactics,' in John Lynn (ed.), *Tools of War: Instruments, Ideas and Institutions of Warfare, 1445–1871* (1990), pp. 53–73.
8. Mathews to Thomas, 1st Duke of Newcastle, 17 Feb. 1744, Mill St House, Iden Green, Weston papers.
9. Marlborough to his wife, 2 Oct. 1758, BL. Add. 61667.
10. Jedediah Tucker, *Memoirs of Admiral the Right Honourable the Earl of St Vincent* (2 vols, 1844) I, 67–8.
11. Sam Willis, 'The Capability of Sailing Warships, part 2: Manoeuvrability', *Le Marin du Nord/The Northern Mariner*, 14 (2004), pp. 57–68.
12. Nicholas Rodger, 'Image and Reality in Eighteenth Century Naval Tactics', *MM*, 89 (2003), pp. 281–2.
13. Willis, 'Fleet Performance and Capability in the Eighteenth-Century Royal Navy', *War in History*, 11 (2004), pp. 373–92.
14. Report of 22 Sept. 1756, NA. SP. 92/64.
15. Cabinet Minute, 29 Sept. 1756, BL. Add. 51376 f. 85–6.
16. AE. CP. Ang. 440 f. 26–7.
17. C. Ross (ed.), *Correspondence of Charles, 1st Marquess Cornwallis* (1859), p. 21.
18. Straton to Sir Robert Murray Keith, 14 Jan. 1783, BL. Add. 35527 f. 214.
19. Jan Glete, *Navies and Nations: Warships, Navies and State Building in Europe and America, 1500–1860* (1993), p. 192.
20. D. Davies, 'James II, William of Orange, and the Admirals,' in Eveline Cruickshanks (ed.), *By Force or By Default? The Revolution of 1688–89* (1989), pp. 82–108; A. Pearsall, 'The Invasion Voyage: some nautical thoughts,' in Charles Wilson and D. Proctor (eds), *1688. The Seaborne Alliance and Diplomatic Revolution* (1989), pp. 166–71.

2 To Defend the Revolution, 1689–1716

1. Peter Le Fevre, *Precursors of Nelson: British Admirals of the Eighteenth Century* (2000), pp. 19–42.
2. Instructions from Lords of Admiralty to Rooke, 3 Sept. 1695, William III to Rooke, 27 Jan. 1696, Gloucester CRO. D 1833 X2.
3. Nicholas Rodger, 'Weather, Geography and Naval Power in the Age of Sail,' in Colin Gray and Geoffrey Sloan (eds), *Geopolitics, Geography and Strategy* (1999), pp. 178–209.
4. Jonathan Coad, *The Royal Dockyards 1690–1850* (1988).
5. Michael Duffy, 'The creation of Plymouth Dockyard and its impact on naval strategy,' in *Guerres maritimes 1688–1713* (1990), pp. 245–74, 'The establishment of the Western Squadron as the linchpin of British naval strategy,' in Duffy (ed.), *Parameters of British Naval Power 1650–1850* (1992), pp. 61–2, and 'Edmund Dummer's "Account of the General Progress and Advancement of His Majesty's new dock and yard at Plymouth" December 1694,' in Duffy (ed.), *The Naval Miscellany*, VI (2003).
6. Blathwayt to Stepney, 28 Feb. 1702, Beinecke, Osborn Shelves.
7. A. S. Szarka, 'Portugal, France, and the coming of the War of the Spanish Succession' (PhD. Thesis, Ohio State University, 1975), pp. 245–6, 264, 270–1, 293, 303–5, 356.
8. Memorandum on state of French navy, [1706–7], NA. SP. 78/154 of. 46.
9. Ellis to Stepney, 17 Oct. 1701, BL. Add. 7074 f. 49.
10. Byng to Sunderland, 2 Mar. 1707, BL. Add. 61588.
11. Byng to Sunderland, 24 June 1709, BL. Add. 61588.
12. Duffy, 'The establishment of the western squadron as the linchpin of British naval strategy,' in Duffy (ed.), *Parameters of British Naval Power 1650–1850* (1992), pp. 60–81.
13. Jennings to Sunderland, 16 July 1709, BL. Add. 61588.

14. Jennings to Sunderland, 8 Ap., 16 July, Jennings to Burchett, 8 Ap. 1709, BL. Add. 61588.
15. Byng to Sunderland, 24 June 1709, Minutes of Council of War of Norris' squadron, 14 June 1709, BL. Add. 61588, 58213.
16. Manchester to Sunderland, 3 Feb. 1708, BL. Add. 58213.
17. Jap Bruijn, 'A Little Incident in 1707: The Demise of a Once Glorious Dutch Naval Organisation,' in A. M. Forssberg et al (eds), *Organising History* (2011), p. 121.
18. John Hattendorf, '"To Aid and Assist the Other": Anglo-Dutch Naval Cooperation in Coalition Warfare at Sea, 1689–1714,' in A. F. de Jongste and A. J. Vesenendaal (eds), *Anthonie Heinsius and the Dutch Republic, 1688–1720: Politics, War, and Finance* (2002), pp. 177–98.
19. Nicholas Rodger, 'Form and Function in European Navies, 1660–1815,' in L. Akveld et al (eds), *In het Kielzog* (Amsterdam, 2003), pp. 85–97.
20. Manchester to Charles, Earl of Sunderland, Huntingdon, CRO. DD. M 36/8, p. 10.
21. Chadwick's report, 1 Aug. 1715, NA. SP. 42/14.
22. H. Davis et al (ed.), *The Prose Works of Jonathan Swift* (16 vols, 1939–68), VI, 23.
23. *Ibid.*, p. 22.
24. John Gibson, *Playing the Scottish Card. The Franco-Jacobite Invasion of 1708* (1988).
25. Pearse to Burchett, 11 Oct. 1715, NA. SP. 42/14.

3 Years of Limited Hostilities, 1717–38

1. T. Corbett, *An Account of the Expedition of the British Fleet to Sicily in the Years 1718, 1719 and 1720 under the Command of Sir George Byng* (1739); F. Hervey, *The Naval History of Great Britain from earliest times to the raising of the*

Parliament in 1779 (1779), III, 386–97; John Hattendorf, 'Admiral Sir George Byng and the Cape Passaro Incident, 1718: A Case study in the use of the Royal Navy as a deterrent,' *Guerres et Paix* (1987), pp. 19–39.
2. Reeve Williams, *Letter from a Merchant to a Member of Parliament* (1718).
3. Dalrymple to the Earl of Loudoun, 2 Aug. 1718, HL. Lo. 8344.
4. Daniel Baugh, *British Naval Administration in the Age of Walpole* (1965).
5. Bod. Ms. French e20, p. 1.
6. Craggs to Stair, 2, 9, 16 Ap. 1719, NA. SP. 104/30.
7. Instructions to John Norris, 14 Ap. 1718, NA. SP. 48/61.
8. Count Karl Gyllenborg to Georg Heinrich von Görtz, 23 Oct. 1716, NA. SP. 107/1B f. 172–3.
9. Robert Molesworth, *Observations upon a Pamphlet called An English Merchant's Remarks* (1717), p. 37.
10. Townshend to Stanhope, 26 Oct. 1714, Maidstone, Kent Archive Office, U 1590 0148.
11. Stanhope to John, 2nd Earl Stair, envoy in Paris, 2 Sept. 1718, NA. SP. 78/162 f. 113.
12. Instructions to Norris, 19 Aug. 1718, NA. SP. 48/61 no. 32.
13. NA. SP. 43/61 f. 34.
14. Craggs to Thomas, Duke of Newcastle, 10 Aug. 1719, BL. Add. 32686 f. 137.
15. Craggs to Newcastle, 10, 16 Aug. 1719, BL. Add. 32686 f. 137–9.
16. For ministers conferring with George Anson, the First Lord, on the state of the navy and its plans, Count Viry, Sardinian envoy, to Charles Emmanuel III, 29 Feb. 1760, AST. LM. Ing. 65.
17. James Craggs to James, Earl Stanhope, his fellow Secretary of State, 7 July 1719, NA. SP. 44/269. The Cardinal, Alberoni, was Spain's first minister.

18. Townshend to Newcastle, 11 Sept. 1725, NA. SP. 43/7 f. 10; Memorandum of Lords Justices' meeting on 9 Sept. 1725, BL. Add. 32687 f. 158–9.
19. Townshend to Newcastle, 2 Oct. 1725, NA. SP. 43/7 f. 145–6.
20. Robert Walpole to Newcastle, 31 Aug. 1723, BL. Add. 32686 f. 320–1.
21. Newcastle to Horatio Walpole, 14 Oct. 1726, BL. Add. 32748.
22. Council of War, 3 May 1727, NA. SP. 42/18 f. 539–40.
23. Memorandum presented by Graham, Jacobite envoy in Vienna, to Prince Eugene, Austrian War Minister, 17 May 1726, HHStA., England, Noten, 2.
24. Horatio Walpole, envoy in Paris, to Townshend, BL. Add. 46856.
25. Anon., 'The second report upon the Treaty of Vienna,' 26 July 1725, copy sent to Townshend, 30 July, NA. SP. 103/107.
26. Townshend to William Stanhope, 11 Aug. 1726, NA. SP. 94/98.
27. Mark Hanna, *Pirate Nests and the Rise of the British Empire, 1570–1740* (2015); David Wilson, *Suppressing Piracy in the Early Eighteenth Century: Pirates, Merchants and British Imperial Authority in the Atlantic and Indian Oceans* (2021).
28. Newcastle to Horatio Walpole, 10 Sept. 1727, BL. Add. 32751.
29. Horatio Walpole to Newcastle, 26 June 1726, BL. Add. 32746 f. 296–7.
30. Wager to Robert Walpole, 9 May 1727, Cambridge UL., Cholmondeley Houghton correspondence 1422.
31. George Tilson, Under Secretary, to Waldegrave, 6 May 1729, Chewton.

32. Newcastle to Townshend, 13 June 1729, NA. SP. 43/77.
33. Townshend to Philip, 4th Earl of Chesterfield, envoy in The Hague, 1 July 1729, BL. Add. 48982.
34. Delafaye to Stephen Poyntz, 17 Mar. 1729, BL. Althorp E5.
35. Newcastle to Waldegrave, 24 Ap. 1731, BL. Add. 32772; Captain Smith to Burchett, Secretary of the Admiralty, 12 Aug. 1731, NA. SP. 42/20.
36. Newcastle to John, 2nd Duke of Dorset, 3 Ap. 1734, NA. SP. 63/397.
37. AE. MD. Ang. 24 f. 154.
38. Chavigny to Chauvelin, 9, 30 Ap. 1734, AE. CP. Ang. 385.
39. Sir Charles Wager, First Lord of the Admiralty, to Newcastle, 5 May 1734, BL. Add. 32689.
40. Cobbett, IX, 536–7.
41. Louis XV to M. de St Ovide, 10 May 1735, AN. AM. B 63.
42. Robinson to Horatio Walpole, 26 May 1734, BL. Add. 23845 f. 149.
43. Harrington to Robinson, 16 Nov. 1733, NA. SP. 80/101.
44. Townshend to Wager, 5 Oct., Townshend to Newcastle, 12, 18 July, 12 Sept. 1727, NA. SP. 42/78.
45. John Couraud, Under Secretary in the Southern Department, to James, 1st Earl Waldegrave, envoy in Paris, 31 May 1735, Chewton House, Chewton Mendip, Waldegrave Papers.
46. Andrew Lambert, *Seapower States: Maritime Culture, Continental Empires, and the Conflict that Made the Modern World* (2018).
47. Robert Trevor, envoy in The Hague, to Everard Fawkener, envoy at Constantinople, 6 Sept. 1738, Aylesbury, Buckinghamshire CRO., Trevor Mss, vol. 14.
48. Diary of Sir Dudley Ryder, 6 Oct. 1739, Sandon House, Ryder papers.

4 War: from Problems to Victory, 1739–48

1. Newcastle to Cumberland, 27 Oct. 1747, RA. Cumb. P. 29/145.
2. Richard Harding, *The Emergence of Britain's Global Naval Supremacy: The War of 1739–1748* (2010).
3. Herbert Richmond, *The Navy and the War of 1739–48*, II, 8–57.
4. Matthews to Newcastle, 17 Feb. 1744, Mill St House, Iden Green, papers of Edward Weston. I would like to thank John Weston-Underwood for permission to consult these papers. See also, Brian Lavery, *The Ship of the Line* I, 90.
5. Richard Harding, 'Contractors, Warships of the Royal Navy and Sea Power, 1739–1748,' in Harding and S. Solbes Ferri (eds), *The Contractor State and its Implications, 1659–1815* (2012), pp. 159–74.
6. Fagel to Hendrik Hop, Dutch envoy in London, 25 Aug. 1739, NA. SP. 107/31.
7. Newcastle to Vernon, 26 Mar. 1740, BL. Add. 32693 f. 109–13.
8. E. J. B. Rathery (ed.), *Journal et mémoires du Marquis d'Argenson* (9 vols, 1859–67), II, 304–5.
9. Newcastle to James, 1st Earl Waldegrave, envoy in Paris, 12 June 1740, NA. SP. 78/233 f. 111.
10. Newcastle to Vernon, 28 Aug. 1741, BL. Add. 32697.
11. Matlock, Derbyshire CRO. Catton Collection WH 3429, p. 154.
12. Ryder diary, 2 Feb. 1744, Sandon.
13. Gateshead, Public Library, Ellison Mss. A 31.
14. Stone to Edward Weston, 2 Aug. 1745, Farmington, Connecticut, Lewis Walpole Library, Weston Papers, vol. 16.
15. Frank McLynn, 'Sea Power and the Jacobite Rising of 1745,' *MM*, 66 (1981), pp. 163–71; RA. Cumb. P. 10/17.
16. Newcastle to Cumberland, 12 Dec. 1745, RA. Cumb. P. 8/9.
17. For reports see NA. 84/583, ADM. 1/3830.

18. Bryan Ranft (ed.), *The Vernon Papers* (1958), pp. 539–60.
19. Newcastle to Cumberland, 3 July 1746, BL. Add. 32707 f. 390.
20. Yorke to Marchionness Grey, 27 Oct. 1747, Bedford, Bedfordshire CRO., Lucas papers, 30/9/102/12.
21. BL. Add. 32807, f. 44.
22. Sandwich to Anson, 14 Nov. 1747, BL. Add. 15957 f. 29.
23. G. E. Broche, *La République de Gênes et la France pendant la guerre de la Succession d'Autriche* (1935), p. 114; Cobbett, XIII, 125.
24. Lowther to John Spedding, 6 Nov. 1739, Carlisle, Cumbria CRO. D/Lons/W.
25. Hardwicke to Newcastle, 2 Ap. 1746, BL. Add. 32707 f. 5; A. H. Buffington, 'The Canada Expedition of 1746: Its Relation to British Politics,' *American Historical Review*, 45 (1939–40), pp. 552–80; R. Harding, 'The Expedition to Lorient, 1746,' in N. Tracy (ed.), *The Age of Sail* (2002), pp. 34–54.
26. Duncan Crewe, *Yellow Jack and the Worm: British Naval Administration in the West Indies, 1739–1748* (1993).
27. Nicholas Rodger, *The Wooden World: An Anatomy of the Georgian Navy* (1986).
28. Denver Brunsman, *The Evil Necessity: British Naval Impressment in the Eighteenth-Century Atlantic World* (2013), pp. 222–33.
29. Nicholas Rogers, *The Press Gang: Naval Impressment and Its Opponents in Georgian Britain* (2007).
30. Newcastle to Cumberland, 11 Mar. 1748, RA. Cumb. P. 32/245.
31. Spy report, Lyons, 24 Feb. 1748, NA. SP. 84/445 f. 73.
32. 11, 14 Ap. 1746, Newdigate papers, Warwick CRO. 136 B2539/17, 2522/4.
33. Cobbett, XIV, 158–9.

5 From Peace to Triumph, 1749–63

1. Vernon to Dashwood, 29 July 1749, Bod. Ms. D. D. Dashwood B 11/12/6.
2. Knowles to Edward Trelawny, Governor of Jamaica, 27 Nov. 1750, Washington, Library of Congress, microfilm reels, Vernon-Wager papers, reel 93.
3. Notes on Debate, Warwick, Warwickshire CRO, Newdigate papers, CR 136B 3012/44.
4. Newcastle to Hardwicke, 18 Sept. 1749, BL. Add. 35410, f. 153.
5. Sarah Kinkel, 'The King's Pirates? Naval Enforcement of Imperial Authority, 1740–76,' *William and Mary Quarterly*, 3rd ser. 71 (2014), p. 8.
6. Halifax to Newcastle, 6 Mar. 1751, BL. Add. 32724 f. 165.
7. Clive Wilkinson, *The British Navy and the State in the Eighteenth Century* (2004).
8. Newcastle to Yorke, 26 June 1753, NA. SP. 84/463.
9. Michael Edwardes (ed.), *Major John Corneille, Journal of my Service in India* (1966), p. 55.
10. Newcastle to Keith, 22 Oct. 1753, NA. SP. 80/192.
11. Rochford to Bedford, 1 Oct. 1749, NA. SP. 92/58 f. 177–8.
12. Doohwan Ahn, 'From "Jealous Emulation" to "Cautious Politics": British Foreign Policy and Public Discourse in the Mirror of Ancient Athens, *c.* 1730-*c.*1750,' in *Ideology and Foreign Policy*, ed. David Onnekink and Gijs Rommelse (2011), p. 129.
13. Newcastle to Holdernesse, 11 July 1755, BL. Add. 32857 f. 45–6.
14. Newcastle to Sandwich, 10 Feb. 1747, BL. Add. 32807 f. 90.
15. Boscawen to John Clevland, Secretary to the Admiralty, 9, 21 Ap. 1755, NA. ADM. 1/481 f. 5, 51.

16. Mirepoix to Rouillé, French Foreign Minister, 25 Ap., 6 May 1755, AE. CP. Ang. 438 f. 448, 439 f. 6–10.
17. Hardwicke to Anson, 14 July 1755, BL. Add. 15956 f. 23.
18. Holdernesse to Robert Orme, 14 Oct. 1755, BL. Eg. 3488 fl. 99.
19. Fox to Bristol, 19 Mar. 1756, NA. SP. 92/64.
20. J. J. Krulder, *The Execution of Admiral John Byng as a Microhistory of Eighteenth Century Britain* (2021).
21. Bath to Sir John Rushout, 24 June 1756, Worcester CRO. 705:66 BA 4211/26.
22. Newcastle to Holdernesse, 11 July 1755, BL. Add. 32857 f. 363.
23. William to brother Charles Hotham, 145 Mar. 1757, Hull UL., Hotham papers, DDHo 4/6.
24. Anon., *Observations on the Conduct of the Late Administration; Particularly in regard to our loss of Minorca* (1757), pp. 2–12; Francis Blackburne, Rector of Richmond, Yorkshire, to Theophilus Lindsey, Archdeacon of Cleveland, 25 Jan. 12 Feb. 1757, Dr Williams's Library, MS. 12, 52, 28 and 31.
25. Dayrolle (Brussels) to Fawkener, 20 Ap. 1756, RA. Cumb.P. 47/12.
26. Eg. 12 June 1756, AE. CP. Ang. 440 fols 231–7.
27. Fox to Duke of Devonshire, 31 Jan. 1756, History of Parliament, Chatsworth transcripts.
28. Bedford to Pitt, 29 Aug. 1759, Bedford Estate Office, papers of 4th Duke.
29. George Quarme to Rockingham, 18 Oct. 1757, Sheffield, Archives, Wentworth Woodhouse papers, R1–111; Viry to Charles Emmanuel III, 18 Oct. 1757, AST. LM. Ing. 62; *Monitor*, 10 Dec. 1757.
30. Holdernesse to Mitchell, 5 July 1757, NA. SP. 90/69; Matt Schumann, 'Anglo-Prussian Diplomacy and the Baltic Squadron, 1756–1758', *Forum Navale*, 59 (2003), pp. 66–80.

31. John Bosher, 'The French government's motives in the *Affaire du Canada, 1761–1763,*' *English Historical Review*, 96 (1981), p. 72.
32. Townshend to his mother, Viscountess Townshend, 10 Aug. 1758, BL. Add. 63079.
33. Peter Padfield, *Guns at Sea* (1973), pp. 90–2, 100.
34. Jonathan Dull, *The French Navy and the Seven Years' War* (2005).
35. Captain Edgcumbe to Cleveland, 24 Mar. 1756, Bod. Eng. Hist. c.124.
36. Geoffrey Marcus, *Quiberon Bay: The Campaign in Home Waters, 1759* (1960).
37. Bosher, 'Financing the French Navy in the Seven Years War: Beaujon, Goosens et Compagnie in 1759', *Business History*, 28 (1986), pp. 115–33; James Pritchard, *Louis XV's Navy, 1748–1762. A Study in Organisation and Administration* (1987), pp. 185–202.
38. Mackenzie to Pitt, 22 Nov., 9, 23 Dec. 1758, NA. SP. 92/66.
39. BL. Add. 45662 f. 41.
40. Campbell Dalrymple to William, 2nd Viscount Barrington, Secretary at War, 20 Jan. 1762, NA. WO. 1/19 f. 81.
41. Newcastle to Devonshire, 29 June 1762, BL. Add. 32940 f. 117.
42. Egremont to Bute, --May 1762, Mount Stuart, Bute papers, papers of 3rd Earl, 7/163.
43. Newcastle memorandum, 30 Sept. 1761, BL. Add. 32929 f. 2.
44. David Syrett, 'The Methodology of British Amphibious Operations during the Seven Years and American Wars', *MM*, 58 (1972), p. 277.
45. Rodney to George Lyttelton, 20 Oct., 19 Nov. 1759, *Sotheby's Catalogue of the Lyttelton Papers* (1978), pp. 143–6.
46. John Cresswell, *British Admirals of the Eighteenth Century* (London, 1972), p. 254; Michael Palmer, 'The

"Military Revolution" Afloat: The Era of the Anglo-Dutch Wars and the Transition to Modern Warfare at Sea', *War in History*, 4 (1997), pp. 147–8. The social dimension of naval service can be approached best through Nicholas Rodger's *The Wooden World. An Anatomy of the Georgian Navy* (1986).

47. Edwardes (ed.), *Corneille*, pp. 95–9.
48. Watson to Holdernesse, 7 Oct. 1755, 15 Feb., 10 Mar. 1756, George Thomas to Mr Thomas, 15 Feb. 1756, BL. Eg. 3488 f. 81–2, 140–1, 157–8, 216–7.
49. Denver Brunsman, *The Evil Necessity: British Naval Impressment in the Eighteenth-Century Atlantic World* (2013).
50. Syrett, *Shipping and Military Power in the Seven Years War: The Sails of Victory* (2008); Roger Knight and Martin Wilcox, *Sustaining the Fleet, 1793–1815: War, the British Navy and the Contractor State* (2010); Martini Wilcox, '"This Great Complex Concern": Victualling the Royal Navy on the East Indies Station, 1780–1815', *Mariner's Mirror*, 97 (2011), pp. 32–49.
51. Gareth Cole, *Arming the Royal Navy, 1793–1815: The Office of Ordnance and the State* (2012).
52. Wolfe to Colonel Charles Hotham, 9 Aug. 1758, Hull, UL., Hotham papers, DDHo 4/7.
53. Watson to Robert, 4th Earl of Holdernesse, Secretary of State, 6 Aug. 1754, BL. Eg. 3488 f. 12.
54. Charles Jenkinson, *A Discourse on the Establishment of a National and Constitutional Force in England* (1757), p. 46.
55. Alan McGowan, *HMS Victory: Her Construction, Career and Restoration* (1999).
56. Richard Middleton, 'Naval administration in the age of Pitt and Anson,' in Black and Philip Woodfine (eds), *The British*

Navy and the use of naval power in the eighteenth century (1988), p. 119.
57. Nicholas Rodger, *The Wooden World*, pp. 205–51.
58. Evan Wilson, *A Social History of British Naval Officers, 1775–1815* (2017); A. B. McLeod, *British Naval Captains of the Seven Years' War: The View from the Quarterdeck* (2012).

6 Deterrence and Defeat, 1764–83

1. Hamish Scott, 'The Importance of Bourbon Naval Reconstruction to the Strategy of Choiseul after the Seven Years' War,' *International History Review*, 1 (1979), pp. 17–35.
2. Wolters to Sandwich, 29 Nov., NA. SP. 84/503; Halifax to Weston, 2 Jan. 1764, BL. Add. 57927 f. 133.
3. Guerchy to Praslin, 21 Feb. 1764, AE. CP. Ang. 455 f. 385.
4. Jeremy Black, 'Foreign Policy and the Tory World in the Eighteenth Century,' in Black (ed.), *The Tory World. Deep History and the Tory Theme in British Foreign Policy, 1679–2014* (Farnham, 2015): 32–68.
5. Frank McLynn, *Charles Edward Stuart: A Tragedy in Many Acts* (London, 1988): 474–5.
6. Christian Buchet, *The British Navy, Economy and Society in the Seven Years War* (2013).
7. Egremont to Admiralty, 3 Jan. 1763, NA. SP. 44/231 f. 118.
8. Nicholas Tracy, *Navies, Deterrence, and American Independence: Britain and Seapower in the 1760s and 1770s* (1988).
9. Weymouth to Earl Harcourt, 28 Nov. 1769, NA. SP. 78/279 f. 178.
10. Stormont to Rochford, 31 Mar. 1773, NA. SP. 78/287 f. 150–1.

11. Wager to Norris, 20 Aug. 1734, BL. Add. 28156.
12. Stormont to Rochford, 31 Mar. 1773, NA. SP. 78/287 f. 159.
13. G. Cornwallis-West, *The Life and Letters of Admiral Cornwallis* (1927), pp. 50–1.
14. Jan Glete, *Navies and Nations*, pp. 272–3.
15. Sarah Kinkel, *Disciplining the Empire. Politics, Governance, and the Rise of the British Navy* (2018).
16. J. Gwyn, *Frigates and Foremasts: The North American Squadron in Nova Scotia Waters, 1745–1815* (Vancouver, 2003).
17. NA. WO. 34/112 f. 166.
18. Paul Krajeski, 'The Foundation of British Amphibious Warfare Methodology During the Napoleonic Era, 1793–1815', *Consortium on Revolutionary Europe. Selected Papers 1996* (Tallahassee, Florida, 1996), pp. 191–8.
19. David Syrett, *The Royal Navy in American Waters, 1775–1783* (Aldershot, 1989).
20. George to Robinson, 24 May 1777, BL. Add. 37833 f. 200.
21. Thomas Truxes, *The Overseas Trade of British America* (2021), pp. 294–5.
22. George to Robinson, 6 Mar. 1777, BL. Add. 38733 f. 143; J. M. Price, *France and the Chesapeake* (2 vols, 1973), II, 681–3.
23. P. D. Chase (ed.), *The Papers of George Washington: Revolutionary War Series* 10 (2000), p. 507.
24. John Reeve, 'British naval strategy. War on a global scale,' in Donald Stoker, Kenneth Hagan and Michael McMaster (eds), *Strategy in the American War of Independence* (Abingdon, 2010), pp. 73–99.
25. Fortescue, IV, 30–1.
26. Nicholas Rodger, *The Insatiable Earl. A life of John Montagu, 4th Earl of Sandwich* (London, 1993), pp. 365–77.

27. Rodger, *Sandwich*, pp. 221–3, 266–79.
28. Syrett, 'Home waters or America? The dilemma of British naval strategy in 1778,' MM, 77 (1991), pp. 365–77.
29. Cobbett, XX, 340–1.
30. Cobbett, XX, 332.
31. Nottingham UL., Clumber Papers, 2, 614; HMC *Carlisle*, pp. 387–8.
32. NA. WO. 34/112 f. 3–4.
33. BL. Add. 34416f. 67–9.
34. Nottingham UL., Clumber Papers, 2, 618.
35. Blankett to Shelburne, 2 July 1778, BL. Bowood papers 511 f. 9–11.
36. Blankett to William, Earl of Shelburne, 29 July 1778, BL., Bowood papers 511 f. 9–11. For the role of the weather gauge, not least the contrast between theory and practice, Willis, *Fighting at Sea in the Eighteenth Century. The Art of Sailing Warfare* (Woodbridge, 2008), pp. 113–28.
37. Jonathan Dull, *The French Navy and American Independence: A Study of Arms and Diplomacy, 1774–1787* (Princeton, New Jersey, 1975).
38. WO. 34/119 f. 66; BL. Add. 34416 f. 417–55; Nottingham, UL. Clumber Papers, 2, 634.
39. Nottingham, UL., Mellish papers, 172–111/21.
40. G. F. Jones, 'The 1780 Siege of Charleston as Experienced by a Hessian Officer,' *South Carolina Historical Magazine*, 88 (1987), p. 64.
41. Nottingham, UL., Clumber Mss. 2, 625.
42. NA. PRO. 30/11/68 f. 11–18.
43. Willcox (ed.), *Rebellion*, pp. 532–3.
44. Clinton to Cornwallis, 11 July 1781, NA. PRO. 30/11/74 f. 33.
45. Cornwallis to Clinton, 8 July 1781, NA. PRO. 30/11/68 f. 53–5.

46. Anonymous, *An Answer to that part of the Narrative of Lieutenant General Sir Henry Clinton which relates to the conduct of Lieutenant General Earl Cornwallis* (1783), p. 110.
47. Nottingham, UL., Clumber Papers, 2, 287–8, 290, 297, 303, 599.
48. Roger Knight, 'Devil bolts and deception? Wartime naval shipbuilding in private shipyards, 1739–1815,' *Journal for Maritime Research* (Ap. 2003).
49. Rockingham to Earl of Hardwicke, c. Ap. 1781, Sheffield, City Archive, Wentworth Woodhouse Mss, R1-1962.
50. Roy and Lesley Adkins, *Gibraltar: the Greatest Siege in British History* (2017).
51. Ardeshir Wadia, *The Bombay Dockyard and the Wadia Master Builders* (1957).
52. Narrative of engagement off Cape Dobbs, Hughes' journal, BL. India Office papers H/Misc./126 pp. 6–18, Mss. Eur., F. 27, p. 174.
53. Coote to Lord Macartney, Governor of Madras, 1 May 1782, BL. Add. 22440 f. 16.
54. Macartney to Warren Hastings, 11 July 1781, BL. Add. 22454 f. 6.
55. NA. WO. 34/136 f. 74.
56. Syrett and William Still, *The Royal Navy in European Waters during the American Revolutionary War* (Columbia, South Carolina, 1998), pp. 139–42.
57. Roger Knight, 'The Royal Navy's recovery after the early phase of the American Revolutionary War,' in George Andreopoulos and Harold Selesky (eds), *The Aftermath of Defeat. Societies, Armed Forces, and the Challenge of Recovery* (New Haven, Conn., 1994), pp. 10–25.
58. Collet to Sir Robert Murray Keith, envoy in Vienna, 20 March 1779, BL. Add. 35516.

59. Syrett, 'The failure of the British effort in America, 1777,' in Jeremy Black and Philip Woodfine (eds), *The British Navy and the Use of Naval Power in the Eighteenth Century* (Leicester, 1988), p. 187.
60. Dull, *The French Navy and American Independence* (Princeton, NJ, 1975); James Pritchard, *Louis XV's Navy, 1748–1762: A Study of Organization and Administration* (Buffalo, NY, 1987).
61. Vergennes to Ossun, 29 Aug. 1755, AE. CP. Espagne 577.
62. George III to North, 13 Oct. 1778, RA. GEO/3094.
63. George III to North, 28 Dec. 1778, RA. GEO/3167.
64. Celina Fox, 'George III and the Navy,' in Jonathan Marsden (ed.), *The Wisdom of George the Third* (London, 2005), pp. 291–312; George III to North, 27 June 1779, *Fortescue* IV, 380; Keppel to Rockingham, 19, 20 Aug. 1779, WW-R1-1845-6.

7 Brinkmanship to the Fore, 1784–92

1. Naval intelligence, 24 July 1787, NA. PRO. 30/11/112 f. 180.
2. Walsingham to Pitt, 16 July 1786, Cambridge UL. Add. 6958.
3. Daniel Hailes, Secretary of Embassy at Paris, to Francis, Marquess of Carmarthen, Foreign Secretary, NA. FO. 27/13 f. 7, 26.
4. Vergennes to Louis XVI, AE. MD. France 1897 f. 134.
5. Carmarthen to John, 3rd Duke of Dorset, Ambassador in Paris, 16 Feb., 28 May, 2, 9, 27 July, 10, 20 Aug., 6 Nov., 25 Dec/. 1784, NA. FO. 27/11 f. 134–6, 27/12 f. 79, 135, 149, 183, 238, 271, 27/13 f. 162, 242–3.
6. Howe to Pitt, 25 Dec. 1784, NA. PRO. 30/8/146 f. 172–3.
7. Paul Webb, 'The rebuilding and repair of the fleet,' 1783–93,' *Bulletin of the Institute of Historical Research*, 50 (1977).
8. Webb, 'The Navy and British diplomacy, 1783–93,' (M.Litt. thesis, Cambridge, 1971).

9. George III to --, 30 June 1787, *McDowell and Stern Catalogue no. 27* (1984), p. 5, item 25.
10. Richmond to Sir James Harris, 13 May 1788, Winchester, Hampshire CRO., Malmesbury papers, vol. 180.
11. Dorset to Thurlow, 25 Oct. 1787, Maidstone, KAO. C.189.
12. Grenville to Pitt, 1 Sept. 1780, NA. PRO. 30/8/140 f. 35–6.
13. John Harbron, *Trafalgar and the Spanish Navy* (1988), pp. 42–5, 86, 91–3, 106.
14. Fitzherbert to James Bland Burges, Under Secretary in Foreign Office, 22 Nov. 1790, Bod. BB papers 38 f. 131.
15. Joseph Ewart, envoy in Berlin, to Pitt, 15 Jan., 11, 15 Feb. 1791, NA., PRO. 30/8/133 f. 281–9.
16. Jackson to Burges, 4 Aug. 1790; Drake to Burges, 29 Mar., 15 Ap. 1791, Bod. BB 36, 34.
17. Ewart to Jackson, 24 Mar. 1791, Williamwood 148.
18. Chatham to Ewart, 24 May 1791, Williamwood 157.
19. Diary of Sarah White, 15–27 Aug. 1789, Plymouth, Acc. 3102, Saltram Archival Documents, Box 2; George to Melville, 10 July 1804, NA. PRO. 30/8/104 f. 374.
20. Auckland to Pitt, 22 Dec. 1790, Cambridge UL. Add. Mss. 6958.
21. Edward Gibbon, *The History of the Decline and Fall of the Roman Empire*, ed. D. Womersley, III, 669.

8 To Confront a Revolution, 1793–1802

1. NMM, AGC/J/9.
2. Cabinet Minute, 27 Dec. 1792, BL. Add. 58857 f. 75.
3. Grenville to Auckland, 4 Feb. 1793, BL. Add. 34447 f. 433–4.
4. William Cormack, *Revolution and Political Conflict in the French Navy, 1789–1794* (1995).
5. Michael Duffy, *Soldiers, Sugar and Seapower. The British Expeditions to the West Indies and the War Against Revolutionary France* (1987).

6. Michael Duffy and Roger Morriss (eds), *The Glorious First of June 1794: A Naval Battle and its Aftermath* (2001); Willis, *The Glorious First of June* (2012).
7. Timothy Jenks, 'Language and Politics at the Westminster Election of 1796,' *Historical Journal*, 44 (2001), pp. 419–39.
8. Stephen Taylor, *Sons of the Waves: The Common Seamen in the Heroic Age of Sail* (2020).
9. Niklas Frykman, *The Bloody Flag: Mutiny in the Age of Atlantic Revolution* (2020).
10. R. Morriss, *Naval Power and British Culture, 1760–1850: Public Trust and Government Ideology* (2004).
11. George to George, 2nd Earl Spencer, 1st Lord of the Admiralty, 17 Ap. 1797, BL. Add. 75805.
12. George to Dundas, 21 Ap. 1797, BL. Add. 40100 f. 190.
13. Steven Pfaff and Michael Hechter, *The Genesis of Rebellion. Governance, Grievance, and Mutiny in the Age of Sail* (2020), pp. 136–76.
14. George III to Spencer, 6, 12 July, 3 Aug., 5 Sept. 1800, 19 Feb. 1801, BL. Add. 75839, 75848; Dudley Pope, *The Black Ship* (1963).
15. J. Ross Dancy, *The Myth of the Press Gang: Volunteers, Impressment and the Naval Manpower Problem in the Late Eighteenth Century* (2015). Dancy's claim that this was about four-fifths is based on a methodology that has been seriously challenged, for example by Nicholas Rogers, 'British Impressment and its Discontents,' *Journal of Maritime History*, 31 (2018), pp. 52–73, esp. 67–73; Isaac Land, 'New Scholarship on the Press Gang,' *Port Towns and Urban Cultures*, 3 Aug. 2015; Taylor, *Sons of the Waves*, pp. 202–3, 450 fn. 32.
16. George to Spencer, 8 Jan. 1795, BL. Add. 75779.
17. Gareth Atkins, *Converting Britannia: Evangelicals and British Public Life, 1770–1840* (2019).

18. George to Spencer, 17 Mar. 1795, BL. Add. 75779.
19. George to Pitt, 4 Mar. 1797, NA. PRO. 30/8/104 f. 145.
20. Michael Palmer, 'Sir John's victory: the Battle of Cape Vincent reconsidered,' *MM*, 67 (1991), pp. 31–46.
21. John Leyland (ed.), *Dispatches and Letters Relating to the Blockade of Brest, 1803–1805* (1899–1902), I, xvi.
22. BL. Add. 59281 f. 13.
23. George to Spencer, 17 Ap. 1795, BL. Add. 75779.
24. A. Ryan, 'In Search of Bruix, 1799,' in *Français et Anglaise n Méditerranée 1789–1830* (1991), pp. 83–90.
25. Brian DeToy, 'A Naval Officer in Westminster: The Political Career of George Berkeley, 1774–1814,' *Consortium on Revolutionary Europe: Selected Papers*, 1997, p. 357.

9 Defeating an Emperor and Fighting a Republic, 1803–15

1. George to Viscount Melville, 12 July 1804, BL. Add. 40100 f. 319.
2. J. Ross Dancy and Evan Wilson, 'Sir John Orde and the Trafalgar Campaign,' *Naval War College Review*, 73 (2020), pp. 141–71.
3. Nicholas Tracy, 'Sir Robert Calder's action,' *MM*, 77 (1991), p. 269.
4. Andrew Lambert, *The British Way of War. Julian Corbett and the Battle for a National Strategy* (2021), p. 255.
5. Michael Duffy, '"…All Was Hushed Up": The Hidden Trafalgar,' *MM*, 91 (2005), pp. 216–40.
6. The key work is James Davey, *In Nelson's Wake. How the Royal Navy Ruled the Waves after Trafalgar* (2015).
7. *The Barham Papers* vol. 3 (1910), pp. 59, 96, 103–4.
8. Ken Linch, *Britain and Wellington's Army: Recruitment, Society and Tradition, 1807–1815* (2011).
9. Paul Krajeski, *In the Shadow of Nelson: The Naval Leadership of Admiral Sir Charles Cotton, 1753–1812* (2000).

10. Martin Robson, *Britain, Portugal and South America in the Napoleonic Wars: alliances and diplomacy in economic maritime conflict* (2011).
11. Aberdeen to Wellesley, 15 Feb. 1810, BL. Add. 37309 f. 344.
12. Frederick Maitland, *Narrative of the Surrender of Bonaparte* (1826), p. 99.
13. Stephen Taylor, *Storm and Conquest: The Clash of Empires in the Eastern Seas, 1809* (2008).
14. Hewes to his father, 30 Nov. 1807, Bristol, Record Office, Mss 1257 (8).
15. James Davey, *The Transformation of British Naval Strategy: Seapower and Supply in Northern Europe, 1808–1812* (2012).
16. Fray to Robert Heywood, 19 Jan., 12 July 1812, Bolton, Town Hall, Heywood papers, ZHE/8.
17. Duffy, 'Festering the Spanish Ulcer: The Royal Navy and the Peninsular War, 1808–1814,' in B. Elleman and S. Paine (eds), *Naval Power and Expeditionary Warfare* (2011).
18. P. J. Kastor, 'Toward "the Maritime War Only": The Question of Naval Mobilization, 1811–1812', *Journal of Military History*, 61 (1997), pp. 455–80.
19. J. C. A. Stagg, 'James Madison and the Coercion of Great Britain: Canada, the West Indies, and the War of 1812', *William and Mary Quarterly*, 3rd ser., 38 (1981), pp. 32–4.
20. T. G. Martin, *A Most Fortunate Ship: A Narrative History of Old Ironsides* (2nd edn, 1997).
21. Kevin McCranie, 'Perception and Naval Dominance: The British Experience during the War of 1812,' *Journal of Military History*, 82 (2018), pp. 1067–91.
22. *Naval War of 1812*, II, 183.
23. W. S. Dudley (ed.), *The Naval War of 1812. A Documentary History*, II (1992), p. 11.

24. *Naval War of 1812*, II, 14.
25. *Naval War of 1812*, II, 78.
26. McCranie, 'The War of 1812 in the Ongoing Napoleonic Wars: The Response of Britain's Royal Navy,' *Journal of Military History*, 76 (2012), pp. 1067–94.
27. *Naval War of 1812*, II, 308.
28. H. F. Pullen, *The Shannon and the Chesapeake* (1970).
29. I. Dye, *The Fatal Cruise of the 'Argus': Two Captains in the War of 1812* (2001).
30. G. K. Harrington, 'The American Naval Challenge to the English East India Company during the War of 1812', in J. Sweetman (ed.), *New Interpretations in Naval History* (1993), pp. 129–52.
31. Nicholas Rodger, *The Command of the Ocean. A Naval History of Britain, 1649–1815* (2004), p. 570.
32. Stagg (ed.), *Madison*, 5, 646.
33. R. Malcolmson, 'HMS *St. Lawrence*: The Freshwater First-Rate', MM, 83 (1997), pp. 419–33.
34. *Supplementary Despatches... of ... Wellington* (1862), IX, 425.
35. Alfred Thayer Mahan, *Sea Power in its Relations to the War of 1812* (2 vols, 1918), I, v.
36. J. A. Goldenberg, 'The Royal Navy's Blockade in New England Waters, 1812–1815', *International History Review*, 6 (1984), pp. 424–39.
37. Kert, *Prize and Prejudice: Privateering and Naval Prize in Atlantic Canada in the War of 1812* (1997); A. Gutridge, 'George Redmond Hulbert: Prize Agent at Halifax, Nova Scotia, 1812–14', MM, 87 (2001), pp. 30–42.
38. F. M. Kert, 'The Fortunes of War: Commercial Warfare and Maritime Risk in the War of 1812', *Northern Mariner*, 8 (Oct. 1998), pp. 1–16.

39. T. J. Crackel, 'The Battle of Queenston Heights, 13 October 1812', in C. E. Heller and W. A. Stofft (eds), *America's First Battles 1776–1965* (1986), p. 33.
40. Roger Morriss, *Cockburn and the British Navy in Transition: Admiral Sir George Cockburn, 1772–1853* (1997), pp. 83–120.
41. *Trewman's Exeter Flying-Post*, 2 Mar. 1815.
42. BL. Add. 71593 fol. 134; W. S. Hutcheon, *Robert Fulton, Pioneer of Undersea Warfare* (1981).
43. Viscount Keith to Hotham, 10 July 1815, Hull UL, Hotham papers, DDHO/7/9, cf. 20 July.
44. Popham to Viscount Melville, First Lord of the Admiralty, 27 Nov. 1812, BL. Bathurst Loan 57/108 f. 327.
45. J. Macdonald, *Feeding Nelson's Navy: The True Story of Food at Sea in the Georgian Era* (2004); M. Wilcox, '"This Great Complex Concern": Victualling the Royal Navy off the East Indies Station, 1780–1815,' MM, 97 (2011), pp. 32–49.
46. Morriss, *Naval Power and British Culture, 1760–1850: Public Trust and Government Ideology* (2004) and *The Foundations of British Maritime Ascendancy: Resources, Logistics and the State, 1755–1815* (2011).
47. W. J. Ashworth, '"System of terror": Samuel Bentham, accountability and dockyard reform during the Napoleonic wars,' *Social History*, 23 (2000), pp. 63–79.
48. Robert Sutcliffe, *British Expeditionary Warfare and the Defeat of Napoleon, 1793–1815* (2016).
49. Roger Knight, *Britain against Napoleon: the Organisation of Victory, 1793–1815* (2013), pp. 437–8.
50. Julian Glover, *Man of Iron. Thomas Telford and the Building of Britain* (2017).
51. Timothy Jenks, *Naval Engagements: Patriotism, Cultural Polities, and the Royal Navy, 1793–1815* (2006).

52. Le Faye, 'Mrs Barrett,': 452.
53. *Persuasion* II, 6; *Mansfield Park* I, 6.
54. D. Leggett, "Navy, Nation and Identity in the Long Nineteenth Century," *Journal for Maritime Research*, 13 (November 2011): 151–63.
55. Helen Watt and Anne Hawkins (eds), *Letters of Seamen in the Wars with France, 1793–1815* (2016).
56. Evan Wilson, *A Social History of British Naval Officers, 1775–1815* (2016).
57. Linda Colley, *Britons: Forging the Nation, 1707–1837* (1992).
58. Wilson, *Naval Officers*.
59. *Juvenilia*: 185.
60. *Juvenilia*: 345–6.
61. Ellen Gill, *Naval Families, War and Duty in Britain, 1740–1820* (2016).
62. *Persuasion* I, 8.
63. Samantha Cavell, *Midshipmen and Quarterdeck Boys in the British Navy, 1771–1831* (2012).
64. *Mansfield Park* II, 7.
65. *Mansfield Park* III, 12.
66. *Mansfield Park* II, 13.
67. E. Gill, *Naval Families, War and Duty in Britain, 1740–1820* (2016).
68. Kevin McCranie, '"He shall be properly taken care of," Lord Keith, Patronage, and the Royal Navy, 1761–1823' and '"My dear Father": The Naval Nepotism of Sir Andrew Snape Hamond and Graham Eden Hamond, 1798–1806,' *Consortium of Revolutionary Europe: Selected Papers*, 1999, pp. 391–400 and 2004, pp. 159–69; C. I. Hamilton, 'John Wilson Croker: Patronage and Clientage at the Admiralty, 1809–1857,' *Historical Journal*, 43 (2000), pp. 49–77.

69. Douglas Ronald, *Youth, Heroism and War Propaganda: Britain and the Young Maritime Hero, 1745–1820* (2015); John Morrow, *British Flag Officers in the French Wars, 1793–1815: Admirals' Lives* (2018).
70. *Mansfield Park* I, 2.
71. *Mansfield Park* I, 6, II, 6.
72. *Persuasion* II, 12.
73. Anon., *The Chimera* (1719).
74. Isaac Land, *War, Nationalism and the British Sailor, 1750–1850* (2009); Margarette Lincoln, *Representing the Royal Navy: British Seapower 1750–1815* (2002).

Conclusions

1. Timothy Jenks, *Naval Engagements: Patriotism, Cultural Politics, and the Royal Navy, 1793–1815* (2006).
2. Richard to John Tucker, 11 Feb. 1744, Bod. Ms. Don. C.106 f. 186.
3. Liverpool to Phenias Bond, 23 May 1798, BL. Add. 38310 f. 221.
4. Stormont to Rochford, 30 Mar. 1774 NA. SP. 78/291.
5. BL. Add. 15956 f. 119–22.
6. Fulton to William, Lord Grenville, 2 Sept. 1806, BL. Add. 71593 f. 134.
7. W. S. Hutcheon, *Robert Fulton, Pioneer of Undersea Warfare* (1981).
8. J. D. Davies, 'The Navy, Parliament and Political Crisis in the Reign of Charles II,' *Historical Journal*, 36 (1993), pp. 271–88.
9. Sedgwick to Weston, 24 Jan. 1765, BL. Add. 57929.
10. Norbert Elias, *The Genesis of the Naval Profession* (2007).
11. Eg. *Owen's Weekly Chronicle*, 15 Ap. 1758.
12. Horace Walpole, *Memoirs of King George II*, ed. J. Brooke (3 vols, 1985), II, 70.

13. Daniel Baugh, 'Naval power: what gave the British navy superiority,' in Prados de la Escosura (ed.), *Exceptionalism and Industrialisation. Britain and its European Rivals 1688–1815* (Cambridge, 2004).

Postscript: Routes to Modernity?
1. Keene to Newcastle, 18 Mar. 1737, NA. SP. 94/127.